an illustrated guide to FOSSIL COLLECTING

Richard Casanova

Ronald P. Ratkevich

Books for a better world

Third Revised Edition, 1981
Naturegraph Publishers, Inc.

Library of Congress Cataloging in Publication Data

Casanova, Richard L.
  An illustrated guide to fossil collecting.

  Bibliography: p.
  Includes index.
  1. Paleontology—Collectors and collecting.
  I. Ratkevich, Ronald Paul, 1948-   . II. Title.
  QE718.C37   1981   560'.75   81-18788
  ISBN 0-87961-112-X   AACR2
  ISBN 0-87961-113-8 (pbk.)

1993 Printing

Dedication

With appreciation to the fossil hunters of the 19th and 20th centuries whose writings on their collecting experiences gave the authors much reading pleasure over many years. With thanks to the many paleontologists and fellow-collectors who shared adventures in the field, collecting invertebrates in Europe, Central America, and among the abundant exposures of our North American fossil fields.

Naturegraph Publishers, Inc.
Happy Camp, California
96039

Acknowledgments

No book of this nature can be of widespread value without the generous assistance and counseling of many friends, museum curators, and collectors. Encouraging interest was expressed by many individuals too numerous to mention by name. Various materials, photographs, and publications were made available by the Office of Public Affairs of the American Museum of Natural History and by the Paleobiology Department of the National Museum of Natural History, Smithsonian Institution.

Numerous photographs and articles were supplied by each of the following: The Cleveland Museum of Natural History; Cecil D. Lewis, Jr. and Dennis B. Davies of Dinosaur National Monument, Dinosaur, Colorado; David Douglass of the Prehistoric Life Museum in Yachats, Oregon; Elmore E. Easter of Norwalk, Connecticut; The Oregon Museum of Science and Industry in Portland; The State Museum, University of Nebraska, in Lincoln; *The Illustrated London News;* Richard Lamborn of Erie, Pennsylvania; William L. Manger of the University of Arkansas; the State Department of Natural Resources, Atlanta, Georgia; the Geological Survey of Wyoming, Laramie; Harris M. Richard of Ganado, Arizona; Denver Museum of Natural History; John D. Tea of the Petrified Forest Wood Company of Phoenix, Arizona; the Kansas Geological Survey, Lawrence; Ward's Natural Science Establishment of Rochester, New York; Anthony G. Zvirblis of Mountain Top, Pennsylvania; Thomas J. Bones of Vancouver, Washington; the George C. Page Museum of Los Angeles; the Royal Ontario Museum, Toronto; the Museum of Natural History, University of Kansas; and, finally, the staffs and directors of the library at the American Museum of Natural History.

Introduction

The simple pleasures (and arduous rigors) of collecting fossils, of the hunt for nature's prehistoric treasures, whether simply a shark tooth, or the tooth of a mastodon, or the imprint of a fern that grew some two hundred million years ago, lie in our curiosity to know our past, to seek the origins of life, to explore the never-ending rite of evolution which has occupied our planet's development for more than three billion years.

What originated as a "gentleman's cabinet of curiosities," during the 17th century, as accumulations of dried animal and bird skins, mummified fishes, shells, "thunder stones," and minerals, eventually was replaced by scientifically-curated museum-research collections of fossilized vertebrates, invertebrates, and plants. Driving the gentleman collector of fossil-oddities, as well as the present-day hobbyist, the student of earth sciences, and the professional paleontologist, is an unquenchable interest in the petrifactions that one may encounter in nearly every part of the world. From the collectors like James Hall of Albany who amassed a half-million specimens in his laboratory, to the young adventurer who finds a cigar box collection suitable for his needs, all find that the study of fossils is not merely an excursion or two out collecting in the field, but a pursuit which offers in the specimens collected a world of biotic associations, populations of millions of years in the past, a science of dating strata and bone, of prehistoric environments, and the pleasures of holding in your own hands ancient forms, rare or common, which you yourself have found. There are thrills in the hunt for fossil specimens, and fortunate are they who enjoy the sport.

Table of Contents

List of Illustrations

CHAPTER 1

THE ROMANCE OF FOSSIL COLLECTING

Set in the Aegean Sea, close to the mainland of Anatolia, lies the island of Cos, the birthplace not only of the Father of Medicine, but of the science of paleontology as well. The birthplace that is, in the sense that a fossil specimen, collected and studied by an ancient Greek, has been preserved there. Here, over two thousand years ago, Hippocrates (460-357 B.C.), Father of Medicine, found the first fossil in recorded history which has come down to us as an actual specimen.

Some years ago, the late Dr. Barnum Brown, of the American Museum of Natural History in New York, digging about the ruins of the Asklepiei, the famous medical school of the time of Hippocrates, dug up the fragment of a small elephant molar. This molar, that of a pigmy form of proboscidean which roamed southeastern Europe during the middle Pleistocene Epoch, is believed to be the first fossil to have been preserved for study. The fact that Hippocrates found and speculated as to the origin of this fossil, we know from a contemporary manuscript written by him that survived the centuries.

Hippocrates was not, however, the first to collect fossils. Many observers before him had picked up random specimens, as we know from the numerous pieces of coral, echinoids and gastropod shells found in Neanderthal burials. While the Greeks may have had a word for it, the science of paleontology, as we know it, was quite unknown to the inhabitants of that distant past. The word "fossil" itself, was not termed until the medieval period when the Latin *fossilis,* meaning "something being dug up," came to be used.

The Heroic Age of Greece saw in its science a mixture of superstition, arising out of their myths and legends, and natural explanation, brought about through careful observation and discussion.

Pliny the Elder was one of these chroniclers of observations and opinions. In his monumental *Natural History* he compiled vast references and notes on plants, animals, and minerals. Pliny was a keen student of volcanic action, and many of his observations were carefully recorded. Unfortunately, it was in the pursuit of scientific knowledge that Pliny lost his life when venturing too close to the scene of the disastrous eruption of Vesuvius in 79 A.D., which destroyed the city of Pompeii. While Pliny was not a fossil collector, he did list many forms of fossils in his works, which he considered "inorganic sports," similar to contemporary animals.

As early as the time of Xenophon of Colophon (430-357 B.C.), we have descriptions of the fossil seashells he found among the hills and valleys of Malta. From these shells he concluded that these creations were left over from some periodical submergence of the land.

Later thinkers of the ancient world followed in this hypothesis, for Xanthus and Herodotus were to find fossils (actually petrified seashells), which they concluded had come from an ancient sea that must have spread over Northern Africa and different parts of Europe. Strabo (63 B.C.–24 A.D.) was a prolific writer on the geography of his time. He wrote many of the "best sellers" of his day, writings which mention many of his experiences in discovering fossils in the rocks of Egypt. He relates the story of one day standing in front of the Great Pyramids of Giza and, on examining pieces of rock which formed the huge blocks of the tomb, finding numerous fossils. On seeing these Foraminifera (*Nummulites*) and seeking an explanation, he was told that these were the remnants of the workers' food turned to stone! Strabo rejected this simple explanation, but failed to suggest any other origin for these large "lentil-like" foraminifers. While Strabo was a far more successful geographer than he was a geologist, he could not help getting on the "bandwagon," so to speak, and joining the philosophers and pseudo-scientists of his age by claiming in his *Geographie* that, at various periods, a great portion of the African mainland had been covered over by an ancient sea. The commonly-found petrified seashells, he felt, were proof of these inundations.

After the decline and fall of the Greek and Roman Empires, such learning as was to survive, was to be found in the monasteries and churches of Europe. The "Dark Ages" were beginning, and with them the Christian Fathers selected from their library manuscript writings which best suited their ecclesiastic philosophies and dogmas. Aristotle was selected as the model of learning, and his teachings and books were actually used to keep the free study of human antiquity and earth science in churchly bondage.

The torch of free thinking and scientific knowledge, however, was kept alight in a part of the world that was considered a land of heretics. Thus, during the nearly five hundred years of Europe's Dark Ages, the torch of science was kept burning by the Arabs. By translating and studying the works of Greece and Rome, the Arabs were to preserve the best that was known in philosophy and such sciences as medicine, mathematics, and astronomy. However, their study of fossils was very limited.

China also contributed to the recorded history of both paleontology and paleobotany. When describing forms of fossilized life, the poetic Chinese compared brachiopods (undoubtedly the common Devonian *Spirifer*) to the outstretched wings of birds, or "stone swallows." The earliest recorded word on "stone fishes" in China occurs early in the sixth century A.D. The classic "dragon bones" unearthed from probable Cenozoic deposits, appeared to be species of rhinoceros, mastodon, *Hippotherium*, and perhaps fragments of dinosaur. Such bone fragments were highly esteemed for medical cure-alls. It is highly improbable that many dinosaur bones were used, due to their solid calcification. "Dragon bones" similar to those dispensed by the Chinese herbal medicine shops gave modern paleoanthropologists their first links to earliest man on the Chinese mainland, with the discovery during the 1920s of Peking Man (*Homo erectus pekinensis* Black, 1927) from deposits of Upper-Middle Pleistocene age, c. 50,000 years B.P. at the caves of Chou-kou-tien, near Peking, China.

The 10th to 15th centuries in Europe were to become known as the "Age of the Diluvialists," who claimed that animal and plant fossils were the remains of animals and plants that perished in the Flood of Noah. In 1452 there was born in Italy a genius who was to plan many inventions which were far ahead of their time, and would become a renowned naturalist, painter, sculptor and inventor. Leonardo da Vinci was his name, and, in his famous notebooks, we find a chapter on the "Origin and Meaning of Fossils."

In his youth da Vinci planned a navigable canal in northern Italy, and, while supervising the work, came upon great numbers of shell, coral, and plant remains. Workers dumped these out on the sides of the canal diggings. Studying these petrified remains, he wrote, "When the floods of the rivers which were turbid with fine mud deposited this upon the creatures which dwelt beneath the waters near the ocean borders, these creatures became embedded in this mud, and finding themselves entirely covered under a great weight of mud they were forced to perish for lack of a supply of the creatures on which they were accustomed to feed. In the course of time the level of the sea became lower, and as the salt water flowed away this mud became changed into stone; and such of these shells as had lost their inhabitants became filled up in their stead with mud, and consequently, during the process of change of all surrounding mud into stone, this mud also which was within the frames of the half-opened shells, since by the opening of the shell it was joined to the rest of the mud, became also itself changed into stone. . . ."

Thus theorizing that the fossils found in the mountains of Italy were not deposited there during the Deluge, he went on to suppose that they came to rest within their strata at a time when seas covered the mountain tops.

Ascribing to the earth a chronological antiquity that bordered on heterodoxy, he assigned to the accumulated sediments brought down by the River Po an age of 200,000 years—this long before stratigraphic chronology had been theorized. Leonardo da Vinci's final geological creativity was to design a map of Italy as he imagined it must have looked in a earlier geological period.

Fracastaro, another Italian, who lived from 1483 to 1553, was a physician at Verona. He, too, collected fossil shells, and, in his study of them, maintained that such fossils were considerably older than the Deluge of Noah, since the Deluge, being of shorter duration, would have scattered the fossils over the surface of the earth, rather than burying them deep within the strata which composed the quarries and mines deep in the mountains. He went on to demonstrate that fossils were once living animals, and regarded as completely absurd the theory of fossils having been formed by "plastic forces."

The 16th century was to see the gradual divorce of science from the ecclesiastic bondage of Churchly dogma. And with the coming of this new century, there came also onto the scene a host of fossil hunters. Aided in their efforts to spread their knowledge and thinking by the printing press, they were to push aside the barriers of a Churchly theology that stated that "the land and sea were separated on the third day of creation, while animal life appeared on the fifth day." Since the days of Avicenna, for an observer to be branded as a heretic, all he had to do was declare his opinions against the teachings of Aristotle and Christian Doctrine. To escape persecution, men who studied fossils stated that such animal evidence was formed by plastic forces deep withn the earth, which formed such "lusus naturae" in imitation of true organisms, but, in reality, were mineral concretions and so-called "sports of nature." The latter was a phrase that was to linger in history until the 19th century.

Among the leaders of the early 16th century to bring the study of fossils out of the dark corners of misunderstanding and prejudice into the brightness of true science was Konrad Gesner (1516-1565), a Swiss naturalist. In 1565 he finished a voluminous treatise entitled *De rerum fossilium lapidum et gemmarum figurus*. While Gesner was one of the first fossil hunters to illustrate his book with plates of fossils, he had no true conception as to the origin of these fossils, which he regarded as being either the remains of animals or productions of some inorganic process. Gesner is best remembered, however, for his *Historia animalium*, which, while taking 36 years to complete, filled five folio volumes with unsystematic accounts of the animal world as known in his time, as well as the many animals of fable and superstition.

The year 1556 was to see printed at Basle in Switzerland, the first study of stratigraphic geology. Georgius Agricola (1494-1555) was the author, and the title of the work was *De re metallica*. This important book was to form the basis for the study of all later metallurgy. Prior to this book, Agricola had written a systematic treatise on mineralogy, which he called *De natura fossilium*. Agricola was a Saxon physician and also professor of chemistry at Chemnitz, which might explain his tremendous interest in forming one of the first "cabinet" collections of fossils. So deep was his interest in collecting fossils and forming a cabinet of them (as collections of all natural history specimens were called in those days), that he carefully compiled all the information he could find both from a study of earlier authors, as well as from examination of his specimens. It was the results of his studies which came forth as *De natura fossilium*. Agricola also had the distinction of being the first scholar to coin the term "fossil," although he used the word for anything which was dug out of the earth. With the further development of the earth sciences, the term came to be restricted only to pre-historic animals and plants, with the use including ancient man by present modern scientists.

In 1579, Pietro Andrea Mattioli entered the stage by writing the first book about fossil fishes, which he had collected at Monte Bolca, Italy. Mattioli is credited with the impression that porous bodies, such as shells and bones, could be turned into stone by being permeated with a "petrifying juice." His volume on the fossil fishes of Monte Bolca serves today as a classic text for this piscine fauna.

The curtain went up on the 17th century with the controversy on earth science and the origin of fossils assuming greater proportions. At this point, one of the most influential of Italy's up-and-coming scientists entered into the conflict, Nicolas Steno (1631-1687). During his travels in Italy, he studied the geology of Tuscany, and, in 1669, published a paper on the results of his studies and observations. The title of this important work was *De salido intra naturaliter contene,* and it included a study of minerals,

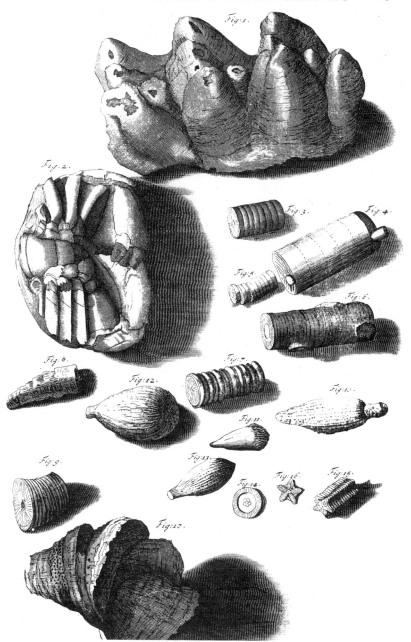

Proboscidean molar-tooth, crab, coral and crinoid stems. From Robert Hooke's "A Discourse of Earthquakes," in *The Posthumous Works of Robert Hooke,* edited by Richard Waller, London, 1705.

fossils, and the composition of crystals. This work made such an impression on the Continent, that an English printing of this book came out in 1671, under the title *The Prodemus to a Dissertation Concerning Solids Naturally Contained Within Solids*. Steno's principles on the formation of the earth created quite a stir in his day, particularly causing a call to arms against his ideas among the Diluvialists. The reason was that Steno's small paper presented principles that "strata has been formed from matter precipitated by water, said matter falling by its own weight to the bottom and this forming a sediment."

One of the most important publications during the Renaissance was *The Posthumous Works of Robert Hooke*. In his writings, Robert Hooke (1635-1703) argues that the Deluge was not of sufficient duration "for the production and perfection of so many and full-grown shells." Hooke went on to say, "the quantity and thickness of the beds of sand with which they (fossils) are many times found mixed do argue that there must needs be a much longer time of the seas residence above the same than so short a space could afford."

Martin Lister (1638-1712) was the first geological worker to introduce the construction of geologic maps. With regards to fossils, he thought of these as curiously shaped stones, which he considered as "never (being) any part of an animal." However, in 1671, he described and illustrated fossil shells with great care and with an eye to detail and even offered illustrations of recent shells for comparison. In his efforts to prove the dissimilarity between fossil and recent shells, he induced many scientists and scholars of his day to discard their Diluvialist theories.

Of much greater importance were his observations upon the different strata and their fossil content. While he was not the first to observe that "quarries of different stone strata" yield quite different species of shells, he was the first to put it down in a printed report. In this same report he goes on to say that "those cocklestones (shells) of the iron-stone quarries of Adderton, in Yorkshire, differ from those found in the lead mines of the neighboring mountains, and both these from the cockle-quarrie (shell-marl) of Wansford Bridge, in Northamptonshire; and all three from those to be found in the quarries about Gunthrop and Beausour Castle." In 1663 he submitted to the Royal Society a series of "mineral maps," through which he proposed to view the correlation and stratigraphy of geological "soil and mineral."

The closing years of the 17th century were again to see the hypothesis of "nature's sports" revived, with a letter published in 1698 by Edward Lhuyd (1660-1709). In this letter, Lhuyd attempted to account for fossils by what he termed "seminal vapour." A translation of his theory runs as follows: "I have imagined they might be partly owing to fish spawn received into the chinks . . . of the Earth in the Water of the Deluge, and so be derived amongst the shelves or layers of stone . . . and whether the exaltations which are raised out of the sea, and falling down in rains, do water the Earth to the depth here required, may not from the seminium, or spawn of marine animals, be so far impregnated with animalcula as to produce these marine bodies. I imagined further that the like origin might be ascribed to the mineral leaves and branches, seeing we find they are for the most part the leaves of ferns and such like plants, whose seeds may be easily allowed to be washed down by the rain into the depths here required."

The curtain comes down on the 17th century with the publication of one of the most important books to be printed up to this point in the history of Earth science. John Woodward (1665-1728) was Professor of Physics at Cambridge. Not only was he the greatest collector of fossils and minerals of his age, but he took such an active interest in the field that he founded a professorship in geology at Gresham College. The England of his day took such a notice of his participation in the fossil-collecting field that many poems and broadsides were written about him. One of the great farces of the day was written about him, and entitled *Dr. Fossil, the man who has the Rare-show of Oyster-whelks and Pubble-stones*. It was a great success on the stage. The literary work which Woodward published in 1695 was to place him among the immortals. Its title was *An Essay toward a Natural History of the Earth and Terrestrial Bodies, especially minerals, as also the sea, rivers, and springs, with an account of the Universal Deluge, and of the effects that is had upon the Earth.*

The theory he promulgated in this long work had it that a great reservoir of sub-surface water, on bursting forth mixed all forms of organic and inorganic matter, which, mingling with sediments, settled in the order of their weight. Thus fossils, being among the heavy substances, forming the lowest layers, were arranged in strata according to their weight. Woodward's collections of fossils are still on exhibition at the University of Cambridge in England, and the Woodwardian Professorship is eagerly sought.

The 18th century, termed the "Age of Enlightenment," was to see tremendous progress being made in evolving a stratigraphical succession among the fossiliferous formations of Europe. This too was a century rich in the learned personalities who flitted across the stage in the courts and palaces of Europe. The battle of ecclesiastical authority versus the freethinkers continued in some countries, though diminished rapidly as scientists were shown royal favor and court privileges. While volume after volume was printed wherein many excellent plates of fossils were to be found, the text still described fossils as "figured stones," or mere sports of nature. This was a thought that was to evaporate in the freshness of a new century. For this certainly was to be a century which took the science of paleontology out of the darkness of dogma and mythology, and turned it into one of the most popular hobbies of the age. The passion for collecting minerals and fossils and the formation of cabinets, or private museums, became the rage of the day.

One such enthusiast was J. J. Scheuchzer of Zurich, who, in the year 1702 published a book on his collections called *Speciman Lithographiae Helveiieae curiosae.* Soon afterwards, Scheuchzer chanced upon a copy of Woodward's essay, from which he saw the error in his previous thinking that such fossils as he possessed in his cabinet were relics of the Deluge. Seeing the light at last, he continued his researches and writings and soon published another volume, this one entitled *Natur Historie des Schweizerlandes,* in which he devoted a section to the description of a number of fossil plants and shells. These two books made him favorably known among scientists; but it was a third book *Homo diluvii testis* that made him famous. Written in 1726, it describes a large salamander-like animal, which he thought to have been human. Writing of this skeleton, he describes it as being from "one of the infamous men who brought about the calamity of the flood." Seems as though way back in his mind, Scheuchzer still was not completely converted from the Deluge theory as far as human fossils were concerned. Actually the storm of protest aroused by the "Homo diluvii" brought forth from every corner of learning in Europe a vast number of writings for and against the book. The Church applauded it, while many scientists criticized it in disbelief.

From Zurich, Switzerland, it is an easy jump to Nuremberg, Germany. In this ancient city, in the years from 1705-1761, lived one of the greatest engravers in all Germany, busily engaged in a devoted effort to prepare a treatise in many folio volumes on all the known fossils. The engraver was George Wolfgang Knorr, and his skill and exact eye for minute detail was to present to the scientist of his day, as to the proud owner of his works today, a rare literary and illustrated masterpiece. For sheer beauty and fidelity of presentation, his illustrations of fossils are unsurpassed. Unfortunately, Knorr died soon after completing the first volume, and another fossil-collecting enthusiast, J. E. Walch (1725-1778), a professor of eloquence and poetry at the University of Jena, took over the task of completing the work of Knorr. Walch was one of those rare individuals who could find poetry and beauty in ordinary rocks, which no doubt played a strong part in the industry and labor he showed in the pursuit of completing the four volumes of text and nearly 300 plates of illustrations of fossils. The work completed was printed under the title of *Lapides Diluvii Universalis Testes-Sammlung von Merck wurdigkeiten der Nattur zum Beweis einer allgemeinen Sundfluth.* It was truly a tremendous title, and a tremendous work, which, with a volume containing systematic tables and an index, issued in 1778, presented an instructive and detailed account of almost all that was geologically known at that time. The printing of this work was to mark a notable advance in the birth of paleontology as a science in its own right. Nevertheless, the work still bore the swaddling clothes of diluvial ideas, and reflected the innocent credulity and abandonment of fossil collecting in those days.

One of the most infamous jokes of the day was played upon a Wurzburg physician, Dr. Johannus Bartholomaeus Adamus Beringer, an ardent collector of the Triassic fossils to be found in his neighborhood, along with crystals, odd-shaped stones and minerals, resembling or imitating organic shapes. Early in 1724, three youngsters from the village of Eibelstadt brought the Doctor several stones bearing on the surface what appeared to be well-preserved figures of scorpions, salamanders, and fish complete with scales. The young fossil dealers began to appear more and more frequently at the Doctor's doorstep, with further exotic petrified figures on stone, as a spider catching a fly, or a pigeon laying eggs. Completely fascinated by these fabrications ("a fossil treasure-trove," he wrote), Beringer hired the boys to assist him in collecting more of these stones, until these "fossil fabrications" reached huge proportions, permitting Beringer to find such God-sent oddities as a slab bearing (in Hebrew lettering, no less) fragments of the Ten Commandments, a slab with a butterfly in flight, comets flashing across the heaven, and, most unusual of all, a sea horse.

In 1726, Beringer had collected over two thousand of these figured stones, which he studied in terms of the theories then prevalent, ranging from the *vis plastica* of post-Aristotelian scholarship, to the *aura seminalis* of the Renaissance. In that year there appeared simultaneously from the printing presses of Frankfurt and Leipzig Beringer's well-illustrated volume of supposed petrified fishes, signs of heavenly bodies, and even Hebrew letters. Beringer's *Lithographiae* was issued in two editions, with numerous plates illustrating all the figments of imagination of the creators, the young fossil dealers, of these "heavenly sent fossils." As with most hoaxes, the bubble burst finally. The fact that a fraud was being perpetrated came to the attention of the Prince Bishop, and the judiciary of the Wurzburg religious body instituted an investigation. Beringer refused to accept the verdict of a hoax and only when further fraudulent specimens were created before his eyes did he accept the untruth of his "fossil trove." But he accepted the providential find of his figured stones and for many years proudly displayed his collection of "divine miracles."

The remainder of the 18th century was to see a host of world famous personalities studying fossils, preparing notable books and maps, and building the famous museums of natural history that house the great fossil collections. One of these men was Ernest Friedrich von Schlotheim (1764-1832), the first German paleontologist to recognize the stratigraphic significance of the occurrence of fossils. In 1813 he printed his *Taschenbuch fur die Gessamte Mineralogie,* in which he described the use of fossils in the geological determination of outcrops.

In 1793, Jean Baptiste Pierre Antoine de Monet, known to us as Lamarck, was appointed Professor of Zoology by the French Revolutionary National Convention. Among his many other interests, Lamarck tackled the study of the *Invertebrata* with imagination and an encyclopedic breadth of vision that was typical of his time. In 1801, he had published a classic that served both the biologist and the paleontologist, the *Systeme des animaux sans vertebres,* in which he laboriously outlined the world of insects, molluscs, worms and chordates, concluding with a portion "On Fossils." In a very lengthy description, he begins by saying, "I give the name of fossil to the remains of living bodies, changed by their long sojourn in the earth or beneath the waters, but whose form and organization are still recognizable."

The 19th century dawned in Europe with fossil discoveries that were to give the science a new emphasis in paleontological researches and publication—studies of fossil specimens beyond the wildest dreams of the medieval fossil collector. In Paris, workers in the gypsum quarries of Montmartre unearthed numerous bones and even complete skeletons of mammals, which were brought to the attention of Leopold Georges Cuvier, the Father of French Science. In the year 1804, a complete skeleton from the quarries in Montmartre was brought to Cuvier at the National Museum for study. The skull, containing twenty-eight molars, twelve incisors and four canine teeth, appeared to resemble the skull of a living tapir, yet the molars were most like those of a rhinoceros. Cuvier named the mammal *Palaeotherium.* More and more specimens were brought to Cuvier, newly unearthed pachyderms, turtles and larger and varied fauna, to each of which he assigned species names as he attempted to describe them. He explained that these creatures had become extinct with the invasion of a sea which covered the freshwater gypsum formation of the Paris Basin.

Alexander Brongniart (1770-1847), famed French mineralogist and zoologist, with Cuvier, established new studies and methods in stratigraphic geology. His *Essai sur la geographie mineralogique des environs de Paris,* issued in 1811, is an important work of reference in the study of the Paris Basin even today.

As the Italy of the 16th century gave birth to Leonardo da Vinci, so did the England of 1769 give birth to William Smith. For not only did the Canal diggings of Italy unfold a story of past earth-history to da Vinci, but a similar revelation was to make William Smith the "Father of English Geology." An advocate of canal navigation, it was while planning and mapping out the course for the Somerset Coal Canal that Smith first noticed the strata lying on top of one another, as he said, "like so many superposed slices of bread and butter." While surveying the cutting of the Canal for six years, he profitably used this time in examining and collecting the fossils he came across in the excavations. Picking up fossils from the waste piles and dumps was not enough for Smith, as he walked uncounted miles over the hills and valleys of Devon and Somerset in search of further fossils. Drawing his own maps as he went along, he began to trace recognized fossils within certain beds, plotting these "index" fossils on his maps, then tracing the beds from one locality to another purely on the evidence of the fossils, noting both the variations and similarities of the beds. His collecting covered several years, and in 1796 Smith began work on a book illustrating his "strata succession principles." While reluctant to publish in haste his observations and faunal notes, the fact that many other European geologists were approaching similar conclusions caused Smith, in 1801, to issue a prospectus of his work and a *Table of Strata.* It was not until 1815 that his momentous volume appeared, *A Delineation of the Strata of England and Wales, with part of Scotland.* Its greatest value lay in the colored geological maps. This classic and, today, very expensive volume, was followed in 1820 by Smith's *A New*

Geological Map of England and Wales, a second edition which proved the value and tremendous interest shown for the 1815 edition.

Smith's correlation maps and fossil illustrations spurred other English geologists into field observation and collecting. Among the most fortunate amateur paleontologists of the era, was Dr. Gideon Mantell (1790-1852), a physician who practised medicine while he hunted fossils. It was while visiting a patient outside Lewes, that the good doctor's wife, bored with the waiting, strolled about the estate, and on the surface of a pile of rocks lying by the roadside, noticed a tooth embedded in a stone. During the ensuing weeks the doctor visited the locality again and again, finding additional teeth, as well as a number of bones. These he studied and described as belonging to the reptile *Iguanodon.* The finding of these fossil vertebrates, as well as many others in the strata of Tilgate Forest, he described in his *Illustrations of the Geology of Sussex,* printed in 1827. In this classic monograph he describes his researches in four of the five genera of dinosaurs known by the time of his death in 1852. The finding of the *Iguanodon* teeth and bones created a great deal of interest in England and throughout Europe, as here was the discovery of the first dinosaurs in England (this was in 1825), although there is one very brief mention of actual dinosaurian remains having been found in Sussex as early as March 1822, when Mantell issued his *Fossils of the South Downs, or Illustrations of the Geology of Sussex.* In this rare work the engraving plates of fossils were executed by Mrs. Mantell.

Whereas Smith founded the principles of stratigraphy and faunal-correlation, and Mantell made important fossil discoveries (as Mary Anning was to do at Lyme Regis), it was during the middle part of the century that historical geology achieved a solid foundation, with the writings of Charles Lyell, Roderick Murchison, Richard Owen, and Charles Darwin.

Sir Charles Lyell (1797-1875), son of a well-to-do Scotch family, was trained for the Law, but interest in geology soon led him to change careers, and the future of paleontology was greatly enhanced by his reluctance to becoming a barrister. In 1818 Lyell graduated from Exeter College, Oxford, having attended lectures in geology, and having mapped the Tertiary and Quaternary rocks of Norfolk. From 1821 to 1823 Lyell did considerable field work in the Mesozoic and Cenozoic geology of Sussex and the Isle of Wight. In 1824 he was at Lyme Regis just as Mary Anning discovered her superb skeleton of *Ichthyosaurus vulgaris.* During 1828 he spent a strenuous two months in the company of Murchison, touring the most geologically interesting districts of the Auvergne, in France. The summer of 1829 Lyell spent in Italy and Sicily observing the Tertiaries, making as he traveled sizeable collections of fossils. By the end of 1829, he published the first volume of his *Principles of Geology: Being an attempt to explain the former changes of the Earth's surface, by reference to causes now in Operation.* This cornerstone volume of historical geology explained the basis of the controversy between geology and cosmogony, tracing the development of the science from the ancients of Egypt and Greece, and ending with the foundation of the Geological Society in London, in 1807. In the second volume of *Principles* (the three volumes of this first edition were issued at different dates) we find Lyell's criticism of the Lamarckian theory of evolution and his firm contention that species were fixed, in the sense that there were limits to the variability of each.

The third volume of the *Principles* is mainly devoted to chapters on stratigraphic and faunal correlation. They include a scheme of Tertiary classification, which he had developed with Paul Deshayes (1796-1875) some years before, the latter having supplied the extensive faunal lists. Although Lyell favored Darwin in his views on descent and evolution, as a Creationist he firmly believed all animal progress to be the design of a Master Creator.

During the late 1700s Lyme Regis was a well-known resort for those visitors wishing to enjoy the sea air and long stretches of beach. Lyme Regis was different from most resorts in that the casual tourist here did not take home samples of "local hand crafts," but something far more venerable and more fascinating— fossils, which weathered out from the exposed cliffs. Mary Anning was celebrated for operating a most unusual shop, a shop that catered solely to the sale of fossils or *Curnua Ammonis,* as ammonites were then called, and which covered any number of species. During her early teens, and in company of her father, who also sold fossils on the side, from his carpenter shop, Mary Anning would walk the beaches and collect fine ammonites and other invertebrates that would be exposed along the cliff-face of the off-shore Jurassic sediments. Upon the death of her father, Mary Anning took up the selling of fossils as a business, selling on a grander scale, and in time became known throughout Europe as "the most eminent fossilist." Although her eventual reputation as a fossil collector reached the greatest paleontologists of her time, who took the opportunity to enrich their private collections and museums with some of the finest specimens to come out of the Lyme Regis outcrops, oddly enough, one of Mary's most exciting finds was made when she was twelve years old. She had located a fine specimen of *Ichthyosaurus,* and had it excavated by some local workmen. Exhibited in London at a quaint "Bullock's Museum at the Egyptian hall in Piccadilly," these valuable fossils "obtained by the indefatigable labours of Miss Mary Anning," so wrote Mantell, eventually reached the British Museum. However, today it is impossible to recognize Mary's own specimens in the museum's vast collections.

Scotland has had its share of fortunate, talented, and very successful fossil-hunters. Northeast of Black Isle and facing Cromarty Firth lies the deserted village of Cromarty, and presently preserved by the National Trust for Scotland, we find the house of plaster and thatch of Hugh Miller. Famed in both literature and fossil-lore, Miller became known as the stone-mason of Cromarty, yet fame brought him a greater calling with the discovery of so many Devonian fossil fishes. His numerous discoveries of the earliest armor-plated fishes, and his numerous books on his finds and observations, brought him to the attention of the London geologists. In 1841, Miller issued in Edinburgh, his now classic *The Old Red Sandstone,* followed in 1847 with *Footprints of the Creator,* and *The Testimony of the Rocks or, Geology in its Bearing on the Two Theologies, Natural and Revealed,* which he published in 1857.

As Lyell was writing the last volume of his *Principles* and Darwin, at his country house at Downe, was gathering notes for his

On the Origin of Species, the British Association met at Dudley Caverns, and before the assembled multitude, the Bishop of Oxford, in a glorious speech is credited with styling Sir Roderick Murchison, "The Silurian King upon his Silurian Throne." "Silurian" happened to be the name given to the bed of rock upon which Murchison happened to be sitting at the time.

Roderick Impey Murchison (1792-1871) was born at Tarradale, Scotland, and was to become one of the most controversial geologists of his day. Murchison had long traced the Silurian System in South Wales in the company of Adam Sedgwick and William Lonsdale, as well as the Devonian System in Devon and Cornwall. With his friend, Sedgwick, he investigated the structure of the Alps, and it was not until the Cambrian-Silurian controversy arose that their friendship was to end. The Rev. Adam Sedgwick, working upward from the "basement rocks," devised the Cambrian System, while Murchison, working downward from the "Old Red Sandstone" (Devonian), set up the Silurian, causing the two systems to overlap. It took Charles Lapworth (1842-1920) through his graptolite studies to settle the dispute in 1879, by proposing the new name "Ordovician" System for the complex series of strata which included both the Lower Silurian of Murchison and the Upper Cambrian of Sedgwick. Lapworth's graptolite studies showed that their use as index fossils could help determine the succession of strata.

Murchison's greatness as a geologist shines brightly from the pages of the folio volume which he published in 1839, after the years he had spent traversing the roads and valleys of Scotland, Wales, Devon and Cornwall, as well as a good deal of European and Russian terrain. His monumental work, known simply as *The Silurian System,* is without a doubt one of the most important cornerstones of fossil studies, and is illustrated throughout with numerous woodcuts of fossils, correlation charts, and a handsome hand-colored geological map.

Prior to the golden era of fossil collecting in England during the middle 1800s, some advances in the discovery and excavation of fossils took place in the United States, particularly where vertebrate fossils were concerned, during the Presidency of

Thomas Jefferson. Early in 1782 Jefferson, in a slim volume entitled *Notes on the State of Virginia* (when the state of Kentucky was still a part of Virginia's western territory) mentioned the now classic fossil locality of Big Bone Lick, situated on the banks of Big Bone Creek, a small tributary of the Ohio River, in Boone County, Kentucky. Returning from a visit to Paris and the museum of natural history there, Jefferson decided to form a collection of Big Bone Lick fossil vertebrates, and arranged for William Clark, of the Lewis and Clark western explorations, already an experienced hand at fossil collecting, to set up camp along the Big Bone Creek and make a comprehensive collection of fossil vertebrates, with the idea in mind of sending a duplicate set of bones to the Paris museum. By the fall of 1807 Clark was able to report to the President that he was successful in making a collection of a fine series of mastodon materials, to include, as Clark puts it, "several heads of Mammoth . . . several pieces of jaw bone with teeth in them, and one with a small tusk." Leaving behind numerous additional specimens too fragile to ship, Clark shipped three heavy boxes of fossils from Big Bone Lick to New Orleans, completing the trip down the Mississippi River in January, 1808. The specimens arrived safely at the White House, and a portion of the collection was prepared for shipment for Paris, while several others were selected by the President for his own personal "cabinet" at Monticello, where they occupied a prominent place among his curiosities.

During Jefferson's years as President of the United States, he continued his interest in fossils, and room was set aside in the White House, where the floor was piled high with fossil bones from the western regions. Although his official duties as President prevented his active participation in the search for fossils, he was to a great extent instrumental in preserving for future study many valuable specimens that might otherwise have been lost.

The American hunt for mastodon remains continued by interested amateurs into the early decades of the 1800s. In 1801 several farmers in the neighborhood of Newburgh, New York, while digging drainage ditches, came across bones of what later were recognized as those of several mastodons which apparently had died while crossing a swamp. These bones came to the attention of Charles Wilson Peale, who operated the celebrated Peale Museum in Philadelphia. Rushing to the farm near Newburgh, Peale supervised the excavation of several mastodon bones from a swamp deposit, by the expedient method of building a treadmill machine for the draining of the water-filled excavation. This mastodon excavation was painted by Peale in 1808 and now graces the mastodon exhibits at the Peale Museum in Baltimore. The mastodon bones were mounted by Peale in his Philadelphia museum. By 1850, the mastodon was exhibited in Barnum's Philadelphia Museum, which burned down in 1851, and the skeleton was assumed lost. In 1954, a report appeared in the *Proceedings of the American Philosophical Society* that Peale's

"Exhuming the Mastodon," by Charles Wilson Peale, 1808. The painting depicts the excavation of the first Peale skeleton on John Masten's farm near Newburgh, New York, in 1801. The treadmill machine drained water from the swamp. *(Courtesy Peale Museum, Baltimore, Maryland.)*

mastodon skeleton had been discovered in a German museum. The article, entitled *The Rediscovery of Peale's Mastodon,* narrates the travels of the skeleton from the Barnum museum in Philadelphia to the German museum in Darmstadt.

The most stupendous fossil hunter of them all was James Hall (1811-1898) of Albany. In 1836, Hall was appointed as an assistant in the recently established State Survey of New York. Within a decade the fossil collections of the New York State Geological Survey were about the largest in the country. Such industrious collecting was to crystallize into the thirteen monumental quarto volumes that Hall wrote describing and illustrating the fossils of New York. In 1875 the American Museum of Natural History in New York purchased a portion of the Hall fossil collection embracing some 80,000 specimens.

January 20th, 1890, was a memorable day in the annals of journalism, involving, as it did, headlines proclaiming the "Battle of Bridger Basin" and the "Uintatheres and Cope-Marsh War." The "war" over fossils, fought by way of slander, innuendo and accusation in which many prominent geologists and scientists of the late 19th century took part, revolved around two of America's most fascinating and misunderstood paleontologists and fossil collectors extraordinaire. Edward Drinker Cope (1840-1897) of Philadelphia, and Othniel Charles Marsh (1831-1899) of New Haven, who have received considerable biographic treatment during the past decade, were mutually antagonistic towards one another in print, in the laboratory, and in the hostility their field-parties shared in the fossil fields of the "Far West." Both were men of exceptional literary ability and major outputters of publications, Cope for *The Vertebrata of the Cretaceous Formations of the West,* and Marsh *The Gigantic Mammals of the Order Dinocerata,* among many other lengthy monographs and hundreds of reports.

The 20th century was to see an equally great collector in the person of Charles D. Walcott of the United States National Museum, who discovered the classic Middle Cambrian Burgess shale of British Columbia. By filing a mining claim on the property, he was able, over a period of years, to "mine" the world's most superb collection of invertebrate fossils.

The Gobi Desert in Central Asia in the first quarter of the 20th century was virtually *terra incognita* as far as paleontology was concerned. A plan for fossil collecting on a grand scale, using motor vehicles and camels for transport, as well as a staff of scientists covering several disciplines, to survey, photograph and make collections in all aspects of natural history, geology and archeology, was presented to the American Museum's President, Henry Fairfield Osborn, by Roy Chapman Andrews, staff zoologist and museum director. Interest in Mongolia and its possible wealth in research materials was sparked by the belief that Central Asia may have seen the origins not only of many mammalian orders, but of the human species as well.

The first Gobi Expedition departed from Peking on April 17th, 1922. By August of the year, members of the expedition were reporting finds of Cretaceous dinosaurs, with the most unexpected find coming in the discovery of dinosaur eggs at the Flaming Cliffs. Actual nests of eggs were located, exposed on the surface of the sedimentaries, some 135 million years old. Andrews in his *On The Trail of Ancient Man,* 1926, relates in great detail the finding of eggs and bones of the dinosaurs (*Protoceratops*), saying, "these eggs could not be those of a bird. No birds are known from the Lower Cretaceous, the geological horizon in which these eggs are found." During this expedition over twenty-five eggs were removed from the sediments, singly, in clusters, and in a nest of nine eggs. Andrews added, "not only did we discover the eggs, but we obtained during our five weeks in this locality a completely developmental series of the parent *Protoceratops andrewsi,* as well as one egg broken in half, exposing the delicate bone of the embryonic dinosaur." An expedition in 1930 saw an end to the motor-camel caravans across the Gobi, with the ensuing political unrest throughout China and Mongolia. Not until 1963 and 1965 did new expeditions explore the Flaming Cliffs again, this time by combined Polish-Mongolian expeditions, which collected over thirty-five tons of fossils, including skeletons of sixty-five foot long sauropod dinosaurs, related to the *Brontosaurus.*

Many students of historical geology consider the passing century as the "Golden Age of Paleontology." Perhaps this is true for vertebrate paleontology in the very extensive collections made throughout our West, Africa, Europe and the Asiatic continent. The invertebrates also came in for a share of the museum wealth they provide. And the names of fossil collectors are legion, for aside from the luminaries mentioned here, there were many, many others, of all nationalities, and all equally important in the field work they accomplished, and in their rich paleontological writings.

Today, fossil collectors, the famous as well as the unknown, abound in every part of the world. Either as professional or as amateur, they continue the quest for the mysterious creatures of the past, always finding strange new treasures in the endless adventure of exploring the ancient rock layers of the earth.

CHAPTER 2

FOSSILS—WHAT ARE THEY?

Whether they be the actual unaltered flesh of a frozen mammoth, or the clamshell petrified with precious Australian opal, or even the trackway of a Paleozoic trilobite, all such remains or traces of life in past geologic ages are considered fossils. Paleontology is the study of fossils, the only remains of ancient life.

Paleontology would be a dry and lifeless science were it not for our imagination which must, if the science is to be real, add flesh, sinew, and movement to the fossils. To accomplish this, all collectors *must* become a little of a biologist, an ecologist, and a geologist, which can only enhance the thrill of finding a brachiopod or trilobite, which are of themselves shards in a very fragile vessel of time.

Fossils often resemble modern organisms. The chitonous shell of a blue crab living in the shallows offshore looks much like the molted crabshell washed ashore during a storm, and still much like the crabshell buried in the sand high above that year's highest tide level. Still similar, yet somehow different, are the crablike arthropods found in late Cenozoic sediments further inland. Even further from the living sea crabs, in the hard Paleozoic rocks of a distant mountain, the strange, unfamiliar ancestral forms of arthropods, 300 million years distant from that blue crab, tempt our imaginations.

Fossils are preserved either by chemical replacement or actual preservation over a long period of time. The word "fossil" comes from the Latin *fodere,* meaning "to dig." From around 1550 to 1700 it was customary to name everything being dug up from the earth—be it mineral, relic or fossil—a "fossil."

By understanding the kinds of fossils a collector will come up with in the field, and their modes of preservation, a collector will gain some insight into the rocks which hold these fossil treasures, therefore making fossil discovery easier.

There are certain geological and environmental conditions which favor the preservation of fossils. (Exceptions exist for all of these.)

1. *Rapid burial in sediments.* Dead animals are usually devoured rapidly by scavengers, or bacteria brings decay. Early burial in moist sediments prevents such happenings.
2. *Rapid burial in volcanic ash.* Similar to sediment burial, volcanic ash, when combined with moisture from rain or as it settles onto water, is an ideal medium for preservation. Organisms, from butterflies to dinosaurs, have been preserved in ash.
3. *Possession of hard body parts.* Having a skeleton or exoskeleton helps an animal become fossilized; but under ideal conditions, plants and worms, even jellyfish, can become fossils.
4. *Presence of highly mineralized ground water.* Since most organisms are built up, in one degree or another, with spongy tissue (even bone and shell have many pores), mineral solutions can rapidly fill these pores, producing a petrified or permineralized condition.
5. *Unusual circumstances.* Animals and plants may be trapped in substances like tar, tar sands, tree resin (amber), icy tundra, or they may be mummified in dry desert climates.

Determined largely by these various conditions, there are a number of specific types of fossil preservation.

1. *Unaltered remains.* Actual preservation, though rare, is possible when bacterial action and decay have been stopped. The baby mastodon uncovered in the icy tundra of Siberia is one classic method of actual preservation. Another frozen mammoth, found in Alaska, can be seen in a refrigerated case in the American Museum of Natural History in New York City. Other animals have been preserved without any chemical or mineral alteration in bogs and oil sands, or in oil seeps like the famous La Brea Tar Pits in Hancock Park, Los Angeles.

2. In fossilization by *mineralization* (technically called "per-mineralization") the porous material in an organism's hard parts become filled with minerals that were dissolved in the water that percolated through the earth. This mineral matter, precipitated out of solution, fills up shell or bone tissue without changing the original shape or substance.

3. *Replacement,* or *petrification,* is a third method of fossilization, and is one of the most common. The original organic substances, shell or skeletal material, are dissolved and replaced by a different type of mineral matter. However, this dissolving takes place so slowly, that every tiny organic structure remains to complete an exact "pseudomorph" of the original material. Common examples of petrification are, of course, petrified wood, dinosaur bone, and agatized shells.

4. *Distillation* or *carbonization* is a process of preservation in which volatile elements in organic matter distill away, leaving a thin carbon film as the only fossil record. Many fossils throughout America are preserved in this way, especially carbon copies of leaves, the flesh of fish, and certain soft-bodied invertebrates such as worms and arthropods.

5. *Footprints* and *trails.* Fossil trackways are an invaluable supplement to the study of ancient life forms. From fossil tracks much more can be learned about an animal's habits than by studying only the actual remains. Dinosaur footprints are widely known, but many prints and trackways of lower vertebrates such as lizards and amphibians are common, as are tracks of invertebrates.

6. *Coprolites.* Casts of excrement preserved as fossils are known as coprolites (from the Greek *kopros* meaning feces). A great deal can be learned by studying fossil food material preserved in such fossils, and the shape alone of coprolites can tell the paleontologist something about the internal anatomy of the long-dead animal. Coprolites can be of invertebrates, reptiles, fish, mammals, and even insects.

CHAPTER 3

CLASSIFICATION OF FOSSIL FORMS

THE PALEOBIOLOGICAL CLASSIFICATION OF FOSSILS

Without utilizing the seemingly complicated method of naming organisms which biologists (and paleontologists) universally rely on, all of us interested in fossils would soon become hopelessly lost in a chaotic tangle of words, with each scientist naming organisms in his or her own, individual style.

Realizing the problems which were inherent in early biological classification systems (which grouped whales with fish, and birds with bats), the eighteenth century Swedish naturalist Karl von Linné (Carolus Linnaeus) devised the system known as *binomial nomenclature.* This "double name" system consists of two parts: the generic name, or *genus,* and the *species,* both being derived from Greek or Latin words or Latinized place names (or Latinized people's names). Greek and Latin words are used in taxonomy (the science of classification) because they are considered dead languages which are not normally changed, and the spelling and meaning of such words are identical in all parts of the world.

UNITS OF CLASSIFICATION

All forms of life on the earth have been classified into five different biological *kingdoms:* Monera (blue-green algae and bacteria), Protista (protozoans and algae forms), Fungi, Plantae and Animalia. Each of these is further divided into smaller groups called *phyla.* The phyla are then divided into smaller groups called *classes;* classes are divided into *orders;* orders into *families;* families into *genera;* and, finally, into the basic units of *species, subspecies,* and, very rarely, varieties or races.

To illustrate the use of binomial nomenclature in the classification of animals, a trilobite, a dinosaur and a clam are each broken down into their Linnean classification in the following table.

Unit	trilobite	dinosaur	clam
Kingdom	Animalia	Animalia	Animalia
Phylum	Arthropoda	Chordata	Mollusca
Class	Crustacea	Reptilia	Bivalvia
Order	Phacopida	Ornichisthia	Eulamellibranchia
Family	Phacopidae	Hadrosauridae	Veneridae
Genus	*Phacops*	*Cortyhosaurus*	*Venus*
Species	*rana*	*casuarius*	*securis*

The genus and the species are written together in italics to form the full scientific name. The gigantic lumbering dinosaur, *Triceratops horridus,* of the Late Cretaceous period might be called, were it not for Linné's system, "The large, erect dinosaur having three cranial horns, with such and such number of toes, measuring so and so inches, etc., etc." Binomial classification obviously allows extremely long descriptions of organisms to be reduced to only two or three words, the meaning of which are known internationally.

Following the *species* name in any taxonomic designation, there follows the name of the author who first described the species, with the year given, in which the species was described. In cataloging genera and/or species, these names are usually followed by the title, date, and name of publication, paging, and illustration figures for the genus or species described.

MAJOR FOSSIL GROUPS OF KINGDOM ANIMALIA

In the pages that follow are inserted, along with the text, a chart that shows the present major phyla and classes of the Animal Kingdom. This chart shows pictures of modern animals in their proper relationships. But in the text are described and pictured fossil animals as they are related to these modern animals (except that some modern phyla, such as Rotifera and Nemertea, are so poorly represented as fossils that they are not mentioned here as part of the fossil record). This will not only help you in classification, but will show you evolutionary relationships between ancient and modern animals. It will also make clear what ancient phyla, classes, and orders of animals have completely disappeared from the earth.

You will note that the more primitive animals are found in the earliest rocks. This is one of the strong proofs of some kind of evolutionary development of animal life. The chart on pages 52-53 shows in very simplified form the development of animals from the simple to the complex (or evolution) as visualized by scientists. This theory of evolution is based on a very great accumulation of evidence that can barely be touched in a small book of this size, but the theory is itself in process of evolution and new discoveries each year bring changes to this idea.

The animal kingdom is divided into approximately twenty-one phyla, and of these only ten are found abundantly in the fossil record. Most of the remaining twelve phyla are rare as fossils because they lack hard parts. A sea scorpion fossil, for example, may be the remains of only one in a hundred thousand individuals which lived in the Paleozoic. Similarly, the multitudes of soft-bodied creatures which lived alongside these scorpions, called *eurypterids,* are mostly gone from the fossil record.

To properly classify the many thousands of different kinds of fossils would take a book vastly larger than this one. Here the aim is to teach the user to classify fossils down at least as far as order or class, and how to identify a few of the very common or unusual fossils down to genus or possibly species. This is sufficient to start a collection of labeled specimens. You can do more complete classification later when you have learned how to use the more technical descriptive literature, or take your fossils to an expert or museum and have them completely classified.

(NOTE: as you read this chapter, refer frequently to page 74 in which the different earth ages are shown in a geologic time chart. This will help you understand the relationship between the fossils described here and their times of recorded appearance in the history of the earth.)

The Invertebrates

Phylum Protozoa

Protozoans are tiny, one-celled animals which are usually single, free-living organisms. The most common living example is the amoeba. Of the uncountable millions of Protozoa forms which have lived over the ages, only a very few subgroups, those which possessed hard parts, are known in fossil form. Of these the most common fossil Protozoa belong to the class Sarcodina and are called Foraminifera, or "forams."

Most fossil Protozoa were microscopic in size, and their tiny coiled shells, called "tests," are extremely abundant in many formations. In the Foraminifera, the shell is made up of calcium carbonate, and consists of numerous microscopic chambers. The blocks of limestone which were used to build the great pyramids of Giza in Egypt are largely composed of the Foraminifer form *Nummulites.* In southern New Mexico, thick formations of Mississippian limestones are composed almost entirely of the foraminifers *Schawagerina,* each specimen about the size and shape of a grain of rice. Many thousands of miles of the sea floor are entirely made up of uncountable numbers of foraminiferan shells. This material is called *Globigerina ooze,* after the most common genus.

Radiolaria, the cone-shaped order in the class Sarcodina, build their shells of silica, and rather than being chambered like the Foraminifera, they occur as globes and pyramids of glass, pierced through by holes and often complicated ornamentations of spines. Radiolarians are often much smaller than Foraminifera, and are, in some areas, much more abundant than their larger cousins. Diatomaceous earth, composed almost entirely of radiolarian tests, is often mined for use as insecticides and as water-filtering material.

Many Protozoa species are very sensitive to slight environmental changes, since they are easily affected by temperature, water salinity, and the nature of the ocean substrate. Also, because of their simplicity, protozoans evolved rapidly and are very useful as index fossils. The term index fossil is used by both the paleontologist and the geologic stratigrapher in designating specific fossil forms. These index fossils serve to correlate similar geological horizons or zones, even if the land layers are continents apart, or of higher or lower altitude.

Phylum Porifera: the Sponges

Poriferans, although they look like plants, are the simplest of the multi-celled animals whose cells are designed to have differing and specific life functions. Sponges are generally aquatic and usually spend their lives attached to objects. Ancient sponges existed in every possible size and shape, but all were characteristically perforated with tiny pores through which water was circulated and in which food particles were trapped and digested.

The soft tissue of the sponge is supported by an internal skeleton composed of hard fibers and/or mineralized rods called spicules (calcium carbonate or silica). Rarely did this soft tissue become fossilized, having rotted before burial. The internal, spicular skeleton, too, disarticulates and eventually settles to the ocean floor in a shapeless mass. Complete fossil sponges are very rarely found as fossils, but spicules can be found in strata from the Cambrian to the present.

The sensitivity of sponges to water current and turbidity (sediment load) makes them a good indicator of paleo-environments, and because forms evolved rapidly, differences in spicule forms provide paleontologists with excellent index fossils.

Phylum Cnidaria: the Corals, Jellyfish & Sea Anemones

Five classes occur under this phylum of comparatively simple animals. The main one which concerns the fossil collector is the Class Anthozoa, or the corals and sea anemones. Of less importance is the Class Hydrozoa, which contains the hydroids, forms of which are known from the Lower Cambrian to the present. The fossils called conulariids are considered possibly related to the Scyphozoa and appear as four-sided pyramids, except when flattened or crumpled by rock pressure in bedding planes. They are known from the Cambrian to the Permian, but are more common from the Silurian on.

Most of the cnidarians are saltwater forms, only slightly more advanced and complex than the sponges. There are two general forms of cnidarians: the medusa, most commonly seen as the bell-shaped, tentacled jellyfish; and the polyp form which resembles a tube with one end closed off and the other end edged with a ring of tentacles used for gathering food. The polyp form of Cnidaria is responsible for most of today's great reef formations, made up of millions of tubes of stony calcium carbonate (calcite) which is secreted by the animals.

Most corals are characterized by forming together in a colonial existence, individual polyps growing upon another polyp to form a rigid mass. There were a few fossil forms which prefered a solitary existence, such as the familiar fossil horn corals.

Class Scyphozoa: Jellyfish

Scyphozoans are primarily the free-floating jellyfish, the medusa forms of cnidarians. They appeared in Lower Cambrian times (Grand Canyon rocks), or possibly before, and lived on to the present where they are common in most bodies of saltwater. The impressions of jellyfish in the rocks are usually so faint that only experts can identify them, but the finds may prove valuable.

One group, however, the conulariids, were unlike the jellyfish in that they possessed shells, and some attached themselves to the sea bottom.

Fossil conulariids are usually cone-shaped or pyramidal and consist of a thin, flexible, chitinous outer "skin" that is usually marked with numerous curved or angular lines.

Conulariids can be found in rocks of Devonian age, mostly in the eastern United States.

Class Hydrozoa: Hydroids

Hydrozoans include both colonial and solitary polyps, as well as medusa forms. Other than having a chitinous covering, the Hydrozoa had no known skeleton. However, a few forms did have a calcareous scaffolding resembling a series of irregular porous layers. An extinct group, the stromatoporoids, built skeletons in mounds or twig shapes, formed in layers on underwater rocks or other animal shells, and became important reef builders in the

Silurian and Devonian periods. Graptolites (class Graptolita) appear in the fossil record as faint "pencil marks" on fine shale. Although their exact biological relationship is questionable, many paleontologists have placed them close to the Hydrozoa.

Class Anthozoa: including Sea Anemones & Corals

The anthozoans are the most important fossil form of cnidarians because all of the members of this class, with the exception of the sea anemone, build stony skeletal structures.

Anthozoan polyps were formed in several shapes: cups, horns or tubes, which might or might not have been joined together into larger masses. Each skeleton is called a "corallum." The polyps exist mainly in a cup-shaped depression at the upper end of the corallum and are attached to a system of radial partitions, called "septa," that run the entire length of the skeleton. In time of danger, the polyp can retract itself into the tube, but its normal position is outside with its tentacles waving in the currents in search of food particles.

All living stony corals belong to the group Scleractinia, a class which ranged no further back than the Triassic Period. During the Paleozoic, corals belonged to the Rugosa and Tabulata groups which became extinct by the early Mesozoic.

The rugose corals built massive colonial skeletons, as well as horn-shaped solitary skeletons, but each corallite was characterized by having a rough (or rugose) outer surface. The tabulate corals were entirely colonial and are characterized by having no septa and having table-like platforms within the coral tubes. These two forms are common fossils in many formations.

Phylum Bryozoa: the Moss Animals

Bryozoans which all belong to one class, Gymnolaemata, are entirely colonial animals living mainly in sea waters. Often seen as encrusting masses on other fossils, the Bryozoa are capable of producing both delicate skeletons, resembling plants or mosses, and thick stone-like formations contributing to the build-up of reefs. Most, however, are delicate and few fossils are found complete, having been scattered by the currents on sea floors.

Like corals, each individual bryozoan forms a tiny polyp, but such similarity is only superficial. The bryozoan's body, called the "zooid," is much more complicated than the simple cnidarian coral polyps.

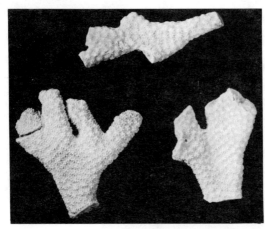

Constellaria florida, an Ordovician, branching type of bryozoan colony.

Bryozoan colonies from Silurian shale near Rochester, New York. Some of them are encrusting other animals, such as brachiopods and bivalves. Notice the lacy appearance.

Many fossil forms of Bryozoa can be identified by surface characteristics, but positive identification usually requires microscopic examination. Usually, thin slices or sections must be prepared to clearly observe the internal structures.

The numerous, small animals work together to secrete calcareous shapes (colonies) which may take various forms. The most common fossil forms show either twig, mound or branching characteristics. Such forms had zooecia covering their surfaces. Other types, such as the ribbon or lacy forms, had zooecia (outer covering which gives structural support) on one surface only and often consisted of long and short branches with a lacy appearance.

The Bryozoa were most common both in variety of species and orders, as well as individual abundance, during early Paleozoic times, particularly in Ohio, Kentucky, Indiana, and Tennessee. But they appear less abundantly from the Silurian to the present day. They form an involved, difficult phylum that needs microscopic study of polished, thin sections in order to determine even genera.

Phylum Brachiopoda: the Lamp Shells

Brachiopods are shelled marine animals which flourished on the bottoms of Paleozoic seas. Only a very small number of brachiopod types exist today, and these have changed very little from their ancestral forms.

There are a great many superficial similarities between brachiopods and their look-alikes, the clams, or bivalves. Most of this is due to the fact that both forms possess two shells, or valves, which enclose the animals' soft bodies. Internally, the animals are quite different. A clam's internal structure is primarily composed of a large muscular "foot" for digging and general locomotion (this foot is what makes clams and oysters so sought after as food), and also a strong set of muscles for closing the shell. The brachiopod's soft parts consist mostly of a bristle-covered feeding structure, called the "lophophore," and a series of complex muscles for shell operation.

Shell differences are used as a simple way to tell brachiopods from clams. The brachiopod's shell is bilaterally symmetrical and unequal in size, but may be divided into two symmetrical halves.

The larger of the brachiopod's two shells is termed the pedicle valve because it bears the long muscular stalk, or pedicle, which is used to attach the animal to rocks or other shells. Some brachiopods, however, lie loose on the sea bottom.

The Phylum Brachiopoda is divided into two classes, the Inarticulata and the Articulata, distinguished by the methods used to articulate, or join, the valves at the hinge.

The articulate brachiopods are characterized by having shell "teeth" in the pedicle valve and sockets in the brachial valve. Most brachiopods belong to the class Articulata.

The inarticulate brachiopods are characterized by the absence of teeth, and sockets usually have only muscles to hold the two shell halves together. Inarticulate brachiopods are among the oldest complicated fossils known. One of these, the *Lingula,* has survived unchanged for more than 500 million years, and is alive in today's waters.

Brachiopods are one of the most common fossil forms in Paleozoic rocks, and, because many forms evolved and became extinct during this time, they are very useful in identifying and correlating Paleozoic formations from all parts of the world.

The phylum Brachiopoda had its beginning in the Cambrian with a majority of inarticulate forms, although several genera of Articulata are known. The most numerous genera and species occurred from Ordovician to the Devonian times. Brachiopods are to be found in just about all fossiliferous shales, limestones, and sandstones from Late Cambrian to Late Jurassic, with a few forms continuing until today.

Phylum Mollusca: The Molluscs

The phylum Mollusca has among its members the most common shellfish in today's seaways. Molluscs have adapted to almost every known environment. There are five classes of molluscs: Gastropoda, Bivalvia, Cephalopoda, Amphineura, and Scaphopoda, all of which have quite different shell structures; but all share very similar soft parts. Only the three most important classes will be discussed here.

Class Gastropoda: including Snails, Slugs, Limpets, Abalones

The gastropods have more than 15,000 different fossil forms, and have worldwide distribution in every environmental niche except that of the air.

The gastropod's shell is usually spiraled, or, as in limpets, is cup-shaped. Several species have an "operculum," which acts as a lid when the animal withdraws into its shell.

The gastropod's soft body is composed of a foot and a head with tentacles, eyes, and a mouth. Most of the soft portion is contained within the shell spirals. The majority of gastropods are scavengers living off whatever dead plant or animal remains they might find, while others are carnivores, boring through the shells of other molluscs to devour soft internal parts. Gastropods ranged from Cambrian to the present, with more of an abundance today, more than 60,000 species, than at any other time in the past. While many of the ancient genera and species have disappeared, a number of the Cenozoic kinds (particularly of the Pleistocene Epoch) still occur today in the warm-water seas.

Class Bivalvia: Clams, Oysters & Scallops

The bivalves, or clams, differ from other members of their phylum in that they develop an external bivalve shell, as do brachiopods. The bivalves are great locomoters, moving readily through the waters, often surfacing, and more frequently burying themselves deep in the sea bottom. Some even dig into solid rock to find shelter. The soft, internal structure of the bivalve is composed mostly of a large, muscular "foot" which is used for movement and for holding the valves closed.

Bivalves ranged from the Ordovician to the present and are evident in most fossiliferous formations, especially marine. They were scarce in some periods, such as the Ordovician, but abundant in others, as in the Cretaceous, when they assumed gigantic and bizarre shapes.

Class Cephalopoda: Squids, Octopods, Nautiloids, Ammonoids

Cephalopods are the most advanced class of invertebrates. All members of the class have well-developed heads, tentacles, eyes, hearing organs, jaws, and sophisticated nervous systems. Cephalopods are also good swimmers, equipped with a marvelous propulsion system which squirts a jet of water from a tube, called a syphon, and propels the animal swiftly through the water. More than 10,000 species of fossil cephalopods have been described.

The soft structures of the ammonoids (extinct) are not well known, because few of these fleshy parts are preserved in the fossil record. Paleontologists assume, however, that such unpreserved parts were similar to those of the living nautiloids which have been studied extensively.

The living genus *Nautilus* lives in a coiled, chambered shell, which is built, chamber by chamber, as the animal develops. The tubular syphon runs the entire length of the shell and functions as a gas regulation device, filling or emptying inner chambers with gases to regulate buoyancy. Where each partition of a chamber joins the outside of the shell, a "suture" is formed. All ammonites of the same species have identical suture patterns.

Nautiloids developed plain suture patterns, while ammonoids developed very complicated patterns. Ammonoids, or ammonites, and nautiloids are among the most beautiful fossils known, often retaining the original pearly, almost metallic, undershell.

In the Cretaceous Period the dying race of ammonites seemed to go into a final splurge, producing fantastic and irregular forms, including many uncoiled or partly coiled types.

The sub-class Nautiloidea ranged from the Cambrian to the present. Though not very common, the nautiloids often reached a spectacular size and were fierce carnivores with long tentacles.

Phylum Annelida: the Worms

The most common of the annelids is the earth worm *Lumbricus* which possessed the most fundamental characteristic of the phylum, the segmented body. Because the body of the annelid worm is composed primarily of soft tissue, entire fossil worms are rarely found in the fossil record. When such fossils are found they are usually preserved as thin carbon films pressed into layers of bedded shale. More commonly found are worm tracks or trails ("trace fossils"), or secreted mineral tubes which were cemented to other fossils or carried with the worm much like the shell of a gastropod. Such tubes are found in rocks of Ordovician age and have changed little if at all into modern times.

Fossil worms belonging to the Polychaeta class had jaws known as "scolecodonts" composed of a chitinous-siliceous material that is frequently preserved in the fossil record. Most of these jaws are tiny, visible only through a microscope.

Phylum Arthropoda

The arthropods, or "jointed leg animals" comprise the largest invertebrate group; living arthropod forms number in the millions, with uncountable millions of species having lived in the geologic past. This is one of the most interesting groups of fossils, containing six classes, and including the famous subclass of trilobites, one of the earliest and most specialized of all invertebrates. Such diverse animals as lobsters, barnacles, crabs, shrimp, centipedes, millipedes, spiders, scorpions, and insects give some idea of the tremendous variety of arthropod forms. All of the above-mentioned forms are living and also have fossil representatives. The trilobites and the eurypterids, which are very important arthropods in the geologic past, are now entirely extinct.

A typical arthropod is elongate and segmented (leading some paleontologists to believe that they evolved from annelid-like animals); they all have jointed appendages, and an exoskeleton, an outer supporting covering. Fossil arthropods are generally rare due to the fragile nature of their skeleton. In some formations, however, arthropod fossils are present in large numbers and leave a fossil record nearly 600 million years long.

Subclass Trilobita

Trilobites are one of the most fascinating of all animal groups. From exceptionally well-preserved specimens, paleontologists have been able to study the remnants of soft internal organs, but usually only the fossil chitinous shell remains. This shell is composed of calcium carbonate plates all jointed together to allow some movement, much like the armor of a knight of the Middle

Ages. The trilobite's shell was comprised of three distinct parts: the cephalon, thorax, and pygidium. On the cephalon are two large compound eyes, composed of hundreds of individual lenses, enabling some blurred sense of sight. The thorax was the largest segment, forming the middle body, and the pygidium, or tail, may have been used for digging in mud. Well-preserved trilobite fossils show that they had numerous jointed legs. In general, trilobites were small, less than two or three inches long, but some became giants of the Paleozoic world reaching twenty inches or more in length. Trilobites were exclusively marine and probably had swimming, crawling, burrowing, or floating habits.

Trilobites appeared in Early Cambrian seas as well-developed, advanced forms, leading paleontologists to believe that the group must have had its origins in the Pre-Cambrian, among the earliest arthropods to appear on earth. They long preceded the crustaceans and the insects. Despite the multitudes of trilobites which lived during the Paleozoic, they never equalled the success of many of the arthropod classes and came to an evolutionary dead end at the close of the Paleozoic. The trilobites left us no descendants, but only a fascinating and diverse fossil record.

Subphylum Chelicerata: Spiders, Scorpions, King Crabs & Eurypterids

This major group of arthropods is characterized by its lack of antennae and by the development of one pair of legs into specialized pincers or fangs. These are the chelicerates, most of which lived on terrain which was not ideal for the preservation of fossils. Some chelicerates closely resemble trilobites, but many paleontologists consider this to be a distant relationship at best. This subphylum is divided into two classes, the Arachnida and the Merostomata. Only the Merostomata are significant as fossils.

Class Merostomata: Horseshoe Crabs & Eurypterids

It is not certain whether eurypterids lived in fresh or marine waters, or even brackish offshore waters. Some of the eurypterids grew to be huge, reaching twelve feet or more, and, during Mid-Paleozoic times, they must have become the terror of the ancient seas. The typical eurypterid body is much like that of the other arthropods, elongated and covered with a thin chitin shell. The head region is equipped with two paired crescent-shaped eyes and numerous legs, two of which developed into paddle-like swimming organs or long pincers. Eurypterids have been found in strata as early as Lower Ordovician, and became entirely extinct at the end of the Permian. Eurypterid remains are well-preserved in limestone quarries in western New York, Ontario, Ohio, and Indiana. They are rarely found abundantly, though a few may usually be found together. Their living cousin, the horseshore crab, *Limulus,* is the sole survivor of this great class of arthropods.

Class Crustacea: Crabs, Crayfish, Lobsters, & Shrimp

With rare exception, preservation of members of this class is impossible because of their soft shells. The few which did grow hard shells can be found as fossils, usually in concretions which prevented crushing. The geologic range of this class ranges from Silurian-Devonian to present.

Subclass Ostracoda: Ostracods

Externally, the shells of these microscopic and nearly microscopic animals resemble clamshells, but internal structures and the presence of jointed appendages show that the ostrocods were true arthropods, a subclass of the crustaceans. Ostrocods are all aquatic (mostly marine) organisms with a geologic range from the Cambrian to the present, and are very common as fossils. Because of this, they are especially useful to the stratigrapher as index fossils.

Class Insecta

The most familiar arthropod group, the winged insects, belong to this ominously prolific class which could, were it not for natural controls, become the dominant animals on the face of the earth. It is ironic that having lived in such great numbers, the insects are very rare as fossils. This, of course, is due to their soft body parts and fragile wings. Most fossil insects occur in deposits which permitted rapid preservation, such as volcanic dust. Superbly preserved specimens of insects have been found completely fossilized in clastic localities such as the lignite deposits under the Baltic Sea which contain amber, fossil tree resins that trapped and entombed the insects, or in the fine volcanic ash deposits of Colorado which have produced insect fossils from creatures as delicate as butterflies.

Phylum Echinodermata: the Spiny-skinned Animals

The common members of this phylum are the starfishes (class Stelleroidea), sea urchins, heart urchins, and sand dollars (class Echinoidea), and less commonly known are the "sea cucumbers" (class Holothuroidea), the cystoids (class Cystoidea) and the sea lilies (class Crinoidea).

Class Crinoidea: the Sea Lilies

This is the most significant fossil group of the Echinoderms. Their extinct cousins, the cystoids, with over 140 genera known in Paleozoic rocks, might at first appear to be a highly successful group of echinoderms, but when we consider the class Crinoidea, which has had a total of over 750 distinct genera, the cystoids pale almost into insignificance. The crinoids, like the cystoids and the extinct blastoids, were primarily bottom-living echinoderms attached to material on deep sea bottoms, although some forms were able to crawl or swim from one place to another. Like their cousins, the crinoids were (and are today) filter feeders which spread their feathery tentacles like flowers in the currents to catch food material.

The crinoid's body is a cup-shaped calyx, and is supported by a long stem, which sometimes has a series of short arms, and by a "root" system which is used for grasping the sea floor. In ancient times, there were also a few free-swimming forms. Being composed of calcite, the crinoids, as with the cystoids, are often well-preserved.

These columnals were so abundant in some portions of the Carboniferous that entire rock beds are made up of crinoidal limestone, sections and plates of crinoid stems. Crinoids ranged from the Ordovician to the present, but were in much greater abundance and variety during Paleozoic times. The crinoids surviving into present times in warm ocean waters are often dredged from ocean bottoms by the tens of thousands.

Class Cystoidea: the Cystoids

Cystoids are an extinct primitive class of echinoderms which looked a great deal like their better known relatives, the crinoids. The cystoids are divided into two major groups, the true cystoids with irregular plate arrangements and an imperfect radial symmetry, and the blastoids which developed a perfect or near-perfect symmetry.

Both groups have structures divisible into two main parts. The stem, a long series of calcite discs connected by muscle fiber, was used to hold the animal to objects on the sea bottom; and the calyx, or body, which is composed of irregular plates that completely enclose the animal's soft internal parts.

The distinctive characteristic of the cystoids is their development of a "diploporid system," consisting of tubes arranged in pairs that open onto the surface of the calyx plates as short grooves through which water passes into the interior of the cystoid. Except for this pore system, the cystoid's adaptation to its environment is nearly identical to that of the crinoids.

The bodies of the cystoids (and crinoids) are composed of calcite, and are usually well-preserved. However, more often than not, the stems and calyxes break apart and are preserved only as fragments scattered throughout the rocks. Cystoids became extinct at the close of the Permian Period, leaving their ecological niche for their cousins, the crinoids.

While cystoids ranged from Cambrian to Permian times, their difficulty of preservation and rarity has not made them common index fossils. But sometimes they are found in clusters.

Class Stelleroidea: the Starfish

Members of the subclass Asteroidea, the starfish, have a star-shaped body with five arms, or a multiple of five, projecting outward like spokes on a wheel. On the underside of the starfish are numerous movable spines which are used to guide food from the arms to the mouth, located at the center of the star. The skeletal plates of the starfish are held together by a leathery skin. When the starfish dies, the skin decays and allows these calcite plates to separate and scatter to the ocean bottom as a formless mass. Because of this, starfish are very rare as fossils and highly prized in any collection. Some large colonies of starfish have been found in the early Paleozoic rocks of New York and Canada. The New York State Museum, for example, has on exhibit slabs of Middle Devonian sandstone bearing on the surface hundreds of specimens of the ancient starfish genus *Palaeaster.*

A second subclass, the Ophiuroidea, are the brittle stars. They are similar in outward appearance to the asteroids but differ greatly in that they have a defined central disc which contains the bulk of the animal's body tissue. Ophiuroids are much more fragile than their cousins, the true starfish, and are the rarest of all the echinoderms in the fossil record.

Class Echinoidea: the Sea Urchins & Sand Dollars

Echinoids are bottom dwellers that can move about on a series of specialized spines. These movable spines are also used for protection, and for wedging the animal into protective crevices in rocks and corals.

Superficially, the bulbous echinoids appear very different from other members of their phylum, but as one observes the animals' detailed structures, the relationships become apparent, and quite remarkable. All echinoids maintain a radial symmetry based on five rays. Like the starfish and the crinoids, echinoids bear a series of skin-covered calcite plates, which, we can be thankful, are joined together more securely than those of either of their relatives. Thus, echinoids are better preserved in the fossil record. Their test (or outer skeleton) is either globular or disc-shaped. Echinoids differ from the crinoids and other classes of the Echinodermata in that they lack arms and a stem, and in having surface spines.

The oldest known echinoid, of the early Ordovician, resembles closely, in many features, the starfish, and many paleontologists believe that echinoids are direct descendants from the asteroid echinoderms.

These ancient sea urchins and sand dollars are not accepted by petroleum geologists as primary index fossils, but their great abundance and range during the Mesozoic and Cenozoic eras is a good indication of warm temperature conditions.

Although they began during Ordovician times and now exist abundantly in all the marine waters of the world, they did not come into prominence until Cretaceous times. The sea urchins and common fossil echinoids, and their remains may be collected by the thousands in the Lower Cretaceous rocks of Texas and Oklahoma.

The Vertebrates

The most advanced forms of the Animal Kingdom are those with a backbone and a spinal cord. These have been placed in the phylum Chordata. All the members of this phylum are characterized by the presence of a structure called a *notochord*. This notochord can be a cartilaginous rod which extends nearly the entire length of the organism and provides support for the body of the chordate. In higher chordates, the notochord has evolved into a body column of articulating vertebrae. The chordates with this backbone are called vertebrates and are often subdivided into two superclasses: Pisces (fishes) and Tetrapoda (the paired-limbed animals).

Protochordates, animals from which true vertebrates evolved, are nearly absent from the fossil record. Graptolites, once thought to be protochordates, are now placed among the class Hydrozoa. The phylum as a whole ranged from the Cambrian to the present.

We can trace the vertebrate lineage through the fossil record, but a meager record remains of the myriad generations of vertebrates which led to mankind. Incomplete as it is, paleontologists know a great deal about vertebrate evolution. Vertebrate fossils are rare, and they are precious, because unlike invertebrates an entire segment of evolutionary history can be lost if one key fossil vertebrate is destroyed.

SEQUENCE OF FISHES

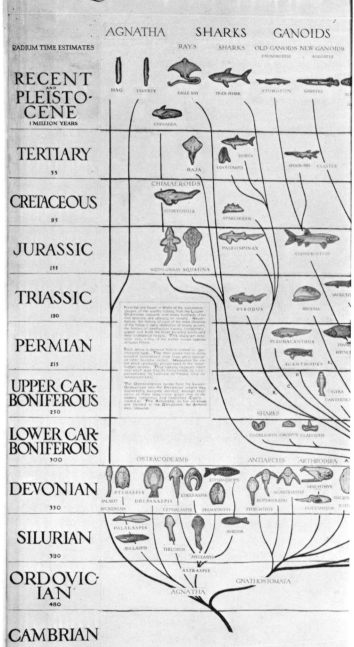

IN GEOLOGIC TIME

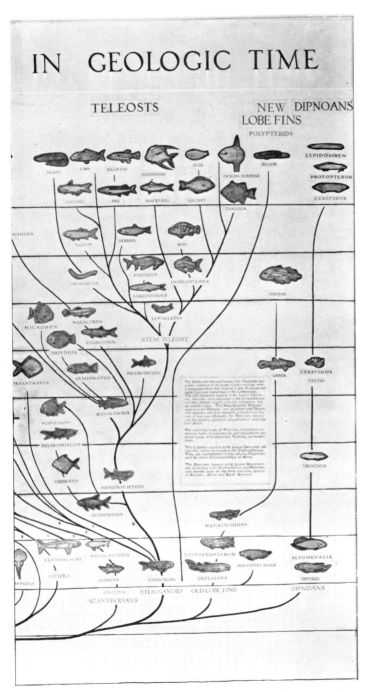

Sequence of fishes in geologic time, from the Agnatha in Ordovician times through existing orders. *(Courtesy American Museum of Natural History.)*

Superclass Pisces

Class Agnatha: Jawless Fishes

We know much about this class of primitive fish because a classic member of the group, the parasitic lamprey of the Great Lakes, is still living. The Agnathas characteristically lack fins and jaws, and for the most part they were well armored (as in the group called ostracoderms). The gills of these fish were supported by bony bars fused to the head armor. These bars were eventually to develop into primitive jaws, while scales on those bars were to become teeth.

Fossils of agnathid fish are usually very fragmentary, often represented by broken, isolated body plates from the head armor. These fossils are found scattered throughout many Paleozoic formations.

Class Placoderma: Extinct Jawed Fishes

This class of primitive, extinct fish, which began in the Silurian and disappeared during the Permian, differs from the Agnatha in that its members developed jaws and had definite fin structures. Like the Agnathas, the Placoderms were armored, and usually only dermal plates were found as fossils. But complete fossil Placoderms are very rare. This class includes the spiny sharks and gigantic, jointed-necked fishes called the arthrodires which were often over 20 feet long. Several large rock layers containing complete schools of such Placoderma have been found in the Devonian and Mississippian rocks of Ohio. One of the best known of these fish is the Devonian form *Ptericthyodes.*

Class Chondricthyes: Sharks, Skates, & Rays

In this class, which ranges from the Devonian to the present, are grouped the living sharks, skates, and rays, a group of fish almost entirely lacking any bony skeleton. The shark skeletons are composed of cartilage, which, under normal circumstances is rarely preserved in the rocks. In some localities, such as the fine-grained Devonian shales near Cincinnati, Ohio, wonderfully preserved fossil specimens are found completely carbonized. Fossil teeth of sharks are very common in some formations, especially in the Cenozoic of the East Coast and in the Cretaceous rocks of the Rocky Mountain region. The shell-crushing, cestraciont sharks of the Mississippian Period probably helped destroy the trilobites. Their fin spines and blunt teeth are often found as fossils in the rocks of this period. By the late Eocene, enormous sharks (*Carcharodon*) roamed the seas, some of them more than 40 feet long.

Class Osteichthyes: Bony Fishes

Everyone is familiar with members of the class Osteichthyes, which includes such fish as the perch, the trout, and the salmon (and many more). All members of this class have bony skeletons.

Primitive members of this class are called the paleoniscoids, which were freshwater forms, usually inhabiting streams which ran through the great Carboniferous fern forests. In some locations, these paleoniscoids are preserved perfectly as carbon residues. Teeth and scales are, however, the more common of their fossil remains.

Paleontologists believe that the amphibians had their beginnings in the Osteichthyes class. Beginning during the Devonian, and so down to modern times, these bony-skeletoned fish have been very successful. The remarkable lung fishes, or *Dipnoi*, belong to this class, and were very common during the latter Paleozoic, when they were probably closely related to the ancestors of the amphibians. They used their so-called "lung bladder" to breathe with during long dry seasons when fish with gills would die.

Superclass Tetrapoda

Tetrapods are paired-limbed creatures, including the amphibians, reptiles, birds, and mammals. The amphibians go back to Upper Paleozoic time. The reptiles began at the end of the Paleozoic, became dominant in the Mesozoic, and faded in strength and numbers in the Cenozoic. A few birds and mammals appeared in the Mesozoic, but reached dominance in the Cenozoic. In general, because land animals infrequently meet the requirements of fossilization, they are rare in the rock record. Fossil collectors should therefore be content to have in their collections fragmentary specimens, such as teeth, isolated bones, etc., which lead professional paleontologists to the complete skeletons.

Class Amphibia: Amphibians

Amphibians are represented today by such creatures as frogs, toads and salamanders, all tied together zoologically by a common need to return to the water to breed. They are all cold-blooded, and breathe (in the adult stage) with lungs. Immature amphibians live entirely in water and breathe with gills.

Although footprints and trails of amphibians have been found in Devonian and Mississippian rocks, their actual remains do not begin until Pennsylvanian time. The clumsy, salamander-like giant labyrinthodonts of the western states are not uncommon fossils. Having heavy bones and thick dermal armor, their skeletons often escaped destruction by the elements. Smaller amphibian fossils, such as those of frogs, are rare, and only occur in fine sediments laid down in optimum conditions. Footprints of amphibians are especially common in some formations, such as the Permian rocks of Arizona and New Mexico.

Class Reptilia: Reptiles

Reptiles are cold-blooded (with the exception of some dinosaurs), relying totally on air or ground temperatures for thermal control. They differ from their ancestors, the amphibians, by being air-breathers from birth, by having a bodycovering of scales, and, primarily, by their development of the amniotic egg (a sac of liquid within the shell in which the embryo develops).

Reptiles have a long and interesting history beginning in the Pennsylvanian Period. They have adapted to all environments, on land, in the air (the pterosaurs), and as completely marine forms, like the mosasaurs.

Of all the reptiles, perhaps the dinosaurs had the most fascinating history. The dinosaurs were, of course, some of the most spectacular reptiles of the past because of their size (though not all were large). Dinosaurs took many bizarre forms and shapes, including sluggish amphibious creatures, peaceful plant-eaters in fantastic armor, great horned monsters, and vicious flesh-eaters. A

Young of Cretaceous dinosaur, *Protoceratops*, hatching from egg. *(Courtesy American Museum of Natural History.)*

weird flying reptile, the pterosaur, belonging to the Archosauria—reptiles which became the first true flying vertebrates (*Pteranodon* and *Rhamphorhynchus* belonged to this group of the Pterosauria)—was not a dinosaur, nor were the fish-eating monster reptiles, such as ichthyosaurs, plesiosaurs and mosasaurs that swam in the warm seas. The synapsids were mammal-like reptiles which ranged from the Permian through the Triassic, and include such strange creatures as *Dimetrodon* and *Coelophysis*, which may have provided the connecting link between mammals and reptiles.

Today, more than a century after their discovery, dinosaurs continue to generate an "instantaneous addiction" to those who study their bones. They also continue to spark controversy: were they cold blooded (ectothermic), being able to maintain a body temperature equal only to the environment, or warm blooded (endothermic), with the ability generally to maintain a constant body temperature? No doubt it will take many more years for vertebrate paleontologists to answer this question.

Two orders of dinosaurs evolved during the Mesozoic: the Saurischia, or lizard hip dinosaurs which were generally meat-eating forms, and the Ornithischia, which evolved from the ancestral carnivorous forms to become generally herbivorous or plant-eating.

Dinosaurs had a geologic range from the Triassic to the close of the Cretaceous, and current theories suggest that dinosaurs, or at least one form of dinosaur, evolved into the birds of today. It is a happy thought for the amateur paleontologist (and to many professionals) that the dinosaur did not die out abruptly with the close of the Mesozoic, but rather adapted to a changing world by developing feathers, "warm blood," and the power of flight.

Class Aves: Birds

Birds are rare as fossils. The earliest and most primitive forms, such as *Archaeopteryx*, were little more than dinosaurs with feathers, and were capable of marginal flight at best. Even today, many zoologists consider the bird to be little more than a "glorified reptile."

The most ancient fossil bird bones have been found in Jurassic formations in North America, but such finds are of isolated bones, and compare poorly with the famous European finds of the last century. Cretaceous birds, however, have been found in the chalk beds of western Kansas and are spectacular in their own right. They are particularly fascinating because they retained the teeth of their reptilian ancestors.

Cenozoic birds of North America are more common, yet are still rarities in the fossil world. Recently, bird eggs have been found in the Oligocene of Nebraska, bird footprints have been excavated from the Eocene of Wyoming, and complete skeletons of giant vultures have been taken out of the La Brea Tar Pits in Los Angeles, California.

Class Mammalia: Mammals

Mammals are warm-blooded animals that bear their young alive, feed them milk, have a body covering of hair, and breathe by

Smilodon species. A large saber-toothed cat of the Pleistocene Epoch in California. The lower jaw was so hinged that it could be dropped out of the way of the great saber teeth that could then be plunged like two knives into the vital organs of thick-skinned elephants, buffalos, or ground sloths. From a mural by Knight in the Los Angeles County Museum. *(Courtesy the Los Angeles County Museum.)*

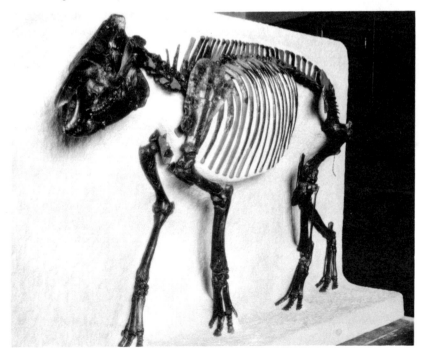

Extinct rhinoceros, *Hyrachius eximius,* of the Middle Eocene Epoch, from Bridger Formation, Uinta County, Wyoming. This was a so-called "running rhinoceros" because of its slender legs and long neck. It did not have true molar teeth. *(Photo courtesy of Smithsonian Institute.)*

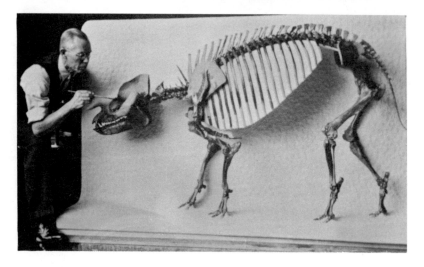

Palaeosyops paludosus, an extinct titanothere mammal from the Middle Eocene, Bridger Formation, Uinta County, Wyoming. This was rather small for a titanothere. Some of these animals later reached very large size and protected themselves with strange-looking horns, but both horns and size apparently proved ineffective against increasingly well-armed predators, and also their comparatively weak teeth and small brains helped bring about their extinction. *(Photo courtesy Smithsonian Institute.)*

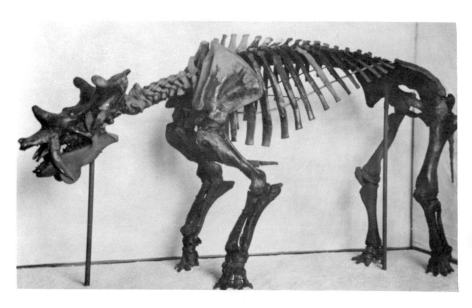

Uintatherium robustum, a Middle Eocene uintathere mammal, Bridger Formation, Uinta County, Wyoming. This was about the size of a large rhinoceros. The bony extensions over the skull, and the large canine teeth were for defense against carnivores, but the small brain and the weakly-developed teeth (good mainly for soft plant foods) led to the extinction of most of such unadaptive mammals by the beginning of the Oligocene Epoch. *(Photo courtesy Smithsonian Institute.)*

means of lungs. As with reptiles, mammal skeletons are rare as fossils. Mammalian origins have their roots in the early Mesozoic, and there is little doubt that their ancestry was tied to the reptiles, or reptile-like creatures. Having a much greater capability of survival in changing climatic conditions, the mammals were able to adapt to all parts of the world, and all environmental niches. Warm-bloodedness, or homeothermy, gave the mammals an evolutionary advantage, and some paleontologists theorize that by the close of the Mesozoic the mammals simply outmaneuvered many reptiles into extinction.

Skeletal characteristics of mammalian fossils include multi-cusped teeth, distinct ball-and-socket joints, and other complex articular joint surfaces. Mammals also developed a much larger and complex brain and nervous system, which can be seen by examining their skeletons.

Tens of thousands of fossil mammal forms have existed since the Triassic Period, but perhaps the most spectacular forms lived during the latest geologic period, the Pleistocene. Commonly called the "Ice Age," the Pleistocene saw the development of the giants of the mammalian world: the mammoths, mastodons, giant sloth, and glyptodonts. Most forms of these Pleistocene giants became extinct at the close of that period in America, and we can speculate as to the effect of man's appearance on their disappearance.

PLANTS

The Plant Kingdom is abundantly represented by a wealth of excellently preserved plant fossils in coal, shales, and sandstones. Beginning in the Pre-Cambrian times as primitive calcareous algae, plants spread onto the land by Devonian times, and reached a marvelous diversity of forms and widespread adaptability during the Pennsylvanian Period when the great coal beds were laid down in thousands of ancient swamps.

Innumerable volumes have been written about plant fossils alone. In a guidebook such as this, only enough detail can be given to acquaint the reader with the major plant divisions (equivalent to animal phyla), and with some of the more interesting and important fossil plants of the different geologic periods. We find that the evolution of plants moved along at about the same pace as that of the animals, from the simple to the complex. Thus, a modern sunflower is probably as complex in its own way as a modern ape.

Division I: Thallophyta

This division includes the one-celled plants, the bacteria and algae, as well as plants such as fungi and lichens, which have few or no hard parts. The fossil record of the lichens and fungi is usually scant.

The subdivision Algae, however, is recorded from the Pre-Cambrian to the present, and occurs abundantly in some Paleozoic horizons (or rock layers) as shapeless masses of algal reefs. The most numerous of one-celled fossil plants belong to the class Bacillarieae, order Pennales, family Diatomaceae, or diatoms. These are tiny plants enclosed in "glass boxes" manufactured by the plant from silica in the water. Such protective coverings take many interesting geometric forms, which are often preserved in the rocks as fossils, sometimes forming huge beds.

The order Charales (the charophytes) are a form of algae that becomes very complex, so much as to sometimes merit classification as a different division. They have apparent leaves and stems, and a small, calcareous fruiting body (like the fruit of higher plants) that enables the plant to reproduce sexually. These hard fruits are solid enough to be fossilized from Pre-Devonian times to the Pleistocene.

The subdivision Fungi, including the mushrooms, the bracket fungi, are found as fossils in Devonian and even older rocks. In Pennsylvanian shales, they have been found preserved as spores.

Division II: Bryophyta

This division includes the mosses and liverworts, which have leaf-like forms (on damp earth, tree bark, or water surfaces), but no true roots or flowers. Although very ancient, their lack of hard parts makes them quite rare as fossils.

Division III: Pteridophyta

This division includes those plants that have vascular tissue (specialized tubes for carrying liquid), as well as leaves, stems, and roots, but that do not possess true flowers, cones, or, with one exception, seeds.

The class Lycopsida, includes the extinct Lepidodendrales, or scale trees, and the Lycopodiales, or club mosses. The latter occur today in our woods as inconspicuous trailing plants. The ancient scale trees, *Lepidodendron,* however, often were over 100 feet high. Their fossils can be identified by the prominent leaf scars patterned regularly over the bark.

The class Sphenopsida includes the modern order Equisateles, or horsetails (also called scouring rushes), which grow two or three feet high, with jointed stems and tiny, scale-like leaves at the joints. But some of the ancient ancestors of these plants, like the Pennsylvanian rushes of the genus *Calamites* (order Calamitales), grew a foot in diameter and more than 35 feet high. Their ribbed and jointed trunks are distinctive when found as fossils. At one time, calamites covered vast swamps, but they died out by the late Permian.

The class Pteropsida has branching stems and large, complex leaves. It includes both true ferns and seed ferns. The order Cycadofilicales, or seed ferns, were wide-spread plant fossils. These plants had leaves or fronds bearing seeds, and often became very large (100 feet tall or more), looking more like palms than ferns. Seed ferns were most extensive in the late Paleozoic, and were the oldest plants with true seeds.

The order Filicales includes the true ferns. These possess well-developed vascular tissues and distinct roots, stems, and leaves. However, they reproduce by means of spores and have no flowers or true fruits. Large collections of fossil ferns lie in the Mazon Creek nodules of Illinois, as well as in most Carboniferous coal-associated shales. Collecting is especially productive along mine dumps or the spoil-banks of strip mines. The major genera found as common fossils are seed ferns of either *Pecopteris* or *Neuropteris.*

Calamites sp. and *Neuropteris* sp., Middle Pennsylvanian. *(Courtesy Joseph R. Kumichitis.)*

Division IV: Spermatophyta

This division includes all the plants with true cones and flowers. The subdivision Gymnospermae includes the modern conifers, ginkgoes, and cycads, as well as some very ancient extinct trees called cordaites, which lived during Devonian and Permian times. These trees were tall with large, strap-like leaves, and with the seeds born naked in open cones.

The ginkgoes (order Ginkgoales) are tall trees with primitive seeds born in pairs and broad, fern-like leaves. They appeared early in the Paleozoic and continue into the present.

The Cycadales include trees of ancient and modern types with short trunks, a palm-like crown, and seeds in large cones. The genus *Sequoia* of the order Coniferales, now famous for the massive redwoods, was very widespread in the Miocene.

The subclass Angiospermae includes the true flowering plants.

TRACE FOSSILS

The study of trace fossils (Ichnology, or Echnology) offers an extra challenge to the paleontological sleuth. In many cases the originator of traces is unknown in the living stage. "Ichnofossils" include ripple marks, raindrop imprints, feather imprints of Jurassic birds, chew marks on bone, both molluscan and annelid borings and burrows, scars of parasitism, sponge borings (*Cliona sp.*), paleopathological traces of illnesses on animal and fossil human remains, trilobite trails and nests, crawl or drag tracks of crustaceans (i.e. *Mesolimulus,* a fossil horseshoe crab), gastroliths, and coprolites (fecal pellets). For students of the vertebrates, tracks play an important part in taxonomic deduction by indicating size, stride, and width of the once-living creature. Possible identification may also be deduced from belly or tail drag marks, and from imprints of the skin, even when the actual skeletal remains of the animal may be unknown.

Several systematic determinations from such traces have located Triassic dinosaurs in New Jersey and the Connecticut

Valley. Fucoids and *Chondrites,* trace fossils previously assumed to have been plant remains, are known to be the burrows of worms which lived in the mud, similar to modern helminthoids which create feeding burrows in sediments today. A hundred years ago, Sir William Dawson identified organic growth in Pre-Cambrian rocks of Canada, which he identified as *Eozoon canadense,* but which, after many years of study and controversy, were definitely labeled inorganic.

Facies indicators are represented by trilobite furrows or genal spine grooves, and resting excavations are widesprad in the Lower Paleozoic sediments of Africa, North America, and Europe. In the ichnogenus *Cruziana* we have remains representative of furrowing traces made in the mud on the ocean floor and preserved by deposits of overlying beds of mud or sand. *Rusophycus* on the other hand, made by the identical trilobitomorph, is accepted as the trace remains of the trilobites resting excavation. *Rhizocorallumm,* a Jurassic trace fossil found in association with its fecal pellets, has been found both as a suspension-feeder and a deposit-feeder. Aside from the vast series of worm-track, trilobite-traces, and the miscellaneous assortment of other ichnofossils, ranging from the Pre-Cambrian through the Neocene, we find a number of exotic fossil forms which are not classified in the usual phyletic orders, as fossil pearls, which occur as blisterous growths on mollusc shells. Fossil pearls are not as rare as one might think, since they occur throughout the geological record in numerous formations from the Cretaceous to the Pleistocene. We have found examples of numerous fossil pearl blisters on shells of *Ostrea sculpturata* (Pliocene, Waccamaw formation of North Carolina). Peter Thorne of Vancouver, Canada, who has examined fossil pearls for many years reports their occurrence in marine deposits from Mongolia to North America. In Kansas, the Niobrara and Benton formations produce numerous pearls. (The Sternberg Memorial Museum in Hays, Kansas, has one of the finest fossil pearl displays in the country.) In Texas, *Exogyra costata* is one of the most common molluscan forms collected, with the largest number of pearls for the Texas Comanchean series.

Another unique "fossil" is the preserved blood cells in dinosaur bone. A number of dinosaur bones from the Jurassic of Utah has produced a remarkable series of preserved cell-type structures which might well be fossil blood-cells.

Mention has been made in Chapter 1 on the historical finds in the Gobi Desert of the fabulous nests of Cretaceous dinosaur eggs. During 1979, the news media reported the finding of several nesting sites in north-central Montana, which contained the well-preserved skeletons of young dinosaurs, and egg-nests containing over 40 eggs, these being 6 inches long and 4 inches wide. While dinosaur eggs have been known for many years from the Gobi and France, such a discovery in North America is extremely rare. The pioneer dinosaur hunters, Marsh, Cope and others, never mentioned finding eggs in their years of collecting.

Finally, we have fossils within fossils. Although not trace fossils in the literal sense, examples are the specimens of the Upper Cretaceous gastropod *Turritella*, which is found near Wamsutter, Wyoming. The chambers of this small spiral gastropod have been found to contain tightly packed masses of ostracods.

CHAPTER 4

A SHORT HISTORY OF LIFE ON EARTH

PALEOECOLOGY: FOSSILS AND THEIR NEIGHBORS

A fossil considered by itself, without reference to its immediate neighbors or its particular place on the evolutionary scale, is of little importance to the history of life on earth. Some preferred moist areas, some dry; others lived in water, while some lived in caves or crevices. Some were carnivores and ate meat that was freshly killed; others were scavengers of meat that had been dead for some time. Still others were plant-eaters. Some, like wolves and wild dogs, ran down other creatures in packs, while others, like the big cats, would spring on the plant-eaters from hiding. Each showed its adaptation to where it lived and what it did by the shape of its bones or other remains, even as living animals today show what they are by the shape of body, head and teeth. The study of such adaptations to environment is called ecology, while paleoecology is the study of ancient environments.

When we study fossils, we should try to imagine and interpret from their shapes how these animals or plants adapted to life in certain environments and in association with other living things. This makes the study of fossils even more interesting, like studying a puzzle and learning the keys to solve its mystery.

To gain significance beyond its own fascination, each specimen must be considered as an integral part of an ecological scheme which tied all forms of life together in what paleontologists call an "environmental net."

The environmental net is a concept of the interaction of a particular organism, or of many organisms, with their environment. Fossil specimens, together with data on their location, association with other fossil forms, and with environmental indicators such as matrix type (siltstone, sandstone, conglomerate, etc.) are considered together as parts of a "geological universe." By gathering all the information possible from a particular stratigraphic zone, the paleontologist can quite accurately infer the paleoecology of a fossil animal or plant population.

A classic example of an environmental net is the coral reef, a vital community of interrelated species. It is dominated by the corals and the calcareous algaes which build up huge wave-resistant skeletal accumulations. Also dominant, in a different way, are the fish which are adapted to eating the living coral polyps. Sharks become important in this net because they feed upon the smaller fish. Crinoids, too, live on this reef, as do the molluscs and brachiopods, and a myriad of other forms of plants and animals. To understand each of the fossil forms found in association with this reef, the paleontologist must understand the dynamics of the entire reef community.

Here is an example of this kind of analysis. In a recent collecting trip to New Mexico, a series of reptile and amphibian trackways were found in an outcrop of Permian sandstone. On that same sandstone, ripple marks were found superimposed with raindrop impressions. In some cases, the trackways could be followed across the remains of conifer and fern fronds. Interpreting this ecological net is simple: The scene took place in a dry, desert area. (We know this because the lithology of the rock indicated it was oxidized by desert conditions.) There was some water, enough at least to produce shallow pools, or perhaps it was a shoreline where the desert came down to the sea. (This is suggested by the ripple marks.) We know the water was intermittent (because the mud had to dry to preserve each layer of fossils), and we know that it rained. Several different sized tracks show that there was a diverse population of vertebrates. The conifer and fern fossils indicate at least some vegetable ground cover and numerous large, primitive pine trees. Much more about the paleoecology can be inferred, but this would be based on what the paleontologist had observed in modern situations, and from what has been found in related paleoecological situations.

Trilobites, sea scorpions, or eurypterids found together in fossil form in the same rock, with the latter much less numerous, would indicate that the eurypterids were probably hunting the trilobites, which they seized with their pincers to break open the outer armor to get at the soft inside. This would be especially clear if we found a trilobite fossil showing signs of being so broken.

Insects trapped in pine sap that has hardened into clear amber tell another tale. The insects lived in a coniferous forest, which had a fairly cool or temperate climate, as conifers rarely dwell in hot country. If the fossil insects are beetles or their larvae with fairly powerful jaws, they were probably pine borers that lived under the bark and bored into the living tree. If they are ants, we know they probably climbed the trees hunting for smaller insects to catch and eat.

This sort of mental game makes collecting fossils even more interesting, and more educational.

GEOLOGIC TIME AND STRATIGRAPHY

It seems odd to paleontologists that for many people the word "fossil" brings to mind only the notion of a dry, lifeless, and very complex science. True, paleontology is complex, but it is far from lifeless. It studies a part of the earth's history which is far less abstract than the physics of this planet's earliest origins, or the chemistry of what scientists believe to be the preludes to life.

Paleontology is a biological science tied to a geologic counterpart. To discuss fossils, and to understand them in the context of the geologic ages in which they lived, it becomes necessary to understand the *geologic column* and the *geologic time scale*.

The *geologic column* is to the geologist what a sequence of pages is to a writer. Just as pages of a story progress logically from the earliest events to the climax, so do sedimentary rocks deposited on the earth's surface. The geologic column includes rocks from the early Pre-Cambrian period to the Pleistocene. Geologists rely on previously determined geologic columns and the *index fossils* (fossils specific to one and only one age) to determine what age they are exploring in the rocks.

The *geologic time scale* is made up of a sequence of arbitrarily named time units which coincide with the rock units of the geologic column, and represent the various ages of the earth's history. The time scale, worked out through various physical dating methods, is an invaluable tool for paleontologists who must communicate their research; but because of the scale's artificial nature and because the science of geologic dating is constantly being refined, there exists no single published time scale which is precisely correct.

The largest unit of geologic time is called an *era.* Each era is divided into *periods,* and each period into *epochs.* Each of these units represents a change in life forms from those of the preceding unit, and each has been given a name which describes its characteristic stage of biological development. For example, Paleozoic means *ancient life,* a name describing the simple and ancient stage of development of life forms in that era.

Each time unit derives its name from the geographical area in which it was *first* studied. For instance, here are some Paleozoic examples: Cambrian—from the Cambria region of England; Pennsylvanian—from the state of Pennsylvania.

The smallest units are called *formations.* Formations are rock layers which generally share common environments of deposition, are relatively contemporaneous in age, and are similar in mineral content. Some examples of formations are the Santa Fe formation of New Mexico, the Redwall limestone of Arizona (named from its characteristic red, cliff-forming sandstone), and the Green River shale of Wyoming.

Boundaries exist between divisions of the geologic time scale not only because of paleontological differences, but also because of changes in geology. Limits to the usefulness of this scale become obvious when we see that geologic events were not taking place simultaneously all over the world, and that animals may have evolved at different rates in different places.

Fossil forms found on the boundaries between time periods often have characteristics of animals in both units; this occasionally causes some confusion. However, for the sake of

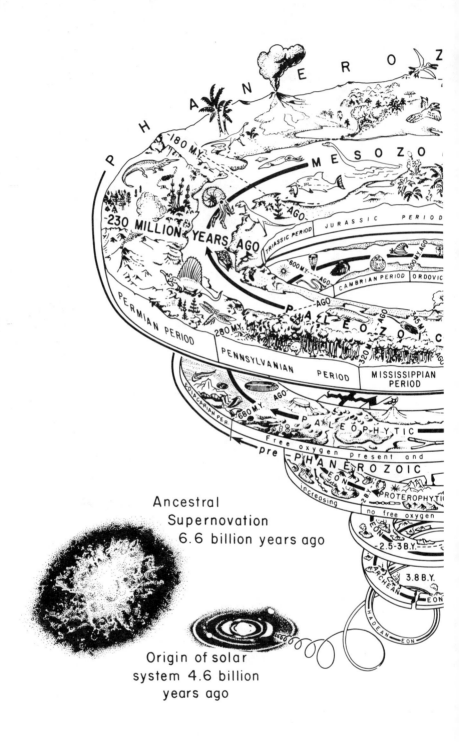

Ancestral
Supernovation
6.6 billion years ago

Origin of solar
system 4.6 billion
years ago

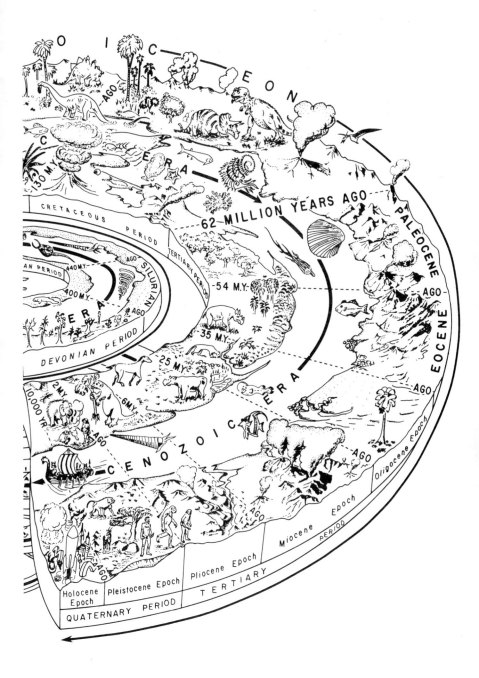

Capsule view of our earth's geological history. *(Courtesy of U.S. Geological Survey, Department of Interior.)*

ERA	YEARS AGO	PERIOD		EPOCH	CHARACTERIZED BY
Archeozoic	5,000,000,000-1,500,000,000				earth's crust formed; unicellular organisms; earliest known life
Proterozoic	1,500,000,000-600,000,000				bacteria, algae, and fungi; primitive multicellular organisms
Paleozoic	600,000,000-500,000,000	Cambrian			marine invertebrates
	500,000,000-440,000,000	Ordovician			conodonts, ostracods, algae, and seaweeds
	440,000,000-400,000,000	Silurian			air-breathing animals
	400,000,000-350,000,000	Devonian			dominance of fishes; advent of amphibians and ammonites
	350,000,000-300,000,000	Mississippian	Carboniferous		increase of land areas; primitive ammonites; development of winged insects
	300,000,000-270,000,000	Pennsylvanian	Carboniferous		warm climates; swampy lands; development of large reptiles and insects
	270,000,000-220,000,000	Permian			many reptiles
Mesozoic	220,000,000-180,000,000	Triassic			volcanic activity; marine reptiles, dinosaurs
	180,000,000-135,000,000	Jurassic			dinosaurs, conifers
	135,000,000-70,000,000	Cretaceous			extinction of giant reptiles; advent of modern insects; flowering plants
Cenozoic	70,000,000-60,000,000	Paleogene	Tertiary	Paleocene	advent of birds, mammals
	60,000,000-40,000,000	Paleogene	Tertiary	Eocene	presence of modern mammals
	40,000,000-25,000,000	Paleogene	Tertiary	Oligocene	sabertoothed cats
	25,000,000-10,000,000	Neogene	Tertiary	Miocene	grazing mammals
	10,000,000-1,000,000	Neogene	Tertiary	Pliocene	growth of mountains; increase in size and numbers of mammals; gradual cooling of climate
	1,000,000-10,000	Quaternary		Pleistocene	widespread glacial ice
	10,000-present	Quaternary		Recent	development of man

Geological Time Chart. *(Reprinted by permission from* The Random House Dictionary of the English Language, *the unabridged edition, copyrighted by Random House, Inc., 1967.)*

convenience, paleontologists have retained this system of time and rock classification and must work around the problems of its artificial nature.

A SHORT HISTORY OF LIFE ON EARTH

The earth is a very old and restless planet, and has gone through many physical changes during its existence. Likewise, life in general has been restless, not content to remain stagnant. Or more accurately, life was forced to change along with the earth. Life had to evolve to cope with environmental conditions unsuitable for particular forms of life. All in all, very few species survived the ravages of time and change. Those that could not adapt were doomed to eventual extinction.

Archaeozoic Era
(4500 to 1500 Million Years Ago)

Geology & Climate

The Archaeozoic Era saw the newly cooled surface of the earth become greatly contorted and metamorphosed. Later in the Archaeozoic, the earth was a lifeless collection of barren mountains, deserts, and abundant, active volcanoes. The rivers and seas formed by condensation of volcanic steam. Many cycles of mountain building and erosion took place during this primitive stage of the earth. Thus, it was during this time that the first soils developed.

Life Record

Most important for our subject, the combination of inorganic elements to form organic molecules took place in the ancient, fiery seas as a prelude to the first simple forms of life. It is possible that this era saw the development of the earth's first cellular life. Archaeozoic microfossils found by electron microscopy in South African chert formations are the oldest known fossils. According to radioactive dating, they are 3.4 billion years old. Life, then, has been around for a very long time!

Proterozoic Era
(1500 to 550 Million Years Ago)

Geology & Climate

What is called the *Laurentian Revolution* occurred during this era, when shrinkage of the earth's crust caused much tension, twisting of the rocks, and mountain building. Ancient metamorphic rocks were formed by the great pressures and heat, which also destroyed much of the Proterozoic fossil record. But there were also long periods of quiet erosion and the formation of warm seas where life could grow.

Life Record

This era of "first life" set the stage for later, more complex forms to develop. Fully-developed, multicellular forms of plants and animals arose from the earlier formless, cellular slime of the Archaeozoic. Although complex, these early marine organisms did not have any hard parts to become fossils themselves. However, nature was on the paleontologists' side, for there is an abundant record of trackways, imprints, burrows, and calcareous algal reefs to indicate a very abundant and diversified ecological situation. The blue-green algae of the primitive oceans secreted immense lime reefs, which later solidified into rocks, usually of dolomitic type such as is found in the Pre-Cambrian shield that covers so much of northern Canada.

To date, geologists have collected rocks containing these very primitive organisms from such diverse regions as Australia, 3.4 billion years old; South Africa, 3.2 billion years old; Greenland, now credited with containing the oldest bacteria-like organisms, 3.8 billion years old, on our planet. These ancient micro-organisms indicate that some of the ingredients necessary for bacterial growth, such as hydrocarbons, were already covering the older sediments and rocks.

Paleozoic Era
Cambrian Period (550 to 480 Million Years Ago)

The Cambrian Period is of great significance to paleontologists, who date everything since as Post-Cambrian, and everything before as Pre-Cambrian. This is the first period of geologic history in which the fossil record is abundant and well-preserved. Animals by this time had developed hard parts: shells and chitinous exoskeletons.

Geology & Climate

At the beginning of this period there was some mountain building, but most of the period was a long quiet time of erosion, during part of which time the sea spread widely over North America. The climate was probably tropical.

Animal Life

This period brought into existence a considerable variety of invertebrate animals, of which the trilobites and brachiopods became the dominant forms. Foraminifera (one-celled animals with calcareous shells), sponges, worms, and other primitive types swarmed in the seas. The trilobites were especially numerous, making up more than 60 percent of the total animal population. No record exists of any vertebrates during this period, but their time was soon (geologically speaking) to come.

Plant Life

The only plant life that left a record during the Cambrian were the algae, which reached their highest development in various kinds of seaweed.

Ordovician Period (480 to 420 Million Years Ago)

Invertebrates became very numerous and varied during the Ordovician Period, but still, it was the trilobite, in its now abundant varieties, that was still dominant.

Geology & Climate

The Ordovician was a very long geologic period, and it was a time of great marine flooding. The sea advanced far over North America, but as it withdrew toward the end of the period, the Taconic Mountains were built up in the eastern part of the continent. For a time the ancient seas retreated and sea floors became dry land. The climate is thought to have been warm and tropical.

Animal Life

As this was a stressful period for organisms, changes occurred rapidly in the biological communities. Many forms arose to fill the many available ecological niches. In shallow waters were found sponges (*Receptaculites*), while the first corals grew in colonies attached to the sea floor. Several forms of echinoderms, including the crinoids, cystoids and a few rare, true starfish and blastoids appeared. The bryozoans came into their own with great numbers of species in divergent shapes and sizes. The molluscs were developing, with the cephalopods becoming numerous and dominant, ranging in size from the giant *Endoceras,* with shells

Life during the Ordovician Period. Courtesy Smithsonian Institute.

fifteen feet long, to tiny coiled nautaloids no larger than a dime. Gastropods and bivalves were also present, but few in numbers. The first vertebrates were represented in this period by the bony, armor-plated fish known as Ostracoderms, relatives to the modern lamprey eels or hagfish.

Plant Life

Plants remained as simple seaweeds and other algaes.

Silurian Period (420 to 395 Million Years Ago)

Geology & Climate

The Silurian was a relatively short geologic period, lasting somewhat over 20 million years. During this period, the great Taconic Mountains eroded and many new land areas were slowly formed by the addition of erosional silts. It was a period of reduced volcanic activity in the East. Deserts began to appear, especially in the East, with continued alternation of low lands with shallow seas. A mild climate extended to the poles. In the eastern part of the continent, sea invasions were especially common during middle Silurian times. Most of North America was comparatively flat during this period.

Animal Life

Many of the seas were of clear water where conditions favored the prolific growth of such lime-secreting organisms as algae, corals, bryozoans, and brachiopods (including spine-bearing kinds). These were so abundant and prolific that they grew into vast reefs along the sea floor. In the shallower waters where the sea bed was sandy or calcareous there were abundant trilobites (many now ornamented with protective spines) and metoporoids, the hydroid corals. The most common echinoderms in the Silurian seas were the stalked crinoids, or sea lilies, as well as numerous species of cystoids. Starfish, brittlestars, blastoids and the now extinct edrioasteroids (cushion stars) were not so common. Large sea scorpions (eurypterids), which were remotely related to land

Life during the Silurian Period. Scorpion-like eurypterid in forefront. *(Courtesy Smithsonian Institute.)*

scorpions, appeared in estuaries and coastal lagoons, where they ferociously hunted smaller animals such as the trilobites. Some giants reached a length of nine feet. Such animals were the largest of that time. It is believed that the early vertebrates, the armored fish, developed their unusual protection as a defense against these sea-going giants of the invertebrate world. Scorpions and millipedes of the Silurian Period may have been the first air-breathing animals.

One of the most primitive vertebrates was the fish-like *Jamoytius,* similar to the modern *Amphioxus* or lancelet. Ostracoderm fish, with body-plated bodies and a cartilaginous skeleton, became more common in this period. There were yet to be terrestrial vertebrates.

Plant Life

The first known land plants appeared in this period, and were the lycopsids (a kind of club moss) in Australia.

Devonian Period (395 to 345 Million Years Ago)

Geology & Climate

During the 50 million years of the Devonian Period, the sea again advanced over almost half of North America. It gradually withdrew as volcanic action and folding of the earth's crust pushed up the Acadian Mountains in the eastern part of the continent. This was a period of heavy seasonal rains and a warm, tropical climate. Tremendous sandstone deposits were made due to the large-scale erosion of the newly formed mountains. There was a probable land bridge from North America to Europe.

Animal Life

Among the invertebrates appeared new types of animals, including air-breathing forms such as mites, spiders, and wingless insects. Freshwater mussels have been collected in Upper Devonian rocks of New York State. Reef-building corals, stromatoporoids (hydroid corals), clams, and brachiopods developed abundantly. The early ammonites developed with closely-coiled, nautaloid shells and a septum (wall between cavities),

Life during the Devonian Period. Trilobites and corals were the predominant forms. *(Courtesy American Museum of Natural History, New York.)*

which proved a new element among the invertebrates. The graptolites (primitive colonial animals related to the hydroids and corals) had almost disappeared while the crinoids (sea lilies) were now flourishing and continued in even greater abundance and variety. Trilobites still existed during this period, but were rapidly declining in numbers, probably because of competition from more advanced forms such as the vertebrates.

One remarkable feature in the Devonian was the rapid evolution and spread of the vertebrates. The heavily-armored Ostracoderm fishes were numerous, but there now appeared large sharks and the bony fishes. One fish (*Osteolepis,* a corssopterygian) possessed a body covered with scales, while a later fish of this same order (*Eusthenopteron*) could breathe air, had stout fins with which it could move on land, and had conical teeth with much infolding of the enamel. All of these characteristics showed an animal that was in transition from true fish to amphibian. Such a fish could crawl from one shallow river to another, giving it an evolutionary advantage. Toward the end of the Devonian, clumsy, salamander-like amphibians appeared.

Plant Life

During the Devonian, we find evidence of rapid development of land plants, primarily the seed ferns, "scale trees" (lycopods), and true ferns. This period saw for the first time extensive forests spreading over the land. Some of the giant scale trees were even two feet thick through the trunk. Also during this period, the Angiosperms, or seed plants, first appeared.

Mississippian Period (345 to 320 Million Years Ago)

In Europe, the Mississippian Period is not recognized as a separate geological period, but rather it has been combined with the Pennsylvanian Period to form a larger unit of time known as the Carboniferous Period. However, in North America, the ages are still considered separate and their treatment is such here.

Geology & Climate

During the Mississippian, there were widespread tectonics,

movements of the earth's crust. The Acadian Mountains continued to rise, as did mountains in Colorado, Oklahoma, and Idaho, while the sea swept again and again over much of the rest of North America. The eastern swamps laid down coal beds, and the shallow seas deposited considerable limestone. The humid, tropical climate greatly encouraged plant growth.

Animal Life

Great, warm-water invertebrate colonies grew in the shallow seas. Foraminifera (single-celled animals with calcareous shells) became very numerous. Reefs were built by large populations of brachiopods, molluscs, and bryozoans. Corals and trilobites, however, were slowly disappearing from the scene. Crinoids, blastoids, various other echinoderms, and the sharks dominated the seas, as the various cephalopods lost out somewhat in the struggle for existence. The sharks were generally of blunt-toothed, shell-crushing types and must have been responsible for destroying many trilobites.

The brachiopods were especially numerous, and a majority of the forms developed distinctive spines. These were the productid brachiopods. Characteristic index fossils of the period were *Archimedes,* the "corkscrew" form of Bryozoa and *Pentremites,* the blastoid form familiar to most beginning fossil collectors.

Early fishes were abundant, though the armored ostracoderms disappeared. Their successors were the heavily scaled and modern-looking paleoniscoids. On the land, amphibians were still progressing, as is shown by their fossilized skulls, skeletons, and footprints. During the Mississippian they were all small creatures with a stride no longer than 12 inches. Insects dominated the air, appearing in great variety and reaching a greater size than ever before or since in history, including gigantic cockroaches and dragonflies. There were also numerous spiders, land scorpions, and centipedes.

Plant Life

The scale trees (lycopods), ferns and seed ferns were dominant in the Mississippian swamps, while in the sea the lime-secreting seaweeds were building atoll-like reefs.

Pennsylvanian Period (320 to 265 Million Years Ago)

Geology & Climate

One of the most fascinating of the geologic ages was the Pennsylvanian, when the Mississippian seas were gradually lifted to form vast wetlands. During much of the period, North America became a broad, low-lying region of tropical, swampy, coal-producing forests, dominated by the plants and the insects.

Animal Life

During the Pennsylvanian, the amphibians continued their rapid development, some reaching ten feet in length and a weight of more than five hundred pounds. These were sprawling creatures (the labyrinthodonts) with splayed legs, webbed feet, and sharp, widely-spaced teeth. With a tremendous population of giant cockroaches, dragonflies, and other insects, the massive fern swamps of this period would have made a terrible home for man.

The tropical seas of the Pennsylvanian encouraged the continuing explosion of the invertebrate populations, which are represented today in Pennsylvanian deposits that provide some of the most prolific fossil collecting areas in North America.

Reconstruction of Coal-Age forest during the Carboniferous Period (Mississippian-Pennsylvanian). *(Courtesy Field Museum of Natural History, Chicago.)*

But the most exciting event in the Pennsylvanian fossil record was the appearance of the first true reptile.

Plant Life

❧ Typical of the swamp plants of the time were tree ferns, seed ferns, scale trees, giant rushes, and conifers. It was these plants, in their great abundance, which produced much of this nation's massive coal reserves.

Permian Period (265 to 215 Million Years Ago)

Geology & Climate

The Permian was a period of crisis for life on earth, as the climate became colder and drier. Along with much volcanic activity, there was world-wide glaciation, and extensive mountain building, including the Appalachian Mountains in eastern North America. Red rock beds show times when deserts had spread widely, alternating with invasions, of our western lowlands, by the sea. The greatest and most catastrophic climatic changes occurred toward the end of the Permian.

Exposures of Permian rocks in the eastern United States are rare, but rocks of this age in the American West are abundant and provide us with some of the most wondrous natural scenery available anywhere.

These rocks also provide the paleontologist with some of the most remarkable fossils to be found, especially the vertebrate fauna preserved in New Mexico, Texas, and Oklahoma.

Animal Life

Considerable evolutionary changes were in progress on land. A great variety of reptiles, better adapted to the drying climate than the amphibians, began to appear. The majority lived on land, but some were partly aquatic. Most were small, clumsy, waddling creatures, though a few began to develop running agility. The largest grew to be ten feet or more. Some developed beaked jaws, generally living on plants, though a number evolved spiked teeth for flesh-eating. Of special interest are the fin-backed pelycosaurs of Texas, which wore long, flat rows of spines connected by skin, rising like a snail from their backbones. Most advanced were the mammal-like reptiles, the therapsids, with teeth becoming differentiated into canines, incisors, and molars. It is probably from these that the mammals evolved.

During the Permian, insects became smaller in general, and the modern orders began to appear. Conspicuous among these were the true bugs, the cicadas and beetles, the latter with four stages of life. Many were trapped and fossilized in falling ash.

Marine faunas were richest in the shallow seas that remained connected with the oceans. Globular or spindle-shaped Foraminifera (fusulinids) lived so abundantly in these seas that some Permian limestones are entirely composed of their shells. Among the new brachiopods were the highly specialized, spiny productids (which are almost a sure sign of Permian rock beds), and the cup-coral-like *Richthofenia*. The fusulinids and the productids, as well as the rugose corals, the fenestellids (lacy types or bryozoans or moss animals), and the trilobites, which had been so abundant in earlier periods, gradually became extinct with the closing of Permian times.

Plant Life

The swamp-dwelling trees and plants of the Pennsylvanian Period began to die out in the early Permian as arid conditions prevailed. By late Permian, the huge scale trees were all but extinct, as were the cordaites and giant ferns. The true coniferous trees began to take their places, as well as primitive cycadeoids (allies of the modern sago palm). Of the older kinds of trees that lived successfully through most of the period, the *Lepidodendron* (slender scale trees) were the most in evidence.

Mesozoic Era
Triassic Period (215 to 175 Million Years Ago)

Geology & Climate

Much of North America was desert during the 40 million years of this period, as shown by the red oxidized sandstones which make up New Mexico's and Arizona's magnificent scenery. There was considerable volcanic activity, especially in the Northeast. The climate became more arid, with some parts turning into plains covered by dunes and shifting sands. Numbers of temporary lakes or salt pools formed local oases and coal-forming swamps. As it was a transition time between the Paleozoic and the Mesozoic, so too were life forms in transition.

Animal Life

The Triassic Period was the first period in the *Age of Reptiles,* for it was then that reptiles became dominant over all other land animals, being evolutionarily advanced enough to rapidly squeeze out the once dominant labyrinthodont amphibians.

The opening of the Mesozoic Era by the Triassic Period saw the appearance of many new groups of marine life. Invertebrates continued to develop, losing some groups and evolving other new ones. The corals developed a new type, the hexacorals, which still exist today. The brachiopods continued abundantly at first, as new kinds, the rhynchonellids and the terebratullids, appeared and flourished, only to diminish later at the end of the period. Clams and oysters became numerous and larger than ever before. Among the cephalopods, the ammonites continued in abundance, increasing in size and developing shells with marginally-frilled partitions. However, most forms of ammonites died out near the end of the period, probably due to attacks by the new marine reptiles. Extinct relatives of the cuttlefish, the bullet-like belemnoids, flourished.

Arthropods evolved the first lobster-like crustaceans. Sea urchins and starfish were clearly becoming related to more recent types. The first carnivorous fish-shaped reptile, the icthyosaur, appeared, and became adapted to life in the open oceans. Later came the thick-bodied, slender-necked plesiosaur, catching fish by surprise rather than by speed.

Plant Life

Plants were no longer dominated by the ferns, rather it was the conifers which rapidly gained a foothold and spread worldwide. Not many fossil plants are preserved from this period. Ferns, scouring rushes and cycadeoids were found along streams and in swamps (as petrified leaves show in Virginia and the Carolinas), while conifers dominated the uplands along with cycads. Ancient logs at Petrified Forest, Arizona, show fossils of many primitive conifers from this period.

Jurassic Period (175 to 135 Million Years Ago)

Geology & Climate

Eastern North America was gradually eroded during the Jurassic. The area now occupied by the mighty Rocky Mountains was during this period a long seaway tonguing up from Mexico and down from Canada. This deluge was followed eventually by the beginning of the Sierra Nevada uplift. The climate was generally mild, even sub-tropical over wide areas, more humid, producing fewer desert areas than the Triassic.

Animal Life

Along the shores of the western inland seaway, low-lying swamplands harbored a fantastic animal population, the most exceptional members being, of course, the two mighty orders of dinosaurs, the saurischians, including most of the carnivorous forms, and the ornithischians, the plant-eaters. The slow and clumsy amphibians of earlier times were probably killed off by the more aggressive reptiles, but smaller, quicker amphibians, such as frogs and toads, began to appear. Crocodiles and turtles also developed large populations.

Flying reptiles, the pterosaurs, became abundant during this period, having evolved from very primitive forms of the Triassic. Marine reptiles, such as the ichthyosaurs and pleisiosaurs became common in Jurassic seas.

Of primary importance in this period was the development of the first known birds. The European form *Archaeopteryx* is the best known. Bird fossils from the Upper Jurassic have been found in the Morrison formation of Wyoming at Como Bluff.

Mammals, primitive rat-like forms, were lurking just offstage in the drama of Mesozoic life. Such Jurassic forms as the multituberculates (rodent-like Mesozoic animals), condylarths (an extinct mammal order which includes the earliest herbivorous mammals), and tricondonts (an order of Mesozoic mammals, with triple-cone teeth), were eventually to give rise to advance mammals of the Early Cenozoic.

Seas were ripe with invertebrates during the Jurassic. Bivalves, foraminifers, corals, and gastropods were among the many groups to continue from earlier periods. The hexacorals that had started in the Triassic were now abundant, some appearing as simple cup corals, while others were compound. These later grew in such profusion that they formed reefs, usually with numerous associated molluscs.

Crinoids (sea lilies) then, as today, liked to live together in large groups. Some were stalkless and free-swimming, while others were rooted to the sea bottom. Sea urchins were abundant in Europe and Asia, though less common in North America. Ancestral crabs appeared for the first time, while arachnids, of spider and scorpion types, inhabited the shallow waters of Germany, France, and portions of the Middle East.

Primitive bony fishes, some with thick, enamel-coated scales, were much in evidence, along with sharks and skates. The dominant animals in the seas, however, were the aquatic reptiles, which preyed on the fishes and cephalopods.

Insect life included grasshoppers, beetles, dragonflies and termites, as well as the earliest known moths, flies, saw-flies and ants. The freshwater snails were so abundant that they sometimes formed thick limestone or marble beds, most seen in England.

Plant Life

The plants of this period were varied and abundant, with forests consisting of primitive conifers, cycadeoids, cycads, tree ferns, and maidenhair trees (our living ginkgo is a representative of this group). The Jurassic is called the "Age of Cycads" since true flowering plants had not yet appeared, although some of the cycadeoids bore flower-like cones.

Cretaceous Period (135 to 70 Million Years Ago)

Geology & Climate

The Cretaceous was the third and last period in the Mesozoic Era. During the early part of this period, the final great continental submergence took place before the rise of the Rocky Mountains. The mountainous uplift, called by geologists the *Laramide Revolution,* may have been responsible for the extinction of many of the great reptilian orders at the close of the Cretaceous, for it was not just a local geological event, but one of world-wide significance. Climates were altered to such an extent as to affect almost all life. Mighty seaways were drained, setting off a chain reaction of extinctions.

The Early Cretaceous sea over much of North America laid down great chalk, coal, and sandstone formations, although the Sierra Nevada Mountains continued to rise. Clays and sand accumulated also in deltas, swampy plains, lakes, and estuaries. A mild climate appears to have prevailed even far to the north, with some coal-forming swamps still in existence along with subtropical areas.

A general lifting of western plateaus, while the seas retreated southward, accompanied the rise of the Rockies and Sierras. The climate gradually became a little colder, especially in the West, though over vast areas it remained comparatively mild. In the East there was a new rising of the Appalachians. On the Pacific Coast the great island of Cascadia poured rivers into shallow seas where now is dry land.

Animal Life

In the warm, shallow seas, invertebrate evolution saw the arrival of nearly all the modern orders, with molluscs dominant, especially the bivalves, gastropods, and ammonites. The extensive faunal deposits of the vast shallow seas that covered portions of Oklahoma, Texas, and Mexico during the Lower Cretaceous, contain rich beds of echinoids, bivalves, and gigantic ammonites. Reefs of rudistids (clams with lid-like shells) became prominent, as well as huge mile-long reefs of two-valved shellfish.

There are vast foraminiferal zones (of tiny, calcareous, one-celled animals) which contain fossils of the regular echinoderms (starfish and their relatives), and equally large limestone deposits containing irregular echinoderms. Some echinoid forms, like the *Macraster* (a heart-shaped sea urchin) reached massive proportions.

The brachiopods were fading out, with fossils found only in a few North American localities, such as the deposits near Tombstone, Arizona. The bivalves (clams, scallops, etc.) began to assume strange shapes and take more massive sizes. Some forms, like *Exogyra*, had a spiral shape like a ram's horn, while others, like *Gryphea*, became extremely large.

The largest and most abundant marine fossils were the ammonites, which are often used as index fossils in classifying periods in the rocks. While mostly of the coiled type, during the Middle Cretaceous they became straight (as in *Baculites*) or became partly coiled (as in *Acanthoscaphites*). By the end of the Upper Cretaceous they and the squid-like belemnites became extinct.

Crabs, lobsters, and floating crinoids (sea lilies) were common among the muddy sea beds of America, while in Europe they inhabited mainly the chalky sea beds. The rare present-day lungfish, the *Latimeria*, probably had its early ancestry in the Cretaceous along with the coelacanth fish (*Macropora*). Coelacanths were thought to be completely extinct until a remarkable example of this ancient family was captured in 1938 off the coast of Madagascar.

Mosasaurs (scaled marine reptiles that could extend their mouths as the snakes do to swallow large animals) soon took the place of the icthyosaurs of the Jurassic, but the long-necked and clumsy plesiosaurs were still numerous. Both preyed on the abundant bony fishes, similar to our present-day rays, sharks, herrings, and others. The immense turtle, *Archelon*, grew to as much as eleven feet in diameter.

Dinosaurs continued to dominate among land animals of the Cretaceous, in such monstrous forms as *Triceratops,*

Tyrannosaurus, Trachodon, and *Ankylosaurus. Tyrannosaurus* was the most terrible of the flesh-eaters, with a height of nearly 20 feet and a length of about 40 feet, as well as six-inch teeth and powerful claws. *Triceratops* (three-horned) and *Trachodon* were among the immense plant-eaters.

Mammals were inconspicuous, but marsupials and insectivores had both appeared. They were primitive woodland creatures, no bigger than rats. Their teeth were adapted for feeding on insects and fruits, but some may have eaten reptile eggs.

Reptiles also adapted well to flight in this period. What a sight it must have been to see a pterosaur, such as *Pteranodon,* which may have had a wingspread of over fifty feet, gliding silently over the shallow seas of what is now Kansas and Texas.

Pterodactyls, with a wingspan of 20 feet or more, inhabited the coastal cliffs, since their hollow, thin-walled bones and general body shape made it best for them to launch themselves into flight from high places. The Niobrara chalk beds of Kansas have produced numerous pterodactyl fossils, as well as fossil mosasaurs, gigantic fishes, and other forms of marine vertebrates. The early true bird, *Hesperornis,* was a powerful swimmer and diver of these times that caught its fishy prey with long-toothed jaws.

The end of the Cretaceous was marked by what has been called the "great dying." Of the millions upon millions of dinosaurs which must have lived during the Mesozoic, none survived (unless, however, you happen to subscribe to the latest theories that birds are, indeed, the true descendants of the dinosaurs).

The ammonites and some other important invertebrates also began to disappear. A change of climate, due to the Laramide Revolution, may well have caused this decline, but there is a good likelihood that competition from more advanced animals (such as the eating of dinosaur eggs by mammals) contributed as well.

Plant Life

Cycads, conifers, and ferns were still the dominant plants during the Early Cretaceous. In the middle of the period, the higher, flowering plants, the angiosperms, began to appear, until, by the end of the Cretaceous, vegetation was essentially modern. The flowers and fruits brought a vast new food supply to many animals.

Cenozoic Era
Paleocene and Eocene Epochs (70 to 35 Million Years Ago)

The division of geological time which comprises the Paleocene, Eocene, Oligocene, Miocene and Pliocene, are grouped within the Tertiary Period of the Cenozoic, whereas the Pleistocene, the last epoch of time on our geologic time chart, is placed within the Quaternary Period.

Geology & Climate

At the beginning of the Palaeocene the sea floors were raised in many parts of the world. The Rockies continued to grow in height. Volcanoes were active in western North America, and there was continual erosion of the mountains. During the Eocene shallow seas were widespread in the center of the continent and along the Pacific Coast. Tropical conditions reached north to the middle states.

Animal Life

During the Early Cenozoic Era, through the Paleocene and Eocene epochs, animal life, especially the vertebrates, began its long road toward biological modernization. The great inland seas had all but vanished, yet the Rocky Mountains in the West had not uplifted to any great extent. The dinosaurs were universally gone from the planet. With the ecological niches "open up for grabs," evolution of the mammals began with unprecedented speed and variation, fostering the Age of Mammals.

Mammals in the Paleocene at first were small, tiny-brained, and generalized in attributes, like the modern hedgehog or rats. Gradually, especially in the Eocene Epoch, mammals grew larger. As they became more specialized, they dominated the land, with all the modern orders appearing, such as rodents, carnivores, primates, etc. What are called "archaic mammals," including some remnants of the Paleocene and the giant, horned uintatheres, survived well into the Eocene.

In many places the ancestors of the elephants, camels, rhinoceroses, horses, cows, and pigs began to appear. All were unspecialized and much smaller than their descendants. The elephants, as a good example, evolved from a pig-sized brute of North Africa and migrated to America. The horse, on the other hand, whose earliest fossils are found in New Mexico and Wyoming, found its way to Europe and Asia, probably meeting the elephants along the same route. This early horse, *Eohippus* or "dawn horse," was no bigger than a fox terrier. Its front feet had four toes, suited to marshy ground, and it was equipped with tiny teeth for forest browsing. The creodonts, or ancestors of the modern carnivores, lived upon the plant-eaters, although they were even more primitive in character, being small-brained and reptile-like.

The toothed birds of the Late Cretaceous had died out, but an equally strange bird, the huge flightless *Diatryma,* roamed in New Mexico and Wyoming. It was the terror of the land, probably feeding on the abundant small-mammal populations.

Florida and California both have extensive Eocene faunal deposits, usually well-preserved in limestone beds. Commonly found within these formations are two unusual groups of fossil mammals which roamed the Eocene seas, the early carnivorous whales (*Zeuglodon*), and the sea cows (*Sirenia*) which fed, and feed today, on seaweed. Among reptiles that survived the "great dying" of the Cretaceous, crocodiles and turtles flourished in the warm lakes and rivers of the Early Cenozoic. These and other herbivores (plant-eaters) are easily identified in their fossil form by their teeth, which were formed in cutting folds with distinctive patterns for each kind.

Commonly thought of for their distinctive vertebrate fossils, these Early Cenozoic periods were also rich with many invertebrate forms. Among them were the *Nummulites* of the class Foraminifera, with their round, flat, calcareous skeletons. Countless millions of their tiny fossil shells built a majority of the limestone in many areas, including that used to form the blocks of the Great Pyramid of Gizeh in Egypt.

Plant Life

Plants of the Early Cenozoic were essentially modern, with many palms, laurels, and magnolias ranging from the southernmost states to the Canadian border and even into southeastern Alaska. The giant redwoods, now confined to the middle Pacific Coast, were widespread.

Oligocene Epoch (35 to 25 Million Years Ago)

Geology & Climate

Uplift of the land continued, while the early Rockies were being rounded down. Asia touched America during this period at Alaska. Volcanoes were active in the West, while much sediment was deposited along the east coast. A warm climate reached far northward.

Animal Life

Perhaps best known for the White River fauna of the Dakota Badlands, the Oligocene was a time of great animal migration into North America over the great land bridge between Asia and Alaska.

The Oligocene was the first epoch in which vast, open grasslands were available to the mammals, that continued their trend toward more modern structures. "Elephants" remained small, about the size of a cow, and developed four tusks, paired in the upper and lower jaws. Primitive horses, such as *Mesohippus,* were evolving rapidly in size, but remained hardly larger than a sheep. Their teeth became modified for grazing, as the trend was away from forest browsing and toward the open grasslands. As seen in the White River deposits, such animals as the giant two-horned titanotheres, saber-toothed cats, giant carnivores, and the multitudes of the sheep-sized plant-eaters, especially the oreodonts, swarmed over the grass-covered plains. Bats made their first appearance during the Oligocene. American camels, deer, and pig-like animals grew in size.

Life classification during the Cenozoic Era. *(Courtesy State Museum, University of Nebraska, Lincoln.)*

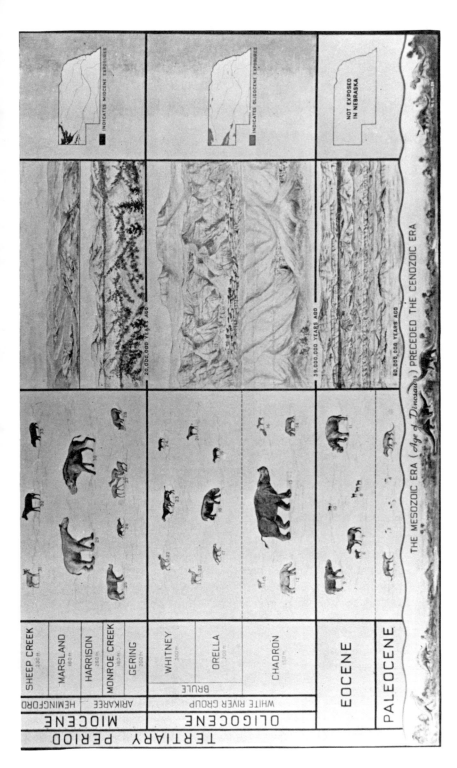

TERTIARY PERIOD	MIOCENE	HEMINGFORD	SHEEP CREEK 230 ft
			MARSLAND 180 ft
		ARIKAREE	HARRISON 250 ft
			MONROE CREEK 180 ft
			GERING 200 ft
	OLIGOCENE	WHITE RIVER GROUP	BRULE — WHITNEY 300 ft
			BRULE — ORELLA 200 ft
			CHADRON 150 ft
	EOCENE		
	PALEOCENE		

20,000,000 YEARS AGO — INDICATES MIOCENE EXPOSURES

35,000,000 YEARS AGO — INDICATES OLIGOCENE EXPOSURES

60,000,000 YEARS AGO — NOT EXPOSED IN NEBRASKA

THE MESOZOIC ERA (*Age of Dinosaurs*) PRECEDED THE CENOZOIC ERA

Invertebrates were common, characterized by the larger Foraminifera, and the reef-building corals and sponges. Echinoids continued to be abundant, with the arthropods such as crabs and barnacles (especially *Balanus concavus*) also much in evidence. Many thousands of bivalve seashells, principally scallops, have been collected from late Oligocene deposits, often with barnacles.

In the Baltic region of Germany, and a few places in America, pine resin hardened to imprison millions of Oligocene insects, representing most of the modern orders. Fossilized remains of termites have been found in freshwater deposits. Land and freshwater snails and slugs were widespread.

Plant Life

Alternating with the grasslands, there were widespread redwoods in Greenland, Alaska, Asia, etc. Hardwoods also spread far to the North. Volcanic dust deposits near Flourisant, Colorado, show a wide variety of hardwood trees, mainly swamp types.

Miocene Epoch (25 to 10 Million Years Ago)

Geology & Climate

During this epoch there was much sedimentation and erosion over most of North America, with tremendous lava plateaus, covering thousands of square miles, in the Northwest, formed by crevice eruptions. As the climate became more temperate, the tropical floras retreated southward.

In North America, rocks of the Miocene Epoch are exposed best in the Great Plains region. Such formations as the Harrison, Sheep Creek, and Rosebud are widely known for their abundant vertebrate fossils. On the east coast, from Maryland to Florida, various formations have produced excellent fossils in great variety. These formations are well-known for their giant teeth of the extinct form of great white sharks, *Carcharodon megalodon,* which grew more than 60 feet in length.

Animal Life

In general, both the vertebrates and invertebrates of the

Miocene appear "modernized" when Miocene specimens are compared to those of the preceding Oligocene. The Miocene was a time of extinction for many of the archaic types of animals, and of advancement for forms destined for later evolutionary strength.

The nautilus *Aturia* attained world-wide distribution, only to become extinct. The echinoderms spread through the warm waters of the world, becoming abundant and diverse. Bony fishes continued in great number and variety, as sharks also diversified.

The air was filled with modern varieties of insect life. Flightless birds reached great size and became fierce carnivores in South America and elsewhere, while primitive penguins, including one species as tall as modern humans, lived in Antarctica.

Miocene horses developed smaller side toes, and teeth with higher crowns, and so were better adapted to the new grasslands. The elephant's ancestors continued their gradual development into larger varieties, spreading from their homelands in Africa and Asia into North America. The small saber-toothed cats (stabbing cats), leopard and lion cats (biting cats), civet cats, bears, and ancestral dogs were among the common carnivores. The largest carnivore was the giant bear-dog, which became extinct during the later part of this epoch.

Plant Life

Swamp cypress, oak, maple, hickory, and redwood were common trees. Grasslands were widespread.

Pliocene Epoch (10 to 2 Million Years Ago)

Geology & Climate

The transition from the Miocene Epoch to the Pliocene in North America is generally thought of as a theoretical zone in the geologic column. For the most part, life forms continued with little change, although several new land animals migrated to North America from Asia.

Toward the end of this epoch there was considerable elevation of the mountains, and much cooling of the climate. This followed a long earlier period of comparative quiet, with a climate as temperate as, or warmer than, today's.

Animal Life

Freshwater, mammal-bearing deposits of the Pliocene often alternate with marine, shell-bearing formations in regions of the western United States. In such deposits, it was first recognized that a true Asiatic animal "invasion" of North America had begun with such fossil forms as ancestors of the modern kudu antelope, *Strepsiceros,* and with true elephants (having evolved from mastodons) appearing here for the first time. The elephants were more numerous and widespread than in any other period, some attaining enormous size.

In the Old World, apes and man-apes had spread widely, some (including *Australopithecus*) learning to come out of the forests and hunt animals in the savannahs.

The horse (*Hipparion*) now had feet in which only the central toe touched the ground, its two side toes having become function-less. Giant buffaloes, wolves and larger saber-toothed cats, and lions began to appear in this epoch. Bears also reached large size.

Interesting evidence points to a general drying up of many areas of North America during this epoch, with prolonged summer droughts. Early in the Pliocene, fossil records indicate that huge herds of large land tortoises began migrating across the Great Plains in search of disappearing water.

In several areas where drought conditions are not considered a factor in animal populations, such as in Florida and Texas, forms such as giant glyptodonts and ground sloths began to appear, having migrated from areas in Central America.

Invertebrate life was very similar to that of today, though there were some warm-water types now extinct. Freshwater molluscs were abundant, especially in the West.

Plant Life

The plants of the Pliocene are little like those of the earlier Miocene, and are more closely related to the plants of the Later

Pleistocene. Plant types, such as the common Mexican oak, fig, beech, birch, and elm are known from California and Nevada, while such forms as sweet gum, soapberry, and laurel have been found as fossils in the East.

There was a general retreat of plant life to the South as the epoch got colder. The *Sequoia*, for example, moved down from the mountains and the north of the California coast.

Pleistocene Epoch (2 Million to About 30,000 Years Ago)

Geology & Climate

This epoch was the time of the great Ice Ages and much mountain building. The Coast Range was formed in the West, as many western volcanoes erupted. Four southward glacial movements and four interglacial stages governed the Pleistocene, each with new faunas.

Until recently, glaciers as thick as two miles covered more than one-third of the earth's land surface. The effects can be seen everywhere in northern latitudes: in the rough-hewn crests of mountain ranges sculptured by small valley glaciers; in lands stripped of soil to bare bedrock, deeply striated by billions of tons of moving ice and abrasive glacier boulders; and in the lakes of America and Canada, which have been gouged out by a gigantic glacial bulldozer. While massive areas have been swept clean of all sedimentary rocks, in other regions glaciers have deposited uncommonly rich, deep soils. In these regions, glacial ice has left its mark not only on the land. Glaciers profoundly affected the history of animal and plant development and distribution, and they, thus, greatly influenced human culture.

Animal Life

During the Ice Ages a land bridge, called Beringia, was formed where the Bering Strait today separates Alaska and Asia. This gateway, with its wide, flat expanses of unbroken tundra, was hospitable to grazing animals of the Pleistocene. Through this gateway, back and forth, must have roamed an endless, concentrated procession of migratory animals, including mammoths and mastodons, horses, bison, deer, elk, and the most fascinating of Ice Age mammals, man.

Some animals adapted to living on or near the ice. Such were the woolly mammoth and the woolly rhinoceros, which have been extinct now for about 10,000 years. During the last glaciation such arctic animals as reindeer, caribou, arctic fox, steppe marmot, and lemmings came as far south as southern England or the central United States. It was during the Pleistocene that the saber-toothed tiger and the giant sloth died out.

Pleistocene birds were mainly of the modern types, with such exceptions as the Great Auk, the *Aepyornis* of Madagascar (a bird as tall as an elephant), and the Moa of New Zealand. At times during the interglacial stages it became so warm that hippopotamuses lived along the Thames and lions ranged as far north as Scotland.

Fossil invertebrates of the Pleistocene are essentially modern. Marine forms are widely exposed in areas along modern coastlines, because sea levels today are lower than extensive fossil beds which were previously off-shore.

Plant Life

Plants were essentially the same as now, but the great ice sheets forced most species far to the South.

Pleistocene deposits are abundant in all areas of North America, carrying numerous fossils of that time. Classic examples of Pleistocene fossil deposits are the La Brea Tar Pits of Los Angeles, the entire state of Florida, and Black Water Draw in New Mexico. There are many other localities across the United States and Canada.

CHAPTER 5

HOW TO COLLECT FOSSILS

PREPARING TO LOOK FOR FOSSILS

Finding likely places to look for specimens is probably the greatest challenge a fossil collector will encounter. The many fossiliferous localities provide collectors, museums, and geology departments with abundant materials for study and display. The localities listed are extensive and not likely to be picked clean or built over. The West is particularly rich in its inexhaustible exposures of sedimentary and limestone rock exposing fossils representative of nearly all the phyla known.

Many museum display collections of fossils, although prepared for students and the general public, are labeled too ambiguously to pinpoint their exact source. An ideal way to find new places to collect fossils is through mineral, fossil or gem clubs, and from earth science instructors in colleges and high schools. Many collectors don't object to letting friends or interested parties in on their "finds," while many others will try to keep their sources a secret. Locate new projects for dams, road cuts, quarrying, marine contruction, and canals.

Fossil localities are invariably listed in paleontological journals, monographs, and geological guidebooks. The time spent in checking over fairly current publications for such locality information is well worth the effort, as locality information can usually be found which best suits a collector for a given area or fossil interest.

United States Geological Survey topographic maps are invaluable in the time they can save a collector by pinpointing roads, rivers, buildings, mines, and other landmarks. State and Federal Survey geological maps of course are a must since they provide the collector with specific geological information for given

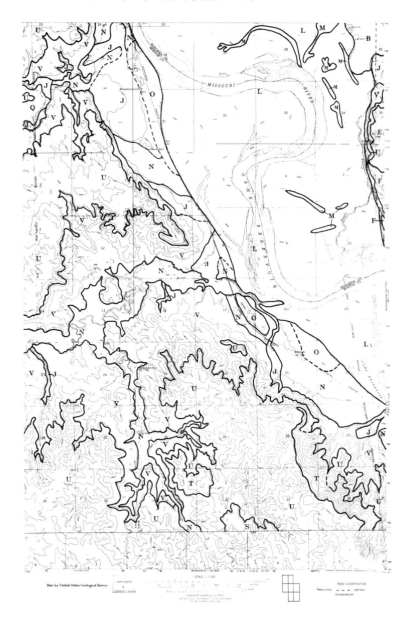

Topographic map, one-fourth of normal size.

Landform map, one-fourth of normal size.

areas. State survey maps can be purchased most reasonably from each state's agency handling these. Addresses are given in Chapter 9. Federal topographic maps and indices can be ordered from the U.S.G.S. Branch of Distribution, Box 2528, Denver Federal Center, Denver, Colorado 80225, or from Publications Division, Branch of Distribution, 1200 South Eads Street, Arlington, Virginia 22202.

Geologic maps are similar to topographic maps except that they use colors to differentiate formations. Fossil localities often are printed on geologic maps. An understanding of the local geology is immensely helpful in successfully predicting where fossils will be found, because certain rock units are known to be more fossiliferous than others. For all practical purposes however, knowledge of fossil localities can best be obtained from collectors who are familiar with the area and can offer good locality data and experience. The best of geological maps, providing excellent formation data, can prove barren of fossils. If you plan a collecting trip of any great distance, acquire as much information as possible from a search of the literature and from other collectors, museum curators, or staff who have worked in that specific area.

Preparations

Before you begin your fossil hunting trip there are several practical things to consider to ensure yourself and your party a safe trip. On long trips into the back country, over dirt roads and far from dwellings or a phone, you should be sure to have a sound vehicle with good tires, a spare, a fan belt, extra water, a jack, sacking, a shovel, and, of course, plenty of gas. Bring along one five-gallon can with water, and one with gasoline. A good emergency first aid kit is a *must*. Cuts and bruises are a hazard of field collecting. It is best to be prepared. Poisonous snakes may be seen frequently, particularly in the western states and Florida. A snake bite kit should be handy, just in case. While high, heavy boots are recommended to prevent blisters and falls, many collectors prefer the far more comfortable tennis shoes. When collecting fossils in quarries with a rock hammer or sledge, always wear protective glasses and a helmet. Collectors should always work in pairs, particularly in any dangerous back-road areas, or in quarries. A CB radio can provide an important backup emergency tool.

Trip Tips

1. Get permission from owner or lessee to collect on any private property. For open quarries or mines, get permission in writing prior to entering collecting areas. You will probably be requested to sign a release form and to assure the operators that you have the proper clothing to wear while in the quarry, i.e. hard hat, metal-toed shoes, glasses.
2. Keep your vehicle off rangelands or cultivated lands. A four-wheel drive vehicle does as much damage to cultivated land as a tractor.
3. Watch out for fires if you smoke or cook out. Carelessness can cause as much grief as any deliberate arsonist.
4. Carry out all trash that you bring into an area. Don't litter roadsides, private property, or quarries. Others should not be required to bury your trash.
5. Be sure to leave all gates as you find them, open *or* closed.

Checklist of Fossil Collecting Equipment

☐ Rock hammer
☐ Chisels
☐ Crowbar
☐ Hand lens
☐ Knapsack
☐ Wrapping paper: toilet tissue and newspaper
☐ Shovel
☐ Pick (railroad or Marsh's)
☐ Dental picks
☐ Glue (Duco type)
☐ Whiskbroom
☐ Old toothbrush
☐ Maps (topographic, geologic, and highway)
☐ Food (sufficient for duration of trip and extra rations for emergency)   *(cont.)*

Checklist (Cont.)

☐ Spare tire(s)
☐ Jack
☐ Work gloves
☐ Protective goggles
☐ Notebook and pencil
☐ Water
☐ Sun hat
☐ Work hat
☐ Snakebite kit
☐ Matches (in watertight container)
☐ Survival kit (many commercial kits are available)
☐ First aid kit
☐ Paper or cloth bags
☐ Small boxes

Where to Look

Paleontologists often say that finding fossils requires more luck than it does skill, but that collecting them requires much skill, hard work, and patience. Where to look often requires a geologic intuition which can only be obtained by experience in the field, by looking carefully at the rocks, and developing a feeling for what can be found where.

Natural Exposures

Fossils are most easily found in areas which have been subjected to long and continual weathering. Weathering by water and frost action causes some degree of matrix disintegration, softening the rock so that it is more likely to break around a fossil than through it. Stream or river cuts, seashore, and lake fronts are good collecting areas, as are naturally weathered slopes of sedimentary hills.

Man-Made Exposures

Highway and railroad cuts make excellent collecting areas. Rock quarries also offer excellent collecting opportunities, but specimens are infrequently found in active quarries because the rocks there are too freshly broken, and specimens have not had the time to weather in relief. Working quarries are also dangerous, prone to slides and the hazards caused by trucks and other machinery.

Fossil-Bearing Rocks

Fossils are most commonly found in sedimentary rocks, but not all sedimentary rocks are fossiliferous. Following are descriptions of rocks which commonly contain fossils.

Sandstones, Siltstones

These medium-textured rocks are usually well bonded by mineral cements. Fossils are extracted from these matrixes with a great deal of effort; sledge hammers and crowbars are often required. Sandstone and siltstone may often contain large numbers of fossils, indicating that they were deposited in environments teeming with life.

Conglomerates, Breccias

Fossils in these rocks are usually fragmentary, and include isolated bones and teeth of reptiles and amphibians.

Shales

Fine-grained shale often contains fossils which are either perfectly preserved or crushed parallel to the bedding plane. Shales can contain vertebrates, invertebrates, and plants.

Limestones

Limestones are usually the most fossiliferous of rocks. Limestones differ greatly in their appearance, and fossils found within such rocks vary in the ease or difficulty with which they can be collected. Massive limestones often require heavy tools, such as five- or ten-pound sledges and crowbars, while silty limestones give up their fossils easily, usually with no tool other than a pocket knife.

Dolomites

Fossils preserved in dolomite are usually molds and casts, and more often than not the preservation is of poor quality. A collector's time is probably best spent elsewhere if possible.

Evaporites

Fossils in evaporites such as gypsum or salt are very rare.

Coal and Coal Shales

Fossils in carbon-rich shales directly associated with coal can often be exquisitely preserved. Usually plant fossils are represented, but vertebrates such as fish, insects, and even dinosaur footprints have been found near coal deposits.

Sand

Many fossils are found in unconsolidated sands. Cenozoic invertebrates and vertebrates are common in such deposits and are usually unaltered.

TECHNIQUES OF COLLECTING FOSSILS

Microfossils

Tiny Foraminifera can be found in many varieties of sedimentary rocks. Because of the great range of sizes in which these Protozoa occur, there are several methods for collection.

Fossils too small to be observed in the field without a high-powered microscope are usually collected "blind," and brought back to the laboratory in chunks of matrix to be examined later. If unsure, a collector often can guess the content of his samples by likely clues which the fingers can sense by rubbing the surface dust: microfossils are infrequently found in clastic rocks (composed of sediments coarser than silt), and frequently found in clay and many shales which feel soapy or talclike, a feeling caused by the millions of spherical specimens rolling upon one another.

Larger "microfossils," such as Foraminifera ranging in size from one millimeter to more than ten centimeters, can be collected much in the same manner as macrofossils. An absolute necessity for collecting such specimens is a 10X or more powerful hand lens. Often obscure, the Foraminifera are best observed on weathered or freshly broken and moistened surfaces. Forams are best observed in the direct sunlight.

Macrofossils

Fossil Sponges

Marine sponges are preserved in every variety of rock type: shale, limestone, and fine-grained sandstone, and they can be preserved as calcite or silica.

Nodules or chert in limestone can indicate the presence of silica sponges, and can be the most common fossils found in such concretions. Delicate, sack-like sponges, are frequently found pressed flat on bedding planes of very fine-grained rocks which were deposited in areas of little water movement. The more sturdy sponges often weather out of the matrix and can be collected whole, or can be collected as cross sections on weathered surfaces.

Sponge spicules, which are commonly preserved, can be etched (if composed of silica) from calcareous rocks with the use of acids such as very dilute hydrochloric or acetic acids. If a collector is lucky, he or she may be able to remove an entire skeletal framework of spicules by using acid treatments. Safety precautions are necessary for the use of acids in the home; a rubber apron, rubber gloves, and glasses should be used in a well ventilated area.

Corals and Other Cnidarians

Corals are preserved often as ridged colonies in many forms of marine sediments. Weathered specimens are easily collected from talus slopes. Whole specimens can be removed from rock ledges with hammer and chisel.

As far as possible, an attempt should be made to remove a specimen whole. If a specimen is found broken, a collector should gather as many fragments as possible and fit them together with glue, or catalog them as a unit.

The most important measurable characteristics of corals occur within the interior of the specimen, so even fragmentary specimens are important. Acid treatment or polishing can be used to expose such features. A. E. Rixon's *Fossil Animal Remains: Their Preparation and Conservation* (Humanities Press, Inc., 1976) offers extensive coverage to the many uses of acid treatment, transfer mounting, and making molds of fossils.

Most other cnidarians, such as the medusae of Hydrozoa (jellyfish) and sea anemones, are rare as fossils and are found only in the finest of clastic sediments such as fine-grained shale or sandstone. If present in a deposit, such specimens can be collected with a hammer and a wide, thin chisel. Residual carbonized films or the cavity of a natural mold of a specimen produce a weak zone within the sedimentary which will allow the rock to nearly always cleave in such a way as to leave the fossil exposed. Such specimens preserved on natural rock bedding planes are easily broken and no attempt should be made by the collector in the field to remove excess material. Corals can usually be cleaned best by immersing them in a pail of Chlorox overnight, and with the use of a brush and running water.

Bryozoans

Fossil bryozoans are often abundant in thin-bedded marine limestones or calcareous shales. (The Cincinnati region produces the greatest variety of bryozoan forms and quantities within the Richmond series of formations.) Fossil bryozoans are rare or absent in noncalcareous rocks such as sandstones or conglomerates.

Most easily collected on weathered surfaces of rock, or talus slopes, bryozoans appear as slender, light, dark gray or yellow branches and fans (within the Paleozoic), or in spherical or massive forms. Many branching forms can be collected without matrix and later etched in very dilute acid to expose detail of frontal walls and pores.

Brachiopods

Complete, well-preserved fossil brachiopod shells are valued in any collection. Their paleontological importance is significant as they shed a great deal of light on the structure of the phylum.

For study purposes, suites of shells should be collected from as many localities as possible, and not just the most complete or most attractive of specimens. The collector must avoid being lured by "pretty" specimens away from the more rare specimens. Usually present, but harder to find, less common species are of great importance to the paleontologist, particularly in taxonomic or stratigraphic studies.

Fossil brachiopods found weathered free in soils composed of calcareous-deteriorated shale are often well-preserved and very easy to collect. Extensive formations may be composed entirely of brachiopods in many eastern and midwestern states. Brachiopods are more commonly found in deposits of massive carbonate rocks. Such rocks often yield silicified fossils in great numbers, with specimens superbly preserved. Specimens in these rocks usually stand out in relief and can be freed by use of a rock hammer and chisel.

Molluscs

Fossil molluscs make up the major portion of any marine faunal assemblage. Consequently, they often are preserved in greater numbers than any other type of marine invertebrates.

Like brachiopods, the shelled molluscs can be collected from weathered soils or they can be broken from matrix with the use of a hammer and chisel. Although many molluscs respond well to the use of acid, care must be used with this method because shells are often incompletely preserved with silica and many dissolve away rapidly while hidden from view by a cloud rising from the dissolving specimen. Most Tertiary and Quaternary molluscs are collected as unreplaced specimens, and washed with a stiff brush.

Annelids

Complete fossil annelids are very rare, usually preserved as carbon impressions upon the bedding planes of fine-grained shales. Such specimens can be collected by splitting such rocks with a wide-blade chisel.

The conodont's exact biological relationships are unknown, but are thought by some paleontologists to be the preserved jaw parts of carnivorous annelid worms. They are minute microfossils that may be bar-, cone-, or blade-shaped. Conodonts are composed of concentric layers of calcium metaphosphate and are translucent amber-brown in color when unaltered, or gray to white when altered by other minerals.

Conodonts are best collected in blocks and returned to the laboratory to be etched from the matrix with acid, or in a bath of kerosene, which acts to dissolve poorly cemented clastic rocks. Conodonts are common in many marine rocks from the Cambrian through the Triassic periods.

Arthropods

The arthropod's exoskeleton is composed essentially of a chitin-protein structure (much like our fingernails) which rapidly disintegrates after the animal's death. Only in ideal sedimentary conditions do the remains of these animals occur as fossils. Because of this, a good fossil of a trilobite, eurypterid, insect, or crustacean is highly prized in any collection.

Arthropod fossils usually occur on the bedding planes of sedimentary rocks. The chitinous shells, carbonized residue, or molds and casts weaken their bedding planes, causing the rock to split and expose fossil specimens.

Fossil chitin and carbonaceous residues tend to chip and spall when exposed to air. Although not recommended by many paleontologists, the use of a thin layer of lacquer is often needed to preserve a specimen from rapid disintegration. A thin coat of hairspray will be of great help. Too thick a film of preservative may change color over time or even shrink and pull away from the specimen, causing irreparable damage.

Most often, the arthropod's chitinous exoskeleton is replaced by other minerals such as calcite or silica. In such cases, the collector should rely on techniques described for other invertebrates.

Fossil Fish

Well preserved fish are among the most highly prized fossil specimens. Their remains lie most commonly in shales, with fragmentary fossils such as teeth and vertebrae found in unconsolidated silts, marls, and conglomerates.

With few exceptions, fossil fish are compressed. Although the bones may be well preserved, they are often distorted by water current action prior to burial and by rock pressure. The flesh of fish is often preserved by carbonization, though a great many "complete" fossil fish are merely impressions.

Although fossil fish are more common than many other types of vertebrate remains, they are by no means easy to find. Even if fossil fish are known to occur in a particular rock unit, prospecting blind for specimens can take up much of a collector's day or weekend. Since fish fossils are rarely distributed evenly throughout a particular formation, a collector should check the paleontological literature of an area before he goes out with the intention of collecting fossil fish.

Fossil fish are collected in much the same manner as plant remains. Overburden, or capping, should first be removed from above a known fish bed allowing the collector to "lift" large slabs of shale. Thus, when the slabs of shale are split with a flat chisel, a good possibility exists that specimens obtained will be complete. Specimens in shale or mudstone usually need little if any stabilization in the field, and can be easily transported to the laboratory. Large specimens, several feet in length, require methods of collecting beyond the scope of the amateur collector and professional help should be sought at a nearby museum or college geology department.

Plants

Fine-grained non-marine sedimentary rocks of nearly every kind can contain fossil plants, and even some marine sediments may contain such specimens. Good plant specimens can be collected from the dark, non-marine shales which are often associated with coal. The rock beds directly above coal layers are usually more productive than beds between or below these zones.

Plant fossils found in loose float or on talus slopes are usually of poor quality and not valuable to the collector. A collector should make every effort to find the strata from which these specimens are weathering.

Once the proper stratigraphic layer has been located, the collector's objective is to quarry as large a slab of fossiliferous rock as possible. Ideally, rock strata lying above the fossiliferous zone

Thomas Bones and students at the Clarno fossil plant beds, Oregon. *(Courtesy Oregon Museum of Science and Industry, Portland.)*

should be removed with pick and shovel and discarded down slope. (This method is often disregarded by collectors because of the time and trouble required for quarrying, and so is responsible for the many fragmented specimens in both amateur and professional collections. The average collector finds surface hunting the best method for building up a collection of fossil plants. By cutting specimens to manageable sizes, attractive and scientifically important collections can be made.)

Split the quarried strata along bedding planes. In plant deposits, this process is easily accomplished because of the natural cleavage produced by the plants themselves. Various wide-edged chisels and putty knives are best for splitting most plant fossil-producing rocks.

If specimens are found in damp strata and if they tend to break apart during preparation, stack the specimens in open plastic bags in the laboratory to dry over several days. In this way, specimens normally unrecoverable, make good, hard additions to a fossil collection.

The classic Mazon Creek fossil plants and a large number of associated organisms occur in the well-known nodules. In opening nodules containing fossil fishes or plants, or other invertebrates (i.e. Mazon Creek nodules), the nodule is split lengthwise, with a light tapping across the top edge, which should split the nodule into two pieces across the bedding. The fossil contained therein will then also be split in half across the length of the specimen, with a cast on one half, and the preserved portion on the other. One half therefore is merely a trace of a fossil, while the other is the preserved or mineral-replaced portion. These fossil-bearing nodules when collected in the field, should be wrapped individually in newspaper and packed in cartons. In the laboratory make repairs to any damaged specimens.

Fossil arthropods such as insects and eurypterids, as well as fossil fish often associate with plant fossils preserved in the thin-bedded sediments from lagoons behind barrier reefs or in lake deposits. Never look for a single kind of fossil. For every kind of animal or plant found, there are others which are ecologically bound to it. Well-known plant deposits in Ohio, Pennsylvania, and

Nova Scotia contain a number of small amphibians in association with the remains of tree trunks. Those are rare finds indeed.

Tetrapod Vertebrates

In areas which have been subjected to little exploration by collectors, or in regions such as badlands or seashores which are continually ravaged by natural erosion, fragmentary fossil remains of tetrapod vertebrates, including amphibians, reptiles and mammals, are not uncommon, though they are usually fragmentary. (Tetrapods are any of the four-footed, land-dwelling vertebrates.)

The nonprofessional collector or student should be content to collect isolated bones or teeth of tetrapods, leaving professionals to the complete skeletons which require years of experience to properly remove from the strata. Fossil bones, no matter how hard and well preserved, have been subjected to continual earth and soil shifting. They often are broken into hundreds of pieces, held together in a seemingly stable shape only by the surrounding matrix.

A fossil skeleton requires many days or weeks of work to collect. Often, novice collectors only begin to realize the time required after a single day's attempt. At that point, they become frustrated, begin pulling bones from the strata, and all too frequently end up with a pile of useless fragments.

Fossil bones recovered from the Cenozoic marls are not "petrified," and are much more likely to break during excavation and transportation. Again, the collector must be advised to seek professional assistance if he or she believes that a find is of some major importance. Sometimes, unfortunately, a collector cannot find a paleontologist at the corner supermarket, and must proceed without help to extract bone material as carefully as possible. The following recommended procedure works as well in recent Florida bone-beds as in the Badlands where you may hunt geologically older game.

Bone Collecting

Having made a discovery of a complete or nearly complete vertebrate tetrapod fossil, the collector should sit down, relax, and go over in his mind the proper steps to follow.

1. Using hand tools, such a pocket knife or awl, investigate the extent of the fossil exposed. If bone has weathered down-slope, bone fragments should follow upslope until the bone can be observed in place, and the extent and nature of the find is known.

2. All fragments should be collected and coated with shellac, Duco, Glyptal, or some other nitrocellulose cement which later can be thinned with solvents.

3. Extremely hard dinosaur bone seldom requires careful packing, except for crating in large sections for transportation. However, more fragile bone material will require considerable attention: plaster jacketing is suggested.

   a. Coat entire area of exposed bone with any of the preservatives suggested above.

   b. Apply a few layers of soft tissue paper to the bone, coating several layers at a time with a thin glue.

   c. When dry, coat all bone surfaces with damp toilet tissue.

   d. Dig a trench all around the specimen, well away from the farthest extent of the fossil, and about three times the depth of the specimen.

   e. For the plaster jacket you will need old burlap sacks (or any sturdy cloth), a plastic pail, and plaster. (Molding or dental plaster is best, as it sets faster than wall plaster.) Cut the burlap into strips three inches wide and long enough to provide support, six to twelve inches. Soak the strips in plaster of a soupy consistency and wrap them onto the specimen block, overlapping ½ to ¾ of an inch. Make sure that the plaster and burlap are worked thoroughly into every irregularity of the surface. When the specimen is completely covered with plaster and burlap, you now can worry about removing the specimen from its hole. This is the critical part of the entire vertebrate fossil collecting operation, for if the specimen has been packed loosely within the plaster jacket, or if the jacket does not have a firm hold of undercuts under the block, the specimen can easily end up as "shale and fossil hash" filling the hole. Always cut far enough under a specimen so that it stands on a pedestal or toadstool if possible. Then break or cut the block from its pedestal. One hopes it now can be turned without all of the inside material within spilling out the newly exposed side. The jacket is then continued around the block, and it is ready for transport.

Plastering fossil bone in the field prior to packing and shipping. *(Courtesy Denver Museum of Natural History.)*

This is a simplification of a very complicated and risky procedure. It is strongly suggested that the collector get a copy of A. E. Rixon's *Fossil Animal Remains: Their Preparation and Conservation* (Humanities Press, New Jersey, 1976) and carefully study the section on tetrapods, which includes a detailed description of plaster jacketing techniques. Or write to us in care of Naturegraph Publishers for detailed methods of bone extraction, preparation, packing, and laboratory procedures prior to identification and display.

CHAPTER 6

CATALOGING, PREPARING, AND DIS-PLAYING YOUR FOSSILS

CATALOGING YOUR COLLECTION

Cataloging your collection is one of the most important parts of fossil collecting, a record keeping procedure which begins in the field. Each separate lot of specimens from each location, formation or zone must be tagged when wrapped or boxed, giving any field data known, particularly the geological formation and precise locality. With good field and laboratory data, the collector and those who might acquire the collection will have proper records containing as much information as possible about each individual specimen or collection.

Information for both labels and catalog cards is derived from field notes, field labels, and the literature references. Samples of various formats for museum specimen labels and catalog cards are shown here (see Pg. 123). A simple catalog card gives the name of the fossil, the name of the collector, geological formation (horizon or zone, if known), precise locality according to topographic, geological or road map, date collected, literature reference, illustrations, and any pertinent data observed in the field. For an accession card system ("accession" being the library science term for recording items in their order of acquisition), the same procedure follows, beginning the numerical catalog system with 100, which can be followed by a year-collected numeral, a locality number, and the numbers of any cross-referenced catalog cards. Some museums use a series of cards for either a single specimen, group of specimens, or entire collections from specific localities or horizons, i.e. locality catalog card, collection catalog card, specimen withdrawn card, accession card, genus and species card, and a more sophisticated IBM computer census card.

UNIVERSITÀ DI PARMA

N.
Arnolus (Variarysium
duodecirlar ellatum
                    (Prorn)
ETÀ ......Sabiaman
LOCALITÀ ...Sabiano-Pecni-

Fonti

MUSEO GEOLOGICO

No.........................

Pecten(Oppenheimopecten)
vogdesi Arnold,1906

Age.Pleistocene.........................
Locality.....Tuberon Island

IST. di GEOLOGIA e PALEONTOLOGIA
UNIVERSITÀ di PISA

Collected by.........................
Identified by.........................

Mollusca from Pliocene
inferiore of Orciano
(prov P.I.S.A.)

Various types of labels used by museums in identifying and cataloging their specimens.

Form of computer card used by both malacologists and paleontologists in the cataloging and recording of specimens. Considerable data can be recorded and retrieved at a later date via print-out systems.

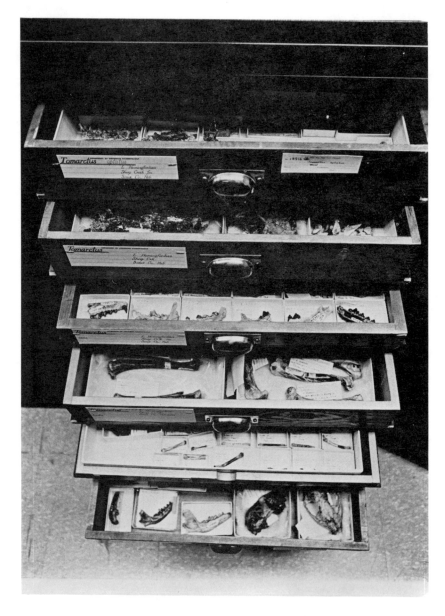

Method of storing specimens in trays and in cabinet drawers, arranged either by geological formation, location, or animal phyla.

DISPLAYING

Storage of collections may follow whatever system best suits the collector, from home-made wood drawers and cabinets to professional storage units from Ward's or Lane Science Equipment Corp. The bottom part of boxes for nylon stockings make excellent trays for vertebrate, plant, or fossil fish specimens. Plastic vials are necessary for very small specimens, with the label enclosed inside the vial. Size and quantity of drawers and cabinets will depend on the size and bulk of the individual collections. Each specimen (depending on size or rarity) should be housed in an individual cardboard or plastic tray or box, with the label either glued to the side of the box or under the specimen. Related specimens for each species or group of species should also be placed in trays.

A collection or group of specimens may be arranged either by the phyla, the geographical locations, or the geological strata, or a combination. We house our reference collection by both geographical locality and geological formation, keeping each series of specimens intact as a single unit, in as many drawers as may be required. In this system, each phylum can follow in biological sequence, allowing a comparative study of several formations from each period, taken from various localities, without disturbing the entire collection.

Field notes are as important, if not more so, than the actual specimens themselves! The following observations should be included in your notes. Personalized field numbers should be applied to each specimen or group of specimens and each series should be bagged and labeled separately. Identify the geological horizon where known from the literature if the site was previously collected. Describe the nature of the site, e.g., spoilbank, quarry, roadside exposure, etc. Give the location according to map reference, topographic landmarks, etc. Photographs of each site to be included with locality cards are very important. Information on the position in which the fossils were found, whether laying in life-like arrangements, broken and scattered in sedimentary layers, tide-washed into drifts, etc., may be included, as well as reference to the bedding of the rock strata, degree of preservation of the specimens, and an estimate of the quantities (i.e. brachiopods abundant; trilobites, few or poorly preserved). Where a collecting trip may occupy several days or weeks, it is well worth the trouble to keep a daily diary of activities, logistical problems, miles covered, localities visited, and fossils or horizons noted and collected. In such a diary, the locality numbers and accession numbers of specimens or collections should be noted for the day involved.

Map, photograph, and diary files may be housed in folders. Each folder may cover a specific locality, including a portion of a map for that area, any photographs of the locality and fossils *in situ,* and the pages from your diary relative to that locality. Such a file would greatly supplement both the collection itself and the catalog card system.

LABORATORY PREPARATION OF FOSSILS

Only rarely can fossil specimens be recovered from the strata with no further preparation required to make them valuable objects for study. Miocene shark teeth, for example, found loose in unconsolidated sands of the east coast, need no preparation whatsoever after collection. Similar fossils found in New Mexico's Dakota Formation, however, are encrusted in hard, cemented sandstone, and must be prepared before study or display.

Each type of fossil presents its own individual preparation problems, and these are compounded by the fact that each and every fossil might have been preserved in entirely different ways. A clam might be preserved in the round, in hard, massive limestone, or p essed flat in thinly bedded shale. A shell might be altered, being permineralized or replaced by opal, pyrite, silica or copper, or it might not be "fossilized" at all. Matrices surrounding the fossil might be unconsolidated silt, shale, sandy shale, shaley sandstone, iron-like silica-cemented sandstone, or conglomerate. The list of possibilities is nearly endless, and it serves well to show that no book, especially one slim chapter in a book such as this, can make a professional preparer out of the amateur fossil collector. Experience becomes the best teacher, and the collector will, over time, learn many tricks of the trade to adequately prepare the fossil he or she finds in the field.

The preceding chapter discussed methods for field collecting, and this chapter deals with the specimen once it is unwrapped and placed on the well-lit, sturdy work bench, which is almost a necessity if one does much collecting and preparing.

Fossil tetrapod vertebrates, including the bones of amphibians, reptiles, mammals and birds, require special techniques in preparation. Many people have spent years learning the various methods used to prepare such specimens for study and display. This short summary acquaints the fossil collector with the simplest procedures. We have omitted methods of mounting articulated skeletons, as well as those procedures involved in preparing problem fossils, requiring methods which are far beyond the scope of this book.

Basic Materials Needed for Home or School Preparation Laboratory

1. Small sandbox. Sand is perhaps the best material available for holding bones together while glue or plaster dries.
2. Plaster. Fast-drying plaster (dental plaster) is an ideal cement for uniting medium to large bones. Plaster is also used for restoration and for duplication of specimens.
3. Rubber mixing bowl, used for mixing plaster.
4. Chisels, a series of various small, sharp chisels ranging from ¼ to ½ inch.
5. Needles.
6. Hammer, small tack type.
7. Nitrocellulose cement such as Alvar, Duco or Glyptal. Since these use acetone as a solvent, they dry fast. Note: use only in well ventilated areas.
8. Plastic clay, used for holding smaller bones together while gluing.
9. Preservative, made from Duco-type glue mixed with acetone.

The process of preparation is simply the removal of matrix from a fossil specimen. The simplicity, however, ends there. Bones

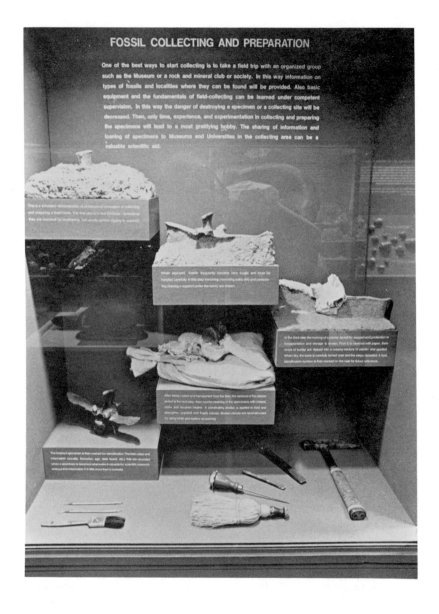

Methods and tools for preparation of fossils.

are normally harder than their surrounding matrix, but they are often brittle, highly fractured, or generally unpredictable, being hard and soft on the same specimen.

Once the fossil bone is removed from its plaster and burlap jacket, it becomes highly susceptible to the effects of drying. As moisture is lost in a vertebrate specimen, bone begins a rapid process of decay. That is, new cracks begin and old cracks expand, resulting in a once good field specimen's becoming a pile of useless fragments sitting on the lab shelf. To avoid this, use preserving materials liberally, with a heavier application brushed on the specimen's surface after preparation is completed.

Matrix is cut away from a bone by using appropriate chisels, needles, and probes. Normally, matrix will separate easily from a specimen, however, in more ancient specimens (for instance, Paleozoic amphibians in hard conglomerate) considerable chiseling may be necessary. Do not become overly concerned if the specimen happens to break while chiseling, but remember always to glue broken pieces together immediately. Let dry, then continue until the specimen is free of however much matrix you as preparer feel necessary.

This is, in fact, all that is basic to preparation of vertebrates. For study purposes, all matrix should be removed. For display, it is often appropriate to leave some matrix as a frame or for support of fragile skeletal parts.

Restoration of missing or damaged parts with molding plaster requires skill and patience. When specimens are new to science (and many vertebrates found by amateurs and students are), an educated imagination is needed to reconstruct skeletal parts. Note: restoration should be left to the expert who is knowledgeable in ancient anatomy and evolution. If attempted by a novice, a specimen could be destroyed by covering important bone surfaces with plaster.

Once the specimens have been washed, sorted and placed in trays for identification, the process takes on a more scientific aspect in that the professional paleontologist takes over the task of formal taxonomic identification, classification, and restoration (or life-like reconstruction) where plants and vertebrates are concerned. Whereas the invertebrates are index fossils to former marine environments, plants and mammals (or reptiles) are important in delineating former environmental and ecological zones.

Fossils in Shale

Many fossils found in softer shales are preserved in the round, especially the molluscs, brachiopods, and echinoderms, and more rarely, the arthropods. Many of these three-dimensional specimens can also be removed completely from the matrix in the lab, though a collector may wish to leave them partly buried in the shale to make an attractive display specimen.

Specimens pressed flat on shale bedding planes usually need preparation only when they are obscured by layers of shale. Certain specimens, such as fossil fish in shale, often need extensive preparation, many hours of tedious work with needles and tiny chisels. Patience and a steady hand are essential for this work, but because such specimens are usually rare, the extra effort and time are well worth spending.

There will almost always be some damage to fossil plants during transport to the laboratory, often because specimens are usually preserved in loosely compacted, fine-grained shales. This is called *friable* rock. Assuming, however, that the plant fossils arrived with a minimum of damage, the specimens should be carefully unwrapped, sorted according to locality, formation, etc., and placed in adequate storage drawers and trays. Every specimen should be quickly numbered and labeled as outlined in this book.

Usually plants need little actual preparation; what is done to a plant specimen consists, for the most part, of chiseling away just enough rock to completely reveal the fossils. This should be done with chisels of various sizes (depending on the matrix) and specimens should always be worked on while the rock matrix is setting firmly on a sand bag to absorb excess vibration.

Fossils in Limestone

Many limestones are among the hardest matrices in which fossils can be found. Limestone is a chemical precipitate formed as a by-product of certain animals' natural metabolism, and by the accumulation of calcium debris from the skeletons of countless microscopic creatures that die and settle into an organic ooze on the ocean's bottom. Like cement, this calcium material hardens over time, trapping the remains of any bottom animals in a stone tomb.

If an organism is replaced by the mineral silica, removal from limestone is simply done by dissolving the matrix away with hydrochloric acid. Fossils in some limestone localities are perfectly preserved, such as the Capatan Reef area of west Texas and southeastern New Mexico. When these are removed from the rock with acid, they retain all spines and the most minute of shell ornamentation.

Acid Treatment: First test samples of fossiliferous matrix to determine if the fossil itself *will not* dissolve in the acid solution, and if the matrix *will* dissolve in the solution. After these two important points have been determined, the sample should be placed in a Pyrex beaker or a large battery jar, with penciled labels giving the contents, locality and horizon, taped to each container. The samples are then covered with 80% technical grade acetic acid, and the container filled with water to the brim. Large specimens can be suspended in the battery jar in stainless steel mesh.

Acetic Acid: Give this acid 48 to 96 hours to exhaust itself, and if, after the solution is poured out of the container, any rock matrix remains, a fresh solution can be used and the process repeated for an additional 8 to 12 hours. When all calcium carbonate (limestone) has been etched away by the acid, the larger specimens are removed and finer organic debris can be washed and screened through a 60-mesh sieve. The remaining shell fragments are usually very fragile, so the washing of the specimens must not be too vigorous. After thoroughly washing the residue in its original beaker or basket, dry it over a radiator or hot plate. This acid process should be done out-of-doors or where some arrangement has been made to carry off the acid fumes.

Hydrochloric Acid: Hydrochloric acid works much faster than acetic acid, but the danger exists that the effervescence caused in the etching matrix will destroy the fossil specimen. Hydrochloric acid must be greatly diluted, in a proportion of about ten parts water to one part acid. Always use metal tweezers or tongs to lift specimens into and out of acid baths, and always rinse thoroughly all specimens and equipment.

Danger—the use of any acid in the preparation of fossil specimens is potentially dangerous, if misused. Acids can cause serious eye and skin damage, and can be deadly if

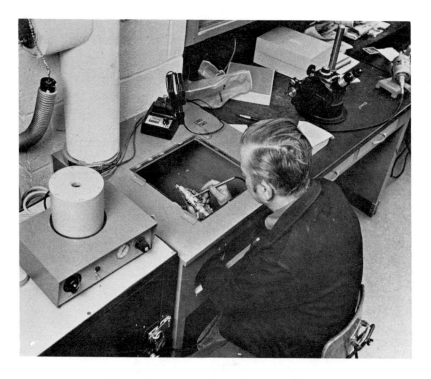

Mechanical method of specimen preparation.

swallowed. Also, fumes from acids can ruin many synthetic clothing materials. Always use caution, and younger collectors should use acids only under the direct supervision of an adult.

Many limestone fossils can be prepared with the use of dental tools. In attempting to free some specimens from compact limestone, shale or sandstone, a small hand drill is effective; coarser drilling or grinding can be done by using a 5 mm. wheel, but the small drill is easier to handle and can be used without causing damage to the specimen itself.

Special Note: Broken pieces of fossils should always be glued back on a specimen at once! There is nothing more frustrating than to loose an important fragment in a pile of worthless matrix scraps piled at your feet.

Collecting Fossils in Metamorphic Rocks

Collectors are often tempted to investigate deposits of seemingly well-stratified layers of undeformed rocks, only to find that the entire fossil content has been severely deformed by the geologic forces of heat and pressure. However, such metamorphic rocks may contain well-preserved fossils in zones of contact with unaltered sediments above or below. Curious associations of trilobites with garnets, brachiopods with chiastolite, or corals with pyroxene are well known, but small fossil forms, or those fossil forms with thin shells, are rarely preserved in such metamorphic contact zones.

In areas of low grade metamorphism, usually in older rocks ranging from Early Cambrian to Early Devonian, fossils in various stages of deformity can be found in rocks such as marble, slate, quartzite, and in water-laid volcanics such as tufa.

Decalcification of rocks caused by old or new circulation of ground water may remove all remnants of shell material. In such situations, molds and casts are the predominant type of fossil and are interesting as specimens.

Dolomitization, or crystalization, of limestone is a metamorphic process which can also destroy fossil specimens. However, organisms with thick shells, and even trilobites or other thin-shelled creatures, have been preserved in dolomite. Usually, fossils in dolomite are of poor quality.

Even though fossils in metamorphic rocks are generally deformed with much of their details obscured, they are very important to paleontologists and stratigraphers. Since many distorted specimens of a particular species may be needed for proper identification, blocks of fossiliferous metamorphic rocks, rather than individual specimens, should be collected. As with all specimens regardless of preservation, little or no preparation should be attempted in the field. As usual, the fossils' own rock matrix makes the best packing material.

Collecting Concretions

Concretions are hard, resistant, irregular, spherical, or discoid rock masses commonly formed in marine shale, chalk, siltstone, and sandstone. Concretions grow by building layers of minerals around an organic nucleus such as shell, bone, or plant material buried in the sediment. Most concretions which contain fossils are composed of siderite and limestone. Other forms of concretions are composed of pyrite and marcasite, and even coal balls can preserve fossils.

The chances of discovering fossils within a formation which contains concretions are better than average, simply because many concretions need an organism on which to form. Recognizing concretions is not difficult. You can see them easily, weathering out on barren or vegetative inclines. They commonly can be found in great accumulations at the base of eroding shale slopes.

There is no special way of attacking a concretion, and generally only hard work with a 4-, 6- or 10-pound sledge is all that is required to crack them. Collectors should bring with them into the field a crowbar to raise the concretions from sedimentary layers. You will also find use for strong bags or packs, glue, and, most important, eye and hand protection.

Often, several blows are necessary to crack or break open a concretion. Concretions which have weathered, however, may be easily broken by striking with a sharp hammer blow on the concretion's lateral edge.

North American Mesozoic formations which contain fossil-bearing concretions are the Pierre, Eagle Ford, Benton, and Bear Paw shales, with prolific fossils being found in concretions of the Fox Hills, Codell, Ripley, and Mancos. Very good Paleozoic fossil concretions with invertebrates occur in such formations as the Antrim and Pomley shales, Mazon Creek of Illinois (more famous for plants and insects). Vertebrate concretions are numerous in the Devonian Kettle Point, Antrim, Marcellus, and Cleveland shales.

CHAPTER 7

FOSSIL COLLECTING LOCALITIES IN NORTH AMERICA

Since numerous publications, including the data from the State Geological Surveys listed here, offer fossil locality information, in these pages only fossil sites known to be productive or located during the 1970's are cited. Many classic localities are no longer available due to construction, owners' restrictions, plant overgrowth, or government restrictions. Numerous vertebrate fossil localities producing dinosaur materials are either claimed as "reserves" by various universities that have set up summer student programs to quarry the materials, or have been turned into national parks. Areas abound where good vertebrate fossils may still be collected from weathered exposures, but these are difficult to reach, some, many miles from highways or secondary roads, and virtually inaccessible except to backpack collectors.

Many of today's remaining classic collecting sites are on private property or in industrial quarries, coal mines, and brickyards. Here it is most important that the collector secure prior permission rom each owner before entering the property. All safety rules and security regulations must be observed, as well as seeing to it that there is no damage done, no refuse left behind, and absolutely no stripping of fossil beds by the overeager collector.

Alaska

In Alaska there is no easy fossil hunting. Most visits to fossil localities involve time, money, and travel. One-day trips are possible; others, however, require several days on various forms of transportation at considerable expense. Collectors have been known to travel by air, swamp buggy, tracked vehicles, helicopter,

horses, boats, etc. The numerous geological reports on the stratigraphy and paleontology of Alaska by the U. S. Geological Survey
provide specific collecting localities for those desiring to collect in
the 49th state.

Alabama

Upper Cretaceous, Mooreville chalk. Creek bed along west
bank of Valley Creek beneath the Jefferson Davis Avenue bridge,
Selma, Dallas County (typical Upper Cretaceous fauna). ● Coal
pits in and around Bessemer have exposed an overburden of
shale in the pits which bear many large slabs covered with
Lepidodendron latifolium, L. obovatum, Calamites suckovi and
Stigmaria ficoides. These occur in the Pottsville shale. ● At
Cedar Bluff, just along the bridge occurs a small exposure of
Conasauga shale of the Cambrian, which contains numerous specimens of *Agnostus* species. ● Goodlight Pool Quarry, ½ mile
northwest of Moulton, Lawrence County, has Gasper limestone,
which contains a rich fauna of Mississippian Age, including gigantic *Pentremites*, brachiopods, and coral fauna. ● In Clarke County,
on the outskirts of Jackson, the Little Stave Creek section contains
a vast exposure, many hundreds of feet long, containing a wealth
of Eocene invertebrates. ● A strip coal mine exposed along
Highway 31, south of Bessemer, will provide the collector with an
abundance of Pennsylvanian ferns and massive specimens of
Calamites, Sigillaria, and *Lepidodendron*. ● At Cedar Bluff,
exposed along the river, is a rich Upper Cambrian trilobite bed.
Agnostids are very plentiful and several genera are known to occur,
as well as the large trilobite, *Tricrepicephalus*. ● Sponges and
trilobites may also be found exposed in tilled fields in the
neighborhood of Center in Cherokee County. Here the fossils are
found in nodules.

Arizona

Ordovician-Tertiary. Several formations present in the exposure at Peppercorn Canyon. From town of Oracle, on Highway
77, drive about 7 miles south to Peppercorn Canyon Campground.
Good collecting for invertebrates from the Ordovician through
Tertiary lake deposits. From the campground, additional collecting

can be done in Stratton Canyon. These are the USNM localities 147 and 152. ● Middle Pennsylvanian, Naco formation, Desmoinesian. Kohl Ranch, 15 miles east-north-east of Payson, Gila County. Collecting site 1.1 miles west of point where Arizona State Rt. 260 crosses Tonto Creek at Kohl Ranch. The locality is a low ridge adjacent to an abandoned road cut (invertebrates with conularids, gastropods, and crinoids).

Arkansas

Silurian, St. Clair limestone. Right side of Dry Creek, ½ mile west of Gilbert, Searcy County (large series of articulate brachiopods). ● Mississippian, Imo formation. Roadcut on the west side of Arkansas Highway 65, 5 miles southeast of Leslie, south of Peyton Creek, Van Buren County (classic crinoid locality). ● Mississippian, Boone formation. Rock quarry 2.1 miles west of Locust Grove, on Highway 14, and second exposure 1.5 miles south of Locust Grove on Highway 21. Collecting extends about 100 feet along road (invertebrates). ● Mississippian, Pitkin, and Imo formations. Chesterian series. Peyton Creek road cut, Van Buren County (very large faunal assemblage of conodonts, ammonoids). ● Mississippian, Pitkin formation; Pennsylvanian, Cane Hill, member of the Hale formation. Pitkin Quarry, Washington County (large fauna of conodonts, bryozoans, and girvanellid blue-green algae). ● Lower Pennsylvanian, Bloyd formation, Brentwood member. Roadcut 0.2 mile north of Woolsey, Washington County (crinoid fauna). ● Pennsylvanian, Atoka formation. Mine dumps 0.9 mile west of Bates, on the Poteau Mountain Tower Road (ferns, rushes, i.e., *Calamites, Annularia, Asterophyllites*). ● Upper Cretaceous, Saratoga chalk. Railroad cut west of Saratoga (large diversified collection of well-preserved sponges, echinoids, molluscs). Bluffs along Ouachita River at low tide, 1.2 miles north of Arkadelphia (molluscs, cephalopods, shark teeth). ● Paleocene, Midway formation. Along railroad cuts of the M.O.P. Railroad east of Grand Glaise (corals, echinoids, molluscs).

Baja California

Upper Cretaceous, La Bocana Roja formation, Campanian. Outcrop south of Arroyo del Rosario, just north of and inland from

Punta Baja (theropod dinosaur remains). ● Upper Cretaceous, Rosario formation, Campanian-Maestrichtian. Sea cliffs along north side of Punta Banda, about 1.6 km. south and 4.3 km. east of summit of Banda Peak on Punta Banda, Todos Santos Bay [molluscs with large rudist (bivalve that forms reef-like accumulations of organic limestones), *Coralliochama*]. ● Paleocene, Sepultura formation. Exposures within the Bahia Santa Eosalia Quadrangle, near El Cardon, on the Pacific side (indeterminate gastropods, bryozoans and algae; most noted finds are species of phymosomatoid echinoids).

California

Lower Triassic, Union Wash formation. South side of Union Wash, 2.5 miles northeast of Owenyo, Inyo Mts., Inyo County (large ammonite fauna). ● Late Jurassic, northeast and southeast of Del Mar, San Diego County (index bivalve locality, *Buchia piochii).* ● Upper Cretaceous, west end and southern end of Point Lomac Peninsula; False Point, south of the La Jolla business district; and on the north side of Mt. Soledad, San Diego County (molluscs, brachiopods, foraminifers, ammonites). ● Eocene, sea cliffs at Torrey Pines State Park, and in Rose Canyon, also exposed in the La Jolla Quadrangle north of San Diego (exposures rich in Mollusca). ● Middle Eocene, Domengine stage. Roadcut on southwest side of California State Highway 78, 5.2 km. southeast of Vista, and 4.8 km. northwest of San Marcos, northern San Diego County (molluscs, corals, bryozoans, and ostracods). ● Middle Eocene, Llajas formation. Arroyo Simi along southern side of Santa Susana, a community at eastern edge of Simi Valley, Ventura County (Mollusca). ● Miocene, Hector formation. Southwest side of Cady Mts., 4 miles north of Hector siding (cattle loading spot) of the Atchison, Topeka, and Santa Fe Railroad line, 14 miles east of Newberry, Mohave Desert (mammalian fauna with oreodonts, camelids, mustelids, and carnivores). ● Pliocene. Exposures from Pacific Beach, and south on Route 8 and east of Route 5, to the International Boundary and southwards, San Diego County (very extensive fauna of molluscs). ● Pliocene, Capistrano formation. Exposures from San Juan Capistrano, discontinuously along the southern California coast from Newport Bay to

San Clemente and inland towards El Toro (extensive foraminifers, ostracods, brachiopods, echinoids, and molluscs). ● Upper Pliocene, Merced formation. Exposures in the Sebastopol region, between Santa Rosa Valley and the Pacific Coast in northwest Marin and southwestern Sonoma counties, 59 miles north of San Francisco (classic molluscan fauna). ● Pre-Cambrian, Wyan formation, Reed dolomite and Deep Springs formation; Lower Cambrian, Campito formation (fossil trails) and Poleta formation, also Harkless formation (archaeocyathids, brachiopods, crinoids, and trilobites; above the Cambrian is found an upper Lower Devonian bed containing a large series of phyla); Lower Cambrian, Latham shale. 50- to 100-foot outcrops exposed widely throughout San Bernardino and Inyo counties in the Providence and Marble Mountains (extensive trilobites, *Aanomalocaris,* brachiopods, *Hyolithes.* See ref. Jack D. Mount, "Early Cambrian faunas from the Marble and Providence Mts., San Bernardino Co.," pp. 1-5, *Bulletin of the Southern California Paleontological Society,* V. 6, No. 1, Jan., 1974). ● Pleistocene. Widely distributed in upper section of cliffs exposed along coastline from Imperial Beach to Pacific Beach on the north, with excellent collecting at Spanish Bight, west of San Diego (large molluscan fauna). ● Upper Pleistocene, Palos Verdes sand. 4700 feet northeast of intersection of Gaffey and Channel streets, at elevation 120 feet above land fill, north side of San Pedro (large and well preserved fauna with over 150 invertebrate genera and species). ● Upper Pleistocene, Bay Point formation. Exposures on low cut on east side of tracks of the Santa Fe Railroad between Morena Blvd. and Interstate 5, Mission Bay, San Diego (large and abundant molluscs). ● Upper Pleistocene, Sangoman. Coastal bluffs 2.5 miles southwest of Goleta, Santa Barbara County, to foot of Camino Majorca Road, Isla Vista, west to Coal Oil Point (over 116 invertebrate species of all taxa collected along this stretch of fossil exposures).

Canada

Ordovician, Chaumont formation, Wilderness stage. Outcrops on Highway 17, 6.5 miles west of Carp turnoff, about 20 miles west of Ottawa, Ontario (corals, brachiopods). ● Middle Ordovician, Trenton limestone, Trenton group, Mohawkian. Quarry 3 miles north of Kirkfield, Victoria County (index form Edrioaster-oidea). ● Middle Ordovician, "Cystid beds," Trenton limestone. Abandoned quarry near entrance to Jackson Park, Peterborough, Ontario (index form Edrioasteroidea). ● Upper Ordovician, Ellis Bay formation. Exposures at Point Leframboise and either side of Ellis Bay, near western end of Anticosti Island, Canadian Gulf of St. Lawrence [extremely rich exposures of corals and coral bioherms (an accumulation of organic remains on the site where the organism lived, e.g. a living oyster reef, or a coral reef with symbiotic association, only found as fossils)]. ● Middle Devonian, Hungry Hollow formation, Hamilton group. Tile Yard, Thedford, Ontario (large coral fauna, brachiopods, gastropods).

Colorado

Lower Cretaceous, Dakota group, Skull Creek shales. South side of Spring Canyon Dam, south end of Horsetooth Reservoir in the northern Front Range Foothills north of Boulder (best exposed sections ranging towards the Wyoming line contain typical Lower Cretaceous fauna with *Inoceramus* the predominant invertebrate, also many *Ostrea facies* and trace fossils). ● Middle late Paleocene, De Beque formation, Atwell Gulch member. "Hell's Half Acre," 6 miles south-southeast of De Beque on the De Beque-Mesa Road, Mesa County (mammal fauna here and scattered in nearby localities, condylarths). ● Middle Oligocene, White River formation, Orellan. Kewis Creek, Logan County (noted locality for reptile skeletal specimens and mammals).

Delaware

Upper Cretaceous, Mt. Laurel formation. Biggs Farm, 1 mile east of St. Georges on the bank of the Chesapeake and Delaware Canal (over 200 species of molluscs, coral, sponges, trace fossils, vertebrates, and crustaceans, including fish and reptilian teeth).

Florida

Eocene, Inglis formation. Pit 2.9 miles south of north limits of Gulf Hammock, southwest of State Road 55 (echinoids and well-preserved molluscs). ● Eocene, Ocala limestone. Exposures along Cross Florida Barge Canal, 1 mile south of Inglis (large echinoid and mollusc fauna). • Eocene, Ocala limestone. Quarry 0.5 mile west of Suwannee River and 0.5 mile north of Florida Highway S-250, in Lafayette County (dredge piles contain an abundant supply of molluscs, ostracods, forams, and echinoids). • Eocene, Ocala limestone. St. Catherine's Rock Company quarry, west of St. Catherine, south of railroad tracks, Sumter County (mollusc casts and echinoids). • Lower Miocene, Tampa formation. Six Mile Creek, between Seaboard Coastline Railroad at Florida State Road 60 and U.S. Corps of Engineers dam south of Orient Park, Hillsborough County (corals and molluscs). • Miocene, Shoal River formation. Shell bed in ravine 300 yards up creek, north bank of Shoal River, 4 miles north-northwest of Mossyhead, Walton County (molluscs). • Miocene, Jackson Bluff formation. High bluff on east bank of Apalachicola River, 4 miles north of Bristol, Liberty County (silty sand with shell fauna). • Upper Miocene, Chipola formation. Farley Creek under bridge on Florida State Road 275, 0.2 mile north of Red Oak Church, Calhoun County (bed of creek made up of highly fossiliferous sand). • Pliocene, Caloosahatchee formation. From Belle Glade west along U.S. 27 to La Belle and Moore Haven (extensive series of roadside, canal cuts, and pit exposures with millions of well-preserved molluscs, corals, and echinoids). • Pliocene-Pleistocene, mostly Caloosahatchee formation. Pit of South Bay Water Plant, South Bay, Palm Beach County (molluscs, corals). • Pleistocene, Pinecrest formation. Warren Brothers' pit, 1 mile east of Sarasota (fauna beds consist of oyster biostromes, molluscs, corals). • Pleistocene, Fort Thompson formation. Lower bank of the Caloosahatchee River, 2 miles east of La Belle, Hendry County, in vicinity of Fort Denaud bridge (molluscs, corals. See ref. *Late Cenozoic Stratigraphy of Southern Florida—A Reappraisal, 1968).*

Georgia

Middle Ordovician, Murfreesboro-Lenoir limestone. Road cut exposures on Georgia Highway 151 north of Ringgold, Catoosa County (invertebrates). • Upper Ordovician, Trenton-Maysville-Sequatchie formations. Exposures along Georgia Highway 143, slopes of Pigeon Mountain, Dade County (typical Cincinnatian fauna, bryozoans, brachiopods, corals, and trilobites). • Silurian,

Red Mountain formation. Road cut on Taylor Ridge east of Ringgold, Catoosa County (bryozoans, brachiopods, and trilobites). • Mississippian, Fort Payne chert. Southeast flank of Taylor Ridge along U.S. Highway 27 near Gore, Floyd County (brachiopods, rare crinoids, and corals). • Mississippian, St. Genevieve, and Gasper formations. Exposures along U.S. Highway 41 in Cherokee Valley, and east side of Cherokee Ridge, 3 miles north of Highway 41, Catoosa County (invertebrates). • Mississippian, between the Chattanooga shale and Lavender shale member. East foot White Mt. along west side of Cherokee Valley Road 0.55 mile north of intersection with U.S. Highway 41, Catoosa County (greenish mudrock containing spherical, phosphatic, nodular masses of plant remains, *Archaeocalamites* and algae *Confervites*). • Mississippian, Lavender shale member of the Fort Payne chert. 1.2 miles east of Ringgold, Catoosa County (trilobites, bryozoans, echinoderms, brachiopods and ostracods). • Pennsylvanian, Vandover, and Rockcastle formations. Mine dumps near Durham, east of Trenton, Dade County (plants, *Annularia,* Cordaites, *Calamites,* etc.). • Upper Cretaceous, Providence sand. One-quarter mile above junction of Pataula Creek and the Chattahoochee River, from Fort Gaines on Rt. 39, 10 miles to small store on north side of Pataula Creek, following dirt road to the Chattahoochee River bank (classic locality for molluscs, ammonites, echinoids, and coral). • Upper Eocene, Ocala formation. Quarry of Penn-Dixie Cement Corp. east side of Rt. 341 at Clinchfield, Houston County (molluscs). • Middle Eocene, McBean formation. Classic locality along west side of Savannah River, historically known as Shell Bluff, 7 miles east of Shell Bluff community, near Waynesboro, Burke County (index location of *Ostrea gigantissima*). • Oligocene, Flint River formation. Chert blocks on State Route 257, 1.5 miles south of Oakfield, Worth County (invertebrates). • Middle Miocene, Hawthorn formation. Good exposures along Rt. 41, both north and south of Valdosta, Lowndes County (invertebrates).

Idaho

Pre-Cambrian. Bonner and Boundary counties, in quarry and U.S. Highway 95 road cuts between Clark Fork and Montana border in northern Idaho (stromatolites). • Cambrian. Lakeview at south end of Pend Oreille Lake in northern part of state; near mouth of Mind Creek 5 miles southeast of Pocatello (fauna primarily trilobites). • Ordovician. Road cuts near Trail Creek Summit about 6 miles east of Sun Valley; road cuts on Bruneau Creek 2 miles west of Clayton, central Idaho (graptolites). • Upper Ordovician, Maquoketa formation, Elgin member. Road cuts along the highway between Clermont and Elgin; dry stream bed along county road "Y" east of Clermont; and the high road cuts along the Turkey River southeast of Elgin (large trilobites and ammonites). • Devonian-Carboniferous. Mackay-Arco area (variety of invertebrates). • Mississippian coral fauna in Fossil Canyon north of U.S. Highway 30, 8 miles east of Soda Springs. • Permian, Phosphoria fauna, many exposures in southeastern Idaho. • Triassic ammonite fauna, Wayan, southeastern part of state. • Triassic bivalve fauna, Hell's Canyon of the Snake River, road cuts 2.03 miles downstream from Oxbow Dam. • Jurassic oyster beds, Mineral, Idaho. • Eocene upland floras, quarries and stream banks near Salmon, Germer Basin, Thunder Mountain, and widespread in Challis Volcanics Complex of eastern and central Idaho. • Miocene, floras common and widespread in western half of Idaho: Coeur d'Alene, Clarkia, Julietta, White Bird, Weiser, Owyhee County. • Miocene fish and insects are common associates with floras of northern Idaho. • Miocene. On the Francis Kienbaum property, 2 miles south of Clarkia, 55 miles northeast of Moscow (laminated lake deposits with a large plant and insect fauna). • Pliocene-Pleistocene vertebrate faunas at Hagerman. • Fish fossils widespread in hills south of Snake River in south-central Idaho. • Fresh-water molluscs in river bluff exposures south of Snake River near Burley.

Illinois

Ordovician, Grand Detour formation, Platteville group. Near Rockford, Winnebago County (typical fauna with brachiopods, bryozoans, trilobites). • Middle Ordovician, Dunleith formation, Galena group, Eagle Point member. From Rockford on Highway 2 northward to Rockton, and west along Highway 75 to Durand,

Winnebago County (exposures afford good series of echinoderms, *Cremacrinus, Mecocrinus, Dendrocrinus, Culupocrinus,* etc.). ● Silurian, Racine formation. Near Grafton, Jersey County (typical Silurian fauna, *Calymene celebra*). ● Lower Pennsylvanian, Caseyville formation, Pounds sandstone member. Creek beds and tributaries, west of Highway 127, Jackson County, 5 miles south of Murphysboro (flora present as sandstone casts, molds, and flattened impressions, *Calamites, Trigonocarpus, Lepidodendron, Syringodendron*). ● Lower Pennsylvanian, Spencer Farm flora of the Caseyville formation. Northeastern Brown County, on the bluff of the La Moine River and along the road that runs NW-SE parallel to the river (a unique and prolific Megalopteris-Noeggerathiales flora with over 29 genera and species that occur abundantly as compression-impressions). ● Pennsylvanian, Carbondale formation. Waste piles, Alden Mine No. 5, Fulton County (black shales and large pyritic and calcareous concretions contain Heteractinid sponges, pyritized *Lepidodendron* scales, orbiculoid brachiopods, fish fragments, and abundant disarticulated phyllocarids). ● Pennsylvanian, Carbondale formation, Oak Grove limestone member. Cutback on Spoon River at Wold Covered Bridge, Knox County (typical invertebrate fauna). ● Pennsylvanian, Bond formation, La Salle limestone member. Southernmost face of Marquette Cement Manufacturing Company quarry, La Salle County (typical Pennsylvanian fauna, shark's teeth, brachiopods, corals). ● Middle Pennsylvanian, Francis Creek shale. Pit 11, Peabody Coal Company, Will County (diversified fauna of invertebrates and vertebrates; numerous brachiopods, tadpoles, and fish have been found here in nodules, as well as hundreds of larval fishes). ● Upper Pennsylvanian, Bond formation, La Salle limestone member. Quarry of Wagner Stone Company, Eppards Point Township, near Pontiac, southern Livingston County, 90 miles southwest of Chicago (remarkably well-preserved crinoids).

Indiana

Upper Ordovician, Waynesville formation, Richmond group, Cincinnatian series. Wash bank, North Branch, Cedar Creek, near Versailles, Ripley County (index forms of Edrioasteroidea *Streptaster*). ● Upper Ordovician, Whitewater formation. North bank of Elkhorn Creek, 500 yards west of bridge on Founts-Road over Elkhorn Creek and 3.9 miles south of center of Richmond, Wayne County (Cincinnatian fauna, brachiopods, and Bryozoa). ● Upper Silurian, Huntington dolomite, Niagara group. H. &. R. Stone Co. Quarry, southeast of Ridgeville, Randolph County (typical Silurian fauna, *Pentamerus oblongus*). ● Middle Devonian, Dundee limestone, Silica shale-Tenmile Creek dolomite, Traverse group. May's Quarry, between Highway 24 and the Maumee River, near Woodburn (these formations produce an extensive series of cnidarians, crinoids, bryozoans, placoderms, trace fossils, brachiopods, trilobites, and ostracods). ● Upper Devonian, New Albany shale. Delphi Limestone Co. Quarry, on the north side of U.S. Highway 421, at the northwest edge of Delphi, Carrol County (conulariid-bearing beds, *Ctenoconularia delphiensis*). ● Mississippian, Glen Dean-Golconda formations, Middle Chester. Road cut exposures along Highway 62, as it descends the west bluff of Little Blue River, ½ mile east of Sulphur, Crawford County (extensive Chesterian macrofauna weathers out all along exposures, but difficult to assign to specific members). ● Mississippian, Glen Dean formation. Mulzer Brothers Co. Quarry, 0.8 mile south of junction of Indiana State Highways 145 and 164, about 2.5 miles north of village of Ekerty, Crawford County (crinoids, brachiopods, bryozoans, blastoids). ● Mississippian, Glen Dean formation. Abandoned quarry 1.8 miles southwest of village of Hillman and 310 feet northwest of Indiana State Highway 56, Dubois County (similar Mississippian fauna). ● Mississippian, Glen Dean formation. Corey's Bluff, along west bank of Sugar Creek, north of Crawfordsville, Montgomery County. This is the classic crinoid locality that produced, from 1858 to 1946, over 104 species of crinoids. Discovered in 1832, the crinoid beds were exposed and thousands of specimens were collected to enrich many museums, as well as the cabinets of James Hall (now the Walker Museum, University of Chicago) and in the Springer Collection at the U.S. National Museum. Corey's Bluff is stated to be grown over with trees and weeds, although traces of the earlier excavations at the crinoidal beds may still be seen. Occasional specimens may still be found here, as well as along other creeks in Montgomery County. Best historical description and illustrations of the crinoids collected here, may be found in the Sant and Lane's *Crawfordsville (Indiana) Crinoid Studies* (1964, The University of Kansas Paleontological Contributious Article 7). ● Pleistocene, Wisconsin stage. Stream bank at Little Cedar Creek, southeast of Brookville, Franklin County, (molluscs, *Vertigo, Pupilla, Columella, Discas*).

Iowa

Upper Ordovician, Maquoketa formation. Graf Station, Dubuque County, at the I.C.R.R. station at Graf, 8 miles west of Dubuque and 1½ miles north of Highway 20 (very extensive series of closely-packed straight cephalopods). ● Upper Devonian, Hackberry stage. Rockford, Floyd County. One-quarter mile south and ¼ mile west of the Rockford Brick and Tile Co. pit on Country Road "D" (brachiopods, gastropods and corals). ● Another Hackberry location at Bird Hill, Cerro Gordo County, 3½ miles west and ¼ mile south of the brickyard. ● Mississippian, Gilmore City limestone. Abandoned quarry of Whelp & McMartin Co., 1 mile west and ¼ mile north of Gilmore City; Hallet Construction Quarry, ½ mile northwest of Gilmore City, Pocahontas County; other quarries within a couple miles around above city (classic and type locality for very extensive beds of brachiopods, bryozoans, and crinoids). ● Mississippian, Pella beds, St. Louis limestone, Meramecian series. Abandoned county quarry west of Harvey, Marion County (index form of Edrioasteroidea *Lepidodiscus*). ● Mississippian, Hampton formation, Kinderhook series. Le Grand quarries 1 mile north of where Highway 30 enters the city limits (finest crinoids collected here, but exceptionally difficult to find. Ref. *The Crinoid Fauna of the Hampton Formation at LeGrand,* by Laudon and Beane, University of Iowa Studies in Natural History, V. 17). ● Mississippian, Gilmore City formation, Kinderhook series. Gilmore City quarries, as above.

Kansas

Upper Pennsylvanian, Stanton formation, South Bend member. South bank of Elk River on both east and west side of county road bridge, 1.5 miles south and slightly west of Elk City, Montgomery County (large coral fauna, *Bibunophyllum* and

Neokoninchophyllum, fusulinids, echinoid spines, brachiopods, and bryozoans). ● Upper Pennsylvanian, Stoner limestone. Quarry south of railroad tracks less than 1 mile south of Benedict, Wilson County (algae, corals, and miscellaneous invertebrates). ● Upper Pennsylvanian, Captain Creek limestone. Small quarry on south side of east-west county road, 4 miles west of Sycamore, Montgomery County (typical Pennsylvanian invertebrates). ● Upper Pennsylvanian, Plattsburg, and Stanton formations. Road cut on Kansas Highway 47, 1.5 miles west of Altoona, Wilson County (large coral fauna, *Archaeolithophyllum,* byrozoans, *Glyptopora,* and brachiopods). ● Upper Pennsylvanian, stratigraphic position undefined. Abandoned limestone quarry 2 miles east of the town of Hamilton, Greenwood County (remarkable fauna of acanthodians, lungfish, palaeoniscoid fishes, sharks, amphibians, scorpions, eurypterids, arachnids, insects, including unusually large cockroaches, and abundant flora of *Walchia,* Cordaites, *Alethopteris,* and *Samaropsis*). ● Upper Cretaceous, Fort Hays member. Road cut along U.S. Highway 183, 1 mile north of Saline River, Ellis County (fauna contains bryozoans, serpulids, molluscs, sponges, shark's teeth and fish scales).

Kentucky

Middle Ordovician, Lexington limestone, Grier member. Type locality, road cut along Shyocks Ferry Road, 1 mile south of Milner, Tyrone Quadrangle, Woodford County (fauna stromatoporoids, brachiopods, bryozoans). ● Middle Ordovician, Cynthiana formation. Hillside exposure west of Kentucky Highway 8, ½ mile south of Carntown (typical brachiopods, Bryozoa, and crinoid *Merocrinus*); road cut exposures west of bridge across Sugar Creek, at divergence of U.S. Highways 127 and 42, Gallatin County (brachiopods, bryozoans, and trilobite *Triathrus*). ● Middle Ordovician, Trenton limestone, Trenton group. 1.5 miles south of High Bridge, Mercer County (index form of Edrioasteroidea *Edriophus*). ● Upper Ordovician, Lower Eden, Cincinnatian series. West of railroad trestle 15, 2 miles west of Million (index form of Edrioasteroidea *Streptaster*). ● Upper Ordovician, Liberty formation through lower limestone of Silurian Osgood formation. Road cuts at quarry 1 mile west of Seatonville on north side of

Seatonville Road, and outcrop on hillside opposite quarry on south side of road, Jefferson County (typical Upper Ordovician-Lower Silurian fauna). ● Upper Ordovician, Arnheim formation through Saluda member of the Whitewater formation. Road cut 7.2 miles southeast of Bardstown Courthouse on south side of Highway 150, Nelson County (corals, bryozoans, and brachiopods). ● Lower Silurian, Brassfield limestone. Abandoned railroad cut midway between Panola and Brassfield, Madison County (typical brachiopod and bryozoan fauna). ● Mississippian, Newman limestone, Haney member. Exposure in drainage ditch on eastbound lane of Interstate 65, 300 feet west of exit ramp to U.S. 60, northeast of Olive Hill; abandoned pit on northeast edge of Kenmore Stone Co. Olive Hill Quarry, 0.3 mile north of junction of Highway 60 and Interstate 64, northeast of Olive Hill; abandoned pit on western edge of Ace Stone Co. Quarry, 1.7 miles east of Olive Hill, all in Carter County; outcrop along Kentucky State Road 1274, 2.2 miles south of junction of Road 1274 and Kentucky State Road 519, south of Morehead, Rowan County (these exposures of the Newman limestone provide a very large collection of Mississippian fauna, including many excellently preserved crinoids, particularly *Agassizocrinus*).

Louisiana

Lower Eocene, Marthaville formation, Sabine group. Numerous exposures around Marthaville, Nathcitoches Parish (fauna, corals *Madracis* and *Haimesiostraea,* bivalves, gastropods, and ostracods). ● Eocene, Moody's Branch formation, Jackson group. Creole Bluff, Montgomery Landing near the Red River, southwest of Montgomery, Grant Parish (over 50 species of Eocene Mollusca). ● Oligocene, Byram marl, Vicksburg group. Railroad cut at Rosefield, Catahoula Parish (large bryozoan fauna).

Maryland

Lower Devonian, Oriskany sandstone, Ridgeley member. Railroad cut of the Western Maryland Railroad near Cumberland, south end of Collier Mt., about 100 yards north of the Potomac River and 300 yards east of Spring Gap P.O. (large brachiopods and gastropods with index forms *Rensselaeria, Costispirifer,* and

platyceratid gastropods. Upper bedding contains a shell coquina).
● Middle Devonian, Marcellus shale. Abandoned slate quarry at
the junction of Maryland State Road 56, and McCay Ferry Road,
near Big Pool, west of Frederick, Washington County (articulate
brachiopods, bivalves, and crinoids). ● Upper Cretaceous, Marshalltown formation. Pit, east of the Penn Central Railroad bridge,
Chesapeake and Delaware Canal and lower slope along main-
tenance road east of the above bridge (abundance of ammonites,
gastropods, and bivalves). ● Upper Cretaceous, Mount Laurel,
Marshalltown, Englishtown, Merchantville, Magothy, and Potomac
formations. All the above formations are well-exposed at one point
or another along the entire length of the Chesapeake and Delaware
Canal (well-preserved bivalves, gastropods, and ammonites).
● Miocene, Choptank formation. One of America's classic fossil
horizons, from which specimens have been known since 1685, is
the famed Calvert Cliffs, on the western shore of Chesapeake Bay,
Calvert County. Here the sands and diatomaceous earth offer one of
the largest and best-preserved selections of Tertiary macro fauna
within the several members of the Miocene Choptank formation.
Mollusca from the Choptank outcrops can be seen in countless
private collections and in museums throughout the world. Fossil
exposures are numerous along the high cliffs. In some places,
collecting is not recommended due to dangerous overhang or high
waters. Much of the land along the Bay is private property. Good
collecting can be found along private beaches, through the
Maryland Geological Survey, or the various geological societies
that have access to selected collecting areas. Listed here are
several excellent areas at which large collections can be
made: ● 1600 feet north of Harper's Creek, 0.9 mile south of
Western Shore, along Calvert Cliffs. ● Type section for the
Choptank formation, 1.8 miles south-southeast of Dover Bridge
(bridge over Choptank River for Maryland Highway 331). ● Across
Choptank River from Frazier Neck, 4 miles southeast of Easton,
Talbot County. ● Natural cliffs in southwestern bank of Patuxent
River. ● Between Cole Creek and St. Thomas Creek, 3 miles
south of Hollywood. ● Across from Boone's Island, St. Mary's
County (locality formerly known as "Drum Cliff" and "Jones
Wharf"). ● At south end of long line of continuous cliffs south of

Flag Ponds. ● Two miles south of Long Beach. (The fauna range from large bivalves and corals, to gastropods, echinoids, and vertebrate fragments. Large colonies of *Balanus concavus* are to be found encrusting large *Lyropecten* shells. Particularly abundant throughout the various members are specimens of *Corbula, Turritella,* the coral *Astrhelia palmata, Ecphora quadricostata,* several pectinid species, and dozens of genera and species of bivalves and gastropods. Shark's teeth are also abundant, as literally millions upon millions of teeth have been strained from the Choptank sands, ranging in size from almost microscopic specimens to giant *Carcharodon* teeth. Ref. Robert S. Gernant, *Paleoecology of the Choptank Formation (Miocene) of Maryland and Virginia,* 1970, Maryland Geological Survey Reports, Investigation No. 12. Also useful is *Miocene (of Maryland),* 1 volume text, 1 volume plates, by the Maryland Geological Survey, 1904, and *Miocene Fossils of Maryland,* by Harold E. Vokes, Department of Geology, 1957, Mines and Water Resources, Bulletin 20.) ● From the Jurassic and Cretaceous of Maryland, dinosaur fragments and tracks have been collected, primarily during mining operations, for well over a century. Fragmentary materials and slabs with tracks and drag-marks are still found occasionally. These recorded sites are all along Highway 1, at Schoolhouse Hill (Baltimore County), Jessup (Anne Arundel County), Beltsville, Marikirk, and Bladensburg (Prince George County). Dinosaurs known from Maryland are *Dryptosaurus, Coelurus,* and *Astrodon.* Among the shark remains found, are the teeth of *Galaeocerdo, Hemipristis, Oxyrhina, Sphyrma, Odontaspis,* and the much sought-after, giant *Carcharodon megalodon.* ● From the Tertiary Period, specimens of deer, horse, mastodons, tapir, and rhinoceros may be found. ● Miocene, Calvert formation. West shore of Chesapeake Bay, 1.5 miles south of Plum Point, Calvert County (molluscan and coral fauna, scarce echinoids, whale fragments, and shark teeth). ● Miocene, Chesapeake group. Along the banks of the Coursey and Killen Ponds near Felton (fauna poorly preserved but representative). ● Pleistocene, Columbia group. State sand and gravel pit just south of Middletown on Highway 896 (plant impressions). ● Pleistocene, Omar formation, Columbia group. Marine deposits abundant where Highway 113 crosses Pepper Creek at Dagsboro.

Massachusetts

Upper Cretaceous, Magothy formation. A dark gray lignitic clay along the beach from road leading to the concession area, Gay Head, Martha's Vineyard Island (cones, family Pinaceae, *Pityostrobus kayei* and *Pseudoaraucaria arnoldii*). ● This state has few fossil localities, mostly consisting of Cambrian strata with some trilobite remaihs. Some dinosaurian remains and tracks can also be found.

Michigan

Middle Devonian, Dundee limestone. Spoil dumps of the Martin-Marietta Quarry, south of Arkona Road and 1¼ miles east of U.S. 523, between Sanford and Godkins Road, and southwest of the Wabash railroad tracks, Augusta Township (typical Silica shale fauna. Ref. *Strata and Megafossils of the Middle Devonian Silica Formation,* University of Michigan Museum, Papers on Paleontology, No. 8, 1975). ● Middle Devonian, Ferron Point formation, Traverse group. Abandoned shale pit of Alpena Portland Cement Co., 7 miles north of Alpena (index forms of Edrioasteroidea, *Krama, Postibulla*). ● Middle Devonian, Charlevoix limestone and Petoskey formations, Traverse group. Dozens of quarries in Charlevoix and Emmet counties, from Charlevoix, on the shores of Lake Michigan, to Petoskey at Little Traverse Bay, expose fossiliferous outcrops of Middle Devonian Petoskey, Gravel Point and Whiskey Creek formations, and the Norwood and Ellsworth shales. Also, abandoned Superior Quarry of Northern Lime Co. near Nine Mile Point, 2 miles west of Bay Shore Quarry; abandoned Northern Lime Co. quarry bordering Little Traverse Bay in eastern part of Petoskey, U.S. Highway 31 traversing the rim of the old quarry; Kegonic Quarry, between U.S. 31 and Michigan 131, 1 mile east of Bay View, between Pickerel Road and the Pennsylvanian Railroad, Emmet County. (The macrofauna within the members of the Traverse group appear to be both abundant and diversified. In all the quarries collected from there appears to be a large series of tetracoral forms, as *Aulacophyllum, Heliophyllum, Hexagonaria,* and others, while the Tabulata are represented by *Aulopora, Favosites, Syringopora,* and *Trachypora,* as well as several other genera. The Brachiopoda are richly represented by such forms as

Athyris, Atrypa, Cyrtina, Leptaena, Mucrospirifer, Productella, Rhipidomella, Spinocyrtia, and many others. The mollusca have fewer forms, as *Euomphalus, Pleurotomaria,* and *Tentaculites,* while the bivalves provide *Aviculopecten, Janeia, Nuculites,* and *Paracyclas.* Cephalopods are found, with the *"Orthoceras"* group fairly abundant, also *Michelinoceras* and *Tumidoceras.* Trilobito-morphs provide about six forms, *Ancyropyge, Cordania, Dechenella, Greenops, Phacops,* and, rarely, *Proetus.* The echinoderms are represented by both crinoids and blastoids, *Megistocrinus* and *Melocrinus, Codaster* and *Pentremites.* The bryozoan beds of the Whiskey Creek formation provide *Dolatocrinus* as well. Ref. Keslling, Segall and Sorensen, *Devonian Strata of Emmet and Charlevoix Counties, Michigan,* Michigan Museum of Paleontology, Papers of Paleontology, No. 7, 1974.)

Minnesota

Upper Cambrian, Franconia formation, Birkmose member. Road cut on State Highway 80 at Wood Hill, Juneau County (trilobite zones, *Camaraspis, Conaspis, Ptychaspis* fauna); road cuts on U.S. 16, 6 miles west of Tomah, Monroe County (typical trilobite fauna, *Maustonia, Parabolinoides*); Hell Hollow, 1.3 miles north of Reno, Houston County (trilobites *Dikelocephalus, Prosaukia, Conaspis, Ptychaspis*); road cut on U.S. 8 and section along Pine Point Trail, 1 mile south of Taylors Falls, Chisago County (trilobites *Conaspis, Wilbernia, Taenicephalus, Parabolinoides* and brachiopod *Eoorthis remnichia*). ● Ordovician, Dunleith formation, Champlainian. Wagner Quarry on U.S. 52, 5½ miles south of Cannon Falls, Goodhue County (brachiopods, bryozoans, and the Belemnocystitil *Scalenocystites strimplei*). ● Middle Ordovician, Rhinidyctia beds, Decorah formation, Mohawkian series. Ford Plant grounds, St. Paul (index form Edrioasteroidea *Foerstediscus*).

Mississippi

Cretaceous, Eutaw formation. Santonian. Banks and bed of the Tombigbee River, 1.2 miles west of the Waverly and along Tibbee Creek, near Tupelo, Lee Co. (Fragments of hadrosaurian dinosaurs, in association with a typical Eutaw assemblage of molluscs. The Eutaw at this locality underlies the Selma chalk which is noted for an abundant invertebrate fauna known to contain varied Mollusca, fish remains, crabs, ammonites, and a very large microfauna.) • Upper Cretaceous, Prairie Bluff chalk. On both sides of Mississippi Highway 6, 2 miles east of Pontotoc, Pontotoc County (echinoids *Hardouinia* and *Hemiaster,* gastropods, bivalves, and vertebrates). • Upper Cretaceous, Demopolis chalk. Agriculture Farm at the northern city limits of New Albany and west of U.S. 45, Noxubee County (typical fauna with *Exogyra costata* and *cancellata,* casts of molluscs). • Upper Cretaceous, Ripley formation. Quarry 450 feet southeast of crossing of the North Prong of Chiwapa Creek by old Mississippi Highway 15, 2 miles south of Pontotoc, Pontotoc County (*Microbacia, Hardouninia, Ostrea, Exogyra, Pecten,* etc. Ref. *The Upper Cretaceous Deposits.* Mississippi State Geological Survey Bulletin 40, 1940). • Upper Cretaceous, Owl Creek formation. Cut on Mississippi Highway 15, northward facing slope of Kings Creek Valley, 3.2 miles south of New Albany, Union County (typical Upper Cretaceous fauna, with molluscs, *Baculites,* shark's teeth, and mosasaur teeth and vertebrae). • Upper Cretaceous, Selma chalk. Pontotoc Road, Mississippi Highway 6, 3.5 miles west of Tupelo, Lee County (echinoids, casts of molluscs, large bivalves). • Paleocene, Clayton formation. Cut on St. Louis-San Francisco Railroad, 4 miles southeast of New Albany, Union County (*Hamulus major* and *onyx, Lima reticulata,* and *Halymenites major*). • Eocene, Yazoo clay. 4.2 miles northwest of U.S. 49 from Cynthia, in Miss-Lite Aggregate Plant pit, Hinds County (gastropods, bivalves, shark teeth, and vertebrae, fragments of whale-like mammal *Basilosaurus cetoides* may be found here). • Eocene, Bashi formation, Wilcox group. Road cuts both sides of Mississippi State Road 19, 16.2 miles north of Tom Bailey Drive in Meridian, Lauderdale County (vertebrates, Mollusca, rare "pavement" type of shark's teeth and snake vertebrae). • Oligocene, Mint Spring marl. Two miles east of Sylvarena Smith County Lime Quarry, east of West Tallahala Creek on State Highway 18 (includes pectinid *Chlamys menthifontis*); 2 miles southwest of Brandon, Marquette Cement Co. Quarry, Rankin County (fauna similar to above locality).

Missouri

Upper Cambrian, Elvins group, Davis formation, and Derby Doerun dolomite. Within a circle ranging from the type locality at Elvins (St. Francis County), Fredericktown (Madison County), Lesterville (Reynolds County) and Belgrade (Washington County), the Elvins shale facies contain a large and varied trilobite and brachiopod fauna. Exposures in this St. Francis Mountains region provide excellent sites of trilobites, with over 50 genera and species. • Upper Cambrian, Bonneterre, Potosi, and Eminence formations. East bank of Big River, 2.7 km. west-southwest of Irondale and 0.7 km. downstream from rhyolite outcrops, north edge of the St. Francis Mountains complex, Washington County [an important site of Upper Cambrian fauna; the overlying formations contain fossil *Monoplacophora hypseloconus,* ancestral to the living deep-sea monoplacophoran, genus *Neoplina* (these are Mollusca with a single valve containing several paired muscle scars; during the Paleozoic they were shallow marine organisms, presently they inhabit abyssal depths)]. • Middle Ordovician, Kimmswick limestone. Goetz Quarry at Glen Park, near Barnhart (trilobites and brachiopods). • Middle Ordovician, Plattin formation. Type locality exposures near the mouth of Plattin Creek in Jefferson County (brachiopods, trace fossils, corals, and bryozoans); Joerling Brothers Quarry, New Melle, St. Charles County (large brachiopod beds). • Upper Ordovician, Bryant Knob formation, Edgewood group. Type section, outcrops west side of State Highway 79, 4 miles south of Clarkville, Pike County (brachiopods). • Mississippian, St. Louis limestone, Salem formation, Meramecian series. South pit, Vigus Quarries Inc., Vigus, St. Louis County (typical brachiopods, corals, stromatolites, conodonts). • St. Genevieve and St. Louis formations. Fort Bellefontaine Quarry, Missouri Portland Cement Co., St. Louis County (large brachiopods, corals, and conodonts). • Middle Pennsylvanian, Burgner formation, Atokan series. Mine dumps, 1.5 miles south of Centerville, Jasper County (crinoids *Synbathocrinus* and *Anchicrinus*).

Montana

Archaeozoic, Belt series. Along Going-To-The-Sun Highway, Glacier National Park (large masses and reefs of algae). ● Upper Mississippian. Heath shale. 2 miles south and 6 miles east of Heath, Fergus County (black, fissile shale, about 8 inches thick, bears crustaceans, many fish, conchastraceans, ostracods, and numerous brachiopod forms). ● Oligocene, Ruby River Basin formation. Paper shales in diggings approximately 13 miles from Alder, between Peterson and Morgan Creek, Madison County (locality noted for diverse insects and plants in the paper-thin shales).

Nebraska

Pennsylvanian, Missouri series, Lansing group. Plattsburg-Vilas-Stanton formation. Dyson Hollow, approximately 1.2 miles southwest of La Platte, Sarpy County (brachiopods, fusulines, and crinoids); abandoned quarry 1 mile southwest of La Platte (fauna similar to above locality); excellent exposures south of Gretna Fish Hatchery on Highway 31, overlooking Platte River, on north side of road, Sarpy County (abundant crinoids, echinoid spines, trilobite *Ditomopyge*, corals, and brachiopods). ● Pennsylvanian, Virgil series, Wabaunsee group. Emporia formation, Auburn formation. At Table Rock, from City Park and water tower proceed north for two blocks to intersection with State Highway 65, turn left (west) and go 1 mile. The outcrop is on right (north) side of road (large deposits with bryozoans, brachiopods, gastropods, and ammonites); outcrop situated both sides of Highway 2, near Unadilla, 0.2 mile from junction of Little State Highway (includes brachiopods, gastropods, ectoprocts, crinoids, and, rarely, trilobites and shark's teeth). ● Pennsylvanian, Virgil series, Shawneed group, Deer Creek formation-Tecumseh formations. From Weeping Water proceed westward along "H" Street for about 0.3 mile to the intersection of county road and Highway 50, turn right (north) and proceed 0.12 mile. The outcrop is situated on the right (east) side of the road (typical crinoids, brachiopods, and corals). ● Permian, Wolfcampian, Matfield shale. Road cut on Highway 8, 2.4 miles east of Barneston, Gage County (rhabdomesid bryozoans and brachiopods). ● Permian, Big Blue series. Chase group. Odell and Grant shales and Winfield limestone. Road cuts south of Odell, along Highway 8, and also 1.6 miles south of Odell, turn left at junction of Highways 8 and 112, then north 1.5 miles to exposure [*Nebraskacrinus, Platyceras, Rhombopora* (crinoids), and abundant brachiopods]. ● Cretaceous, Colorado group, Greenhorn-Graneros formations. From western edge of Gilead to west on U.S. 136 for about 1.6 miles, turn right onto county road from Highway 136, go north, crossing Little Blue River, for 1.7 mile to junction between county roads, exposure is on north side of the east-west road [*Inoceramus, Portheus, Squalicarax, Ptychodus, Belemnitella,* and *Prinocyphus* (bivalves)]. ● Middle Miocene, Runningwater formation. Type section northwest corner of Box Butte County, north side of Niobrara River, 19 miles east of Agate (mammals).

Nevada

Lower Cambrian, Pioche shale. Exposed along western front of Frenchman Mountain, Clark County, approximately 6.5 miles due east of the town of North Las Vegas (trilobites with *Paeduemias, Fremontia, Biceratops,* trace fossils, and *Hyolithes*). ● Several formations in both Lower and Middle Cambrian series, in numerous exposures in and around the town of Eureka. This is a classic trilobite and brachiopod region made famous by the descriptions of the fauna by Charles D. Walcott. ● Upper Cambrian, undefined formation. Exposures located on crest of large spur projecting westward from face of Egan Range, 6 miles north of ranch at Sunnyside. The spur is south of Cave Valley and north of Whipple Cave (brachiopods and trilobites, *Leperditia*). ● Middle Ordovician, Antelope Valley limestone. Extends up and across Copper Mountain on the north side of Ikes Canyon about 0.5 to 0.7 mile west of canyon mouth, Tonquina Range, central Nevada (classic sponge bed, brachiopods, and rhombiferan cystoids). ● Upper Ordovician, Tank Hill limestone. Ely Springs Range, Pioche Mining district (*Protopliomerops, Kirkella, Memoparia, Asaphellus, Lingulella*); Pogonip group, Lehman formation and Kanosh shale. North Snake Range section, on old U.S. Route 6 (Cowboy Pass route) 7 miles south of Robinson Ranch, 2 miles west of the graded road [*Leperditia, Barrandia,* large *Pseudomera,* receptaculites (a lower Paleozoic sponge with a globular to platter-shaped body), and numerous brachiopods]; Antelope Valley limestone. Meiklejohn Peak on west face of Bare Mountain 6 miles northwest of Beatty (trilobites and articulate brachiopods). ● Upper Devonian, Red Hills bed and Base Devils Gate limestone. Southwest flank of Red Hill, off Red Hill Road, in Horse Creek Valley quadrangle, between Carlin and Eureka, Simpson Park Range, Eureka County (fish remains, *Astrolepis,* brachiopods, tentaculitids, conodonts). ● Permian, 1 mile south-southeast of the Coal Canyon Mine, on a ridge at the 7000-foot contour, east central Elko County (invertebrate fauna). ● Upper Triassic, Grantsville formation. Exposures along the Union District, Shoshone Mountains, 30 miles south of both Eastgate and Campbell Creek Ranch on U.S. 50, about 50 miles southwest of Austin via Nevada State 21, also about 70 miles north of Tonopah, by way of the Cloverdale Ranch and about 40 miles east of Gabbs by way of Lodi Valley and Burnt Cabin Summit. This is lonely country, sparsely settled and difficult to get around in, but a very rich selection of brachiopods and ammonites makes the trip worthwhile.

New Hampshire

Exposures here are extremely rare and difficult to find, with fossils deformed by folding and metamorphism. Late Lower Silurian fossils from the Sillimanite Zone have been collected near Claremont, while Middle Paleozoic invertebrates, as well as Silurian brachiopods, are reported from metamorphosed rocks in the western part of the state.

New Jersey

Upper Cretaceous, Merchantville formation, Matawan group. Along west bank of Matawan Creek, north of Matawan, Monmouth County (*Belemnitella americana, Choristothyris plicata, Exogyra costata, E. cancellata*). ● Upper Cretaceous, Navesink marl. Exposures along west bank of Crosswicks Creek, Ocean County (*Belemnitella americana, Exogyra costata, Inoceramus, Cucullaea, Lunatia halli*); spoil banks around irrigation pond on property of Oscar Damninger, where Jackson Road crosses boundary between Mantua and Harrison Township, Gloucester County (bone fragments of plesiosaurs in association with typical Navesink fauna. Ref. *The Cretaceous Fossils of New Jersey,* New Jersey Department of Conservation and Development, 1958, 2 vols.). ● Eocene, Umpqua formation. Road cuts along Road 3406 adjacent to Snouth Creek, between 2.5 and 3 miles east of Agnes (decapod fauna, *Raminoides washburnei* and *Plagiolphus weaveri*).

New Mexico

Devonian. Along New Mexico Highway 90, 14 miles east of Santa Rita, and 30 miles west of Kingston (typical fossiliferous Devonian shales; steep hills have many weathered silicified Silurian brachiopods). ● Pennsylvanian. U.S. Highway 64, from Taos to Eagle Nest; road cuts along U.S. Highway 60 west to Scholle; along New Mexico Highway 63, north of Pecos, in the Pecos River Canyon (all of these exposures provide abundant brachiopods, molluscs, and bryozoans); Jemez Springs, on New Mexico Highway 4, about 20 miles north of San Ysidro. Hills and stream behind ruined mission, Jemez State Monument (extensive Pennsylvanian fauna); Tijeras Canyon, near Albuquerque, about 5 miles south of the junction with Interstate 40, New Mexico Highway 10 passes through a series of cuts in Pennsylvanian limestone (brachiopods, bryozoans, and trilobites); along New Mexico Highways 44 and 536 to the crest of the Sandia Mountains near Albuquerque, and along the crest of the mountain (brachiopods, bryozoans, and crinoid stems); Madera formation. Shale bed exposed over an area of ½ acre west of State Highway 10 and 8.5 miles south of its intersection with U.S. 66, Bernalillo County (long known for its excellently preserved palaeoniscoid and acanthodian fishes, also producing tetrapod amphibians, among them *Lafonius lehmani*). ● Permian, Yeso formation. Along U.S. Highway 380-70 between Hondo and Roswell (typical Permian fauna). ● Cretaceous, Greenhorn limestone. Along U.S. 85, south of Springer (typical Cretaceous fauna with numerous shark teeth); on U.S. Highway 380 between San Antonio and Carrizozo; at Carthage, 8 to 10 miles east of San Antonio; in several road cuts 3 to 5 miles farther eastward (Permian formations containing scaphopods, ammonites, clams).

New York

Lower Cambrian, Neopagetina macrofauna. Deep road cut on Columbia County Route 32, 1 mile west of Malden Bridge, Malden, (trilobites, *Olenellus, Paedeumias, Senodiscus, Acediscus*). • Middle Cambrian, Nassau beds. Exposures along New York Central Railroad tracks at Stockport Station, Judson Point, Hudson North quadrangle (trilobites, *Beltagnostus, Bathyuriscus, Centropleura, Hypagnostus*). • Ordovician, Chaumont formation, Black River group. Jones Quarry, 1 mile south of Chazy (brachiopods, gastropods, corals); Napanee limestone, Kings Fall limestone. Between Watertown and Utica, roadside exposures around Deer River, Roaring Brook, Turin, Trenton Falls, Ingham Mills, in north-central New York State (abundance of brachiopods, ectoprocts, trilobites, ostracods, crinoids, cystoids, asteroids, corals, conodonts, sponges, algae, and trace fossils, with over 200 species); Cobourg limestone, Trenton group. Exposures along bed of Stony Creek where it crosses U.S. 11, at Talcott Falls, Jefferson County (brachiopods, corals, and bryozoans); Lowville limestone, Black River group. East wall of quarry in Camp Drum, about 850 feet west of LeRaysville Cemetery, south of the Camp Drum-Evans Mills Road, Jefferson County (bryozoans, brachiopods, gastropods, orthoceracones, crinoid stems, ostracods); Chaumont formation, Black River group. Quarry 1 mile east of Champion Huddle, Jefferson County (corals, cephalopods, gastropods). • Middle Silurian, Lockport formation, Gosport member. Railroad cut on the east side of "The Gulf," 1.3 miles west on Route 31 from intersection with Route 78 from Lockport (extremely fossiliferous exposures with tabulate and rugose corals, crinoids, brachiopods); Herkimer formation, Upper Clinton group. Steel Creek, Ilion Gorge, Winfield quadrangle (brachiopods, gastropods, bivalves). • Lower Devonian, Esopus formation. Quarry 1.2 miles west of Cotterville, northwest of Rosendale (ammonite fauna, *Eso poceras*). • Devonian, West Hills flags and shales. Large gully at head of Italy Hollow, Yates County (ophiuroids, *Klasmura mirabilis*). • Middle Devonian, Ludlowville formation, Ledyard shale member. Spring Creek at the town of Alden, between the Alden-Crittenden Road and Route 20, Erie County (pyritized fossils, brachiopods, gastropods, bivalves, cephalopods, and trilobites, large colonies of *Phacops rana*);

Onondaga limestone. Abandoned LeRoy Quarry, north 2.2 miles on Route 237 from intersection with Route 5 in village of Stafford, turn left, go 2.6 miles to east end of Britt Road, cross Lehigh Valley Railroad tracks north into entrance road to quarry (corals *Heliophyllum, Favosites, Cystiphylloides*); Moscow shale, Windom and Kashong members. Cazenovia Creek, near Northrup Road, Spring Brook; Penn Dixie Cement Co. quarry near Big Tree Road, Bayview; Eighteen Mile Creek, between railroad bridge and mouth of Lake Erie shore south of Eighteen Mile Creek, all in Erie County (large and abundant classic fauna, brachiopods, corals, cephalopods, bivalves, and trilobites); Ludlowville formation, Hamilton group. Brown's Creek, 1 mile west of York (typical Hamilton fauna of brachiopods and trilobites). ● Upper Devonian, Chadakoin formation, Dexterville and Ellicott members. Abandoned shale quarry at Jamestown, Chautaugua County (*Pugnoides, Aviculopecten, Cyrtispirifer, Productella, Leptodesma*); Sonyea formation, Cashgue shale member. 130 yards upstream from railroad bridge, Eighteen Mile Creek, 0.5 mile northwest of North Evans; below road culvert at intersection North Davis Road, and Conley Road northwest-flowing tributary to Cazenovia Creek, 0.8 mile south of Spring Brook; Parris limestone. About 900-foot elevation in third stream crossed by Griesa Hill Road north of intersection with New York Route 21, 3 miles northeast of Naples; Geneseo formation, Geneseo shale member. Fall Brook, 1.5 miles south of Geneseo; Penn Yann shale member. Near the foot of Falls in Lodi Glen, 1.7 miles west of Lodi, Seneca Lake (all Upper Devonian localities noted for extensive sites of ammonoid *Probeloceras* and related forms in association with typical Upper Devonian fauna).

North Carolina

Eocene, Castle Hayne formation. Quarry 0.7 mile west of Carlton, Duplin County (molds and casts of molluscan fauna, well-preserved pectinids, echinoids, and, rarely, fish teeth and ostracods). ● Lower Miocene, Trent formation. Pit on east side of highway 0.2 mile southeast of Silverdale, Onslow County (shell gravel on clayey coquina); quarry of the Superior Stone Co. at Belgrade, Craven County (*Busycon onslowensis, Calyptraea aperta, Crepidula, Oliva, Arca* and several other forms); Duplin formation. Left bank of Lumber River, 2 miles east of Lumberton, and exposures from 2 to 4 miles along Highway 221, Robeson County (large collection of Miocene fauna with Mollusca and corals. Ref. *Geology of the Coastal Plain of North Carolina,* by Horace G. Richards. Transactions American Philosphical Society, Philadelphia, new ser., V. 40, 1950); classic locality pit about 500 yards southeast of Matthews Farm, 1.7 miles southwest of Magnolia, Duplin County (classic Mollusca, echinoids, and Bryozoa); Yorktown formation. South bank of Tar River, 0.5 mile downstream from North Carolina Highway 42 at Old Sparta, Edgecombe County (shell bed 15 feet below top of bluff, classic molluscan site); Pungo River and Yorktown formations. Texas Great Sulphur Co. Lee Creek Phosphate Quarry, near Aurora. Site is located on southern shore of Pamlico River east of mouth of Lee Creek, Beaufort County (aside from typical massive Mollusca of Yorktown age, cetacean remains have been found of *Squalodon tiedemani*). ● Miocene-Pleistocene, Duplin to Pamlico formation. Strip mine operations of Texas Gulf, Inc., east of Suffolk Scarp, near Aurora, off Lee Creek, Beaufort County (phosphate mining operations have exposed beds ranging from late Miocene through late Pleistocene, with fossils typical of those horizons, index macrofaunas, and trace fossils). ● Marina excavations of the Carolina Shores Development Co., 0.3 mile south of Calabash, Brunswick County (an extremely rich exposure in quarrying operations with *Glycymeris americana* and *Mercenaria tridacnoides* the most abundant forms, also *Chione, Ostrea, Anadara, Chlamys, Busycon, Dentalium,* and *Septastrea*).

North Dakota

Upper Cretaceous, Fox Hills formation, Timber Lake member. North-facing cutback on Beaver Creek in Seeman Park, 1 mile southwest of Linton, Emmons County (bivalves, ammonites, gastropods, decapod crustaceans, and echinoids); Logan County near town of Burnstead, road cut exposures (bivalves, gastropods, and ammonites); best outcrops in south-central part of state, extending across Sioux, Morton, and Emmons counties (macrofossils in limestones and sandstones, concretions and lenticular sandstone, fauna largely scaphites, bivalves, annelid worms,

arthropods, fish, crocodiles, and turtle fragments, trace fossils, cirripides, linguloid brachiopods, index form *Ophiomorpha*).
● Paleocene, Cannonball formation. Sand blow-out west side of road, 5 miles west and 1.1 mile south of Moffit, southern Burleigh County (decapod crustaceans, *Camarocarcinus arnesoni*); southwest facing exposure 0.5 mile west of Little Missouri River, 15 miles north-northeast of Marmarth (typical Cannonball fauna with foraminifers, corals, bryozoans, molluscs, ostracods, crabs, trace fossils, amphibians, reptiles, and a large oyster bed of *Crassostraea*); Ludlow formation. Dark clay bands running from Golden Valley County to Slope County (oyster bedstone to two feet thick, freshwater fauna, turtle plates and bone fragments, champosaurus bones, fragments of ganoid fishes, and abundant lignitized plants).

Ohio

Middle Ordovician, Point Pleasant limestone, Cynthiana formation, Trenton group. Quarry section on Bear Creek Road, 0.1 mile north of intersection with Route 52, 3 miles east of Neville, Clermont County (index form Edrioasteroidea, *Carneyella*). ● Upper Ordovician, Kope formation, Edenian. Creek bed on north side of Twelve Mile Creek, east of Twelve Mile Road, east of Moreland Cemetery, 4 miles northeast of New Richmond (extensive crinoid calyxes and crowns, *Heterocrinus, Ectocrinus,* and *Merocrinus,* in association with trilobites *Triarthrus, Isotelus, Flexicalymene,* and abundant bryozoans); McMillan formation, Corryville member, Maysville group. Creek level, south of bridge over Stone Lick Creek, 1 mile west of Newtonsville (index form Edrioasteroidea, *Isorophus*); Liberty formation, Upper Richmond group. Road cuts along U.S. 12, 4.6 miles south of Camden (*Glyptorthis, Hebertella, Plaesiomys, Protarioa, Strophomena*). ● Lower Silurian, Brassfield limestone, middle Llandoverian, Small creek about ½ mile east of bridge over Ohio Brush Creek, 1 mile northeast of Dunkinsville, Adams County (brachiopod and bryozoan fauna). Greenish clay shales at stream level of the Elkhorn (Upper Ordovician) are exposed overlying the gray limestone termed the "Belfast Beds," with conodonts and scolecodonts. Upper beds are the Brassfield; Sevenmile Creek, 2 miles south of Eaton, on U.S. 127 (typical Brassfield fauna); road cut on the north side of Ohio Highway 41, north of Little Fork Church, at West Union, Adams County (while this is a classic Silurian conodont locality, a large Brassfield fauna may also be seen). ● Middle Devonian, Silica formation, Traverse group. South quarry, Medusa Portland Cement Co. (The fauna of the Ohio-Michigan Silica formation are some of the best preserved and abundant fossils of the entire Devonian Period. From massive brachiopods, *Paraspirifer bownockeri*, to equally large trilobites, *Phacops rana milleri* and *P. rana crassituber-culata*, to malacostracans, *Hebertocaris, Dithyrocaris,* and *Echino-caris,* to a large assemblage of crinoid species, bryozoans, corals, bivalves, edrioasteroids, and asteroids. Ref. *Strata and Mega-fossils of the Middle Devonian Silica Formation.* University of Michigan Museum Papers on Paleontology, No. 8, 1975). Adjacent to Medusa Quarries are the Frances Stone West Quarries, Sylvania Avenue to Brint Road, just west of Centennial Road, with Middle Devonian, Detroit River, and Dundee limestones; also Ten Mile Creek exposures about ¾ mile west of Centennial Road, with Silica shale and Ten Mile Creek dolomite faunas. ● Pennsylvanian, Columbiana formation, Allegheny group. Abandoned mine of the Sterling Coal Co. east of Franklin Square and north of Route 344, Salem Township, Columbiana County (representative brachiopods, *Lingula, Orbiculoidea, Derbyia, Juresania*); Putnam Hill formation, Allegheny group. Abandoned strip mine, north side of Route 224, 2 miles west of Canfield, Mahoning County (brachiopods, *Derbyia, Mesolobus, Retocularia, Hustedia, Composita*); Ames formation, Conemaugh group. Exposures along roads in Emerson Hall real estate development along valley northwest of Route 50 and west-northwest of Clairview, Athens County (brachiopods, *Linopro-ductus, Neospirifer, Antiquatonia*). ● Middle Pennsylvanian, Vanport shale and Putnam Hill limestone. Abandoned strip mine of the Keller Mine Co. southwest corner of junction of Oyster and Middletown roads, northeast of Alliance, Mahoning County; abandoned strip mine at norheast corner of road junction at elevation 1014, east of Ohio Highway 93, northeast of Baltic, Holmes County (all these Middle Pennsylvanian locations contain abundant brachiopods, fenestellid bryozoans, gastropods, conu-lariids, and polyplacophorans). ● Lower Permian, Upper Wash-ington formation, Dunkard group. Exposures at Belpre, Washington

County (fish fauna and reptiles, *Pelycosauria*); 653-foot exposure of entire Dunkard group exposed, Clark Hill Road section, along road at north end of Clark Hill near mouth of Opossum Creek, beginning 0.8 mile due south of road junction to Valley Methodist Church, Salem Township, Monroe County (extensive assemblage of invertebrates, plants, fishes).

Oklahoma

Middle Ordovician, Bromide formation, Simpson group, Pooleville member. Rock Crossing, Criner Hills, Arbuckle Mountains (classic locality for Bromide trilobites with over 30 species, including index forms *Ceraurus, Plimerops, Amphilichas, Lonchodomas, Vogdesia*). ● Silurian, Clarita formation, Fitzhugh member. Type locality, Lawrence uplift, 2 miles southeast of the Lawrence Quarry, Ideal Cement Co., Pontotoc County (large series of invertebrates); Henryhouse formation. West side of U.S. 77, Murray County, also extending to Cedar Hill, Pontotoc County (Henryhouse formation ranges across Murray and Pontotoc counties with unusually well-preserved specimens of trilobites *Anaspis, Dalmanites, Calymene, Proetus, Kosovelptis, Cheirurus*, and others). ● Lower Devonian, Frisco formation. Outcrops and prospect pits, quarries, and underground limestone quarry of the St. Clair Lime Co. near Marble City, Sequoya County (invertebrates, including extensive brachiopods); Bois d'Arc formation, Cravatt member. Quarry on north side of Oklahoma Highway 61, 2½ miles southeast of Fittstown, Pontotoc County (many brachiopods, *Atrypa, Cyrtina, Leptaena, Meristella*); Haragan formation, Hunton group. Classic site at White Mound, Murray County (surface exposures contain large and varied brachiopods and trilobites). ● Lower Pennsylvanian, Bloyd formation, Brentwood member. Greenleaf Lake spillway, southeast of Braggs, Muskogee County (crinoids); Keough Quarry, north of Fort Gibson, Muskogee County (invertebrates and crinoids); Wapanucka beds. Abandoned quarry east of Clarita, Coal County (crinoids); Morrowan series. Braggs and Brewer Bend limestone members of the Sausbee formation and the Chisum Quarry member of the McCully formation. Chisum Quarry, Muskogee County (ammonoids, conodonts, trace fossils). ● Upper Pennsylvanian, Francis shale, Missourian. Brick Pit, southeast edge of Ada, Pontotoc County (crinoid fauna, *Oklahoma-crinus, Chlidonocrinus, Aesiocrinus* and several other species). ● Permian, Wolfcampian, Havensville shale. Road cut on Oklahoma Highway 14, 4 miles west of junction with Oklahoma Highway 18, 6 miles south of Pawnee, Pawnee County (rhobdomesid bryozoans, brachiopods). ● Lower Permian, Hennessy formation. On property of Floyd Lawson, deposit lies 6½ miles southwest of Grandfield and 3 miles north of the Red River in southern Tillman County, known locally as the South Grandfield vertebrate fossil locality (over 6 species of fish, 2 labyrinthodonts, lepospondyls, and reptiles, represented by *Grantfielddiana, Ectosteorhachis, Tersonius, Lysocophus, Cardiocephalus* and *Hapsidopareion,* as well as several cotylosaurs); Wellington formation. 6 miles west of Waurika, Jefferson County (section about 50 feet of gray shale with abundant vertebrates; reptilia, *Edaphosaurus* and *Dimetrodon;* Amphibia, *Eryops* and *Diplocaulus;* Chondrichthyes, *Diacranodus*); road cut with exposures that contain quantities of bone scrap and large tree trunks, 4.5 miles east of U.S. Highway 183, on a secondary road that passes through center of Manitou, Tillman County (Amphibia, *Eryops* and *Trimerorhachis*; reptilia, *Dimetrodon*; and abundant *Orodus*-type shark teeth); Perry site on tributary of Black Bear Creek northwest of Perry, Noble County (this is one of the richest Permian vertebrate sites with thousands of skulls of *Trimerorhachis* (Permian labyrinthodonts with flattened short-snouted skulls, who lived along river and lake banks and dined on fish), amphibians, and reptiles collected over the years, lungfish burrows containing remains of *Gnathoehiza* also found in these deposits); Chickasha formation. Omega Quarry near small town of Omega, Kingfisher County (vertebrate fauna, caseids, *Cotylorhynchus, Angelosaurus,* actinopterygian fishes); Chickasha formation, Middle Flowerpot member. Exposures along ridge 1.5 miles northeast of Tabler, on south side of U.S. Highway 62, Grady County (vertebrate fauna with numerous amphibians and reptilians).

Oregon

Lower Cretaceous, Days Creek formation. Bank of Cow Creek, just south of Riddle and about 400 yards downstream from bridge,

Douglas County; sandstone exposures 1½ miles downstream from Agness on south side of Rogue River, Curry County (the upper member of the Days Creek formation consists of alternating beds of fine-grained sandstone containing limestone concretions bearing decapod specimens, lobster *Hoploparian riddlensis,* and a series of ammonoid species). ● Eocene, Coaledo formation. Cape Arago State Park, coastal headland southwest of Coos Bay, 15 miles from U.S. Highway 101. Trails lead down to the park beaches where the bedrock contains macrofauna of bivalves, gastropods, and echinoids. Crustaceans are found inside hard concretions in the sandstone. ● Middle Eocene, Lookinglass formation. Approximately 2.5 miles east of Agness, southwest Oregon (molluscs, foraminifers, eleutherozoan echinoderms, and crustacean decapods, the latter represented by numerous specimens of *Zanthopsis* and *Lophopanoreus*). ● Middle-Upper Eocene, Yamhill formation, Rickreall limestone member. Oregon Portland Cement Co. quarry, 1½ miles southwest of Dallas, Polk County (gastropod fauna, *Pleurotomaria*). ● Upper Eocene, Clarno formation. Type locality, 1½ miles east of Clarno's Ferry, Wheeler County (plants, large multilobed leaves of *Platanophyllum angustiloba, Lygodium, Anemia, Dryopteris, Woodwardia latiloba;* in addition, fruits, nuts, and silicified wood); Camp Hancock operated by research teams from the University of Oregon, on the John Day River, near Clarno, Wheeler County. This is the locality worked extensively by Thomas Bones, whose magnificent collections of paleobotanical materials have enriched the collections of the U.S. National Museum, the British Museum of Natural History, and the Oregon State Museum. Known as the Clarno nut beds, located about ¼ mile northwest of Camp Hancock, vast numbers of leaves, fruits, and nuts may be broken out of the silicified matrix. The fauna is very extensive and only a partial listing can be included here: (stems, *Equisetum, Ginkgo, Palmoxylon, Quercus;* fruits, *Paleospermum, Magnolia, Lauocarpum, Meliosma;* leaves, *Asplenium, Lastrea, Tetracera, Amesonemon, Cinnamomophyllum.* Ref. *Description and Interpretation of Fossil Woods, Leaves and Fruits from the Clarno Nut Beds, Wheeler County, Oregon.* The Oregon Museum of Science and Industry Technical Reports, V. 4, 1976, pp. 65-102; another Clarno

bed on East Birch Creek, 10 miles southeast of Pilot Rock, Umatilla County (extensive flora also found here. See list and illustrations on page 58, *Plant Fossils in the Clarno Formation,* Oregon State Department of Geology, The Ore Bin, V. 23, June 1961.) • Oligocene, Eugene formation. Numerous exposures for marine fossils may be seen in the Eugene area: small rock quarry at entrance to Hendrick's Park; Smith's Quarry between Millrace and Franklin Blvd.; also, outcrop beneath east end of overpass of Franklin Blvd. over Southern Pacific railroad tracks (extensive fauna with several taxa represented, bivalves *Modiolus, Neocardium, Lucinoma, Diplodonta*; gastropods *Acrilla, Crepidula, Calyptraea*; shark teeh; and the cephalopod *Aturia angustata.* Ref. *The Oligocene Marine Molluscan Fauna of the Eugene Formation in Oregon.* Bulletin No. 16, Museum of Natural History, University of Oregon, 1969).
• Oligocene, Kearsey and Pittsburg formations. Fossiliferous area 35 miles northwest of Portland extends from Mist at the north end to Gaston on the south end, in the Sunset Highway area. An unusual crinoid zone is located in a high cliff on the west side of Nehalem River 0.3 mile south of junction of Oregon Highway 47 and 202 in Mist. The sandstone bluffs along the Nehalem River near Pittsburg in Columbia County bear thickly crowded gastropod beds. An abundantly fossiliferous zone in the Kearsey formation is exposed in the cliffs at both ends of the railroad trestle which crosses Oregon State 47 between Sunset Highway and Vernonia (crinoid *Isocrinus*; decapod *Zanthopsis*; bivalves *Thyasira, Glycymeris, Acila, Delecopecten;* gastropods *Epitonium, Exila, Polinices, Bruclarkia; Dentalium*); Little Butte Volcanic series. Upper Thomas Creek area, 5 miles southeast of Lyons, northwestern Canyon (over 24 flora species, e.g. *Ginkgo biloba, Cunninghamia chaneyi, Sequoia affinis, Pterocarya mixta, Rosa hilliae, Holmskioldia sperrii, Alonguin thomae*). • Middle Miocene, Astoria formation. Exposures in cliffs, road cuts and stream banks, extending 3 miles south and 10 miles north of Newport (gastropods *Chlorostoma, Turritella, Polinices,* and bivalves *Anadara, Macoma, Autia*); Fogarty Creek State Park, 1 mile south of Lincoln Beach Post Office, on U.S. Highway 101 in cliffs along the beach; sea cliffs extending for over 4 miles at Beverly Beach State Park; on Spencer Creek, 6 miles south of Depoe Bay (fauna,

Macrocallista, Acila, Pecten, Marcia, Anadara, Turritella, Natica).
● Pliocene, Empire formation. Fossil Point is a classic collecting
area, which juts out from the west shore of Coos Bay, 1.6 miles by
road north of the east end of the South Slough bridge, or 3.2 miles
south of the right-angle turn in the highway at Empire (over 50
fauna species are present in the Empire, primarily bivalves,
gastropods, scaphopods, echinoids, and crustaceans). ● Pleistocene, early to mid-Wisconsin. Fossil Lake is in the eastern part of
the Fort Rock-Christmas Lake Basin in northern Lake County. The
exposures are in sparsely settled country about 30 miles east of
Fort Rock village, reached by roads from Fort Rock or Silver Lake.
Many of the fossils lie exposed in wind-blown pockets or along
sand dunes or cliffs (recorded are over 23 species of mammals; 68
species of birds, both land and aquatic; fish; freshwater Mollusca.
Carnivora include *Canis, Felis, Arctotherium, Microsus, Thomo-
mys;* edentate *Mylodon harlani;* proboscidian *Elephas columbi;*
perissodactyl *Equus pacificus;* artiodactyls *Antilochopa, Platy-
gonus, Camelops, Eschatius*).

Pennsylvania

Lower Ordovician, Stonehenge limestone. Beekmantown
group. Excellent exposures on northern outskirts of Axemann,
Centre County north of Logan Branch along Route 53 to Bellefonte
(contains pelmatozoans, algal limestone, ophletid gastropods,
orthocerids, trilobites, brachiopods, gastropods, with rare patelli-
form gastropod *Palaelophacmaea criola*). ● Upper Silurian,
Keyser formation, Cayugan series. Double quarry on the southeastern side of Route 96, near Hyndman (index form Edrioasteroidea, *Foerstediscus*). ● Middle Devonian, Mahantango formation, Sherman Ridge member. East side of Mahantango Creek
Valley northeast of the junction of Pennsylvania Route 104 in the
village of Shadle, Snyder County. Landowner is Mr. Marvin Haines
(typical Middle Devonian trilobites, cephalopods, Criconarids,
and several genera of bivalves and gastropods); west side of
Pennsylvania Route 61, ¼ mile north of junction of Routes 61 and
895 in the village of Deer Lake, Schuylkill County, in mine pit of
George R. Lynn, Inc. (brachiopods, bivalves, gastropods, cephalopods, and trilobites); exposures on south side of Township

Road 365, ¾ mile southwest of Suedberg, Schuylkill County within the bounds of proposed Swatara Gap State Park (typical fauna, with bryozoans, brachiopods, numerous genera of bivalves, ostracods). ● Upper Devonian, Brallier formation. Road cut exposed along Route 118, 2½ miles east of Hughesville at the site where a secondary road turns north into Miller Hollow. The exposure extends about 100 yards to the west of the intersection, Lycoming County (fauna represented by molds and casts as all the original material has been dissolved: excellent corals, molluscs, brachiopods, and miscellaneous); Oswayo formation, Fammerian stage. East side of Route 46, 0.6 mile north of the McKean-Cameron County line, near the town of Emporium (red-brown shales with abundant rhipidistian fishes of the crossopterygians, *Eustehnopteron, Hyneria lindae*). ● Mississippian, Pocono formation. Borrow pit on southwest side of Route 153, on Boone Mountain, about 4.1 miles northwest of the village of Penfield, Clearfield County (upper part of pit contains well-preserved plants, *Adiantites* and *Lepidodendropsis,* as well as carbonaceous impressions of plant stems. The lower portion of the pit contains Mississippian brachiopods, bivalves, crinoid columnals, Bryozoa, and the bivalve *Cypricardinia*). ● Middle Pennsylvanian, Llewellyn formation. Allegheny series. Strip mine dump 11 miles south of Wilkes-Barre, at town of Wanamie, also excellent strip mine exposures along Route 6, south of Carbondale (typical coal flora of *Neuropteris, Pecopteris, Alethopteris, Ptychocarpus,* Sphenophyllum). ● Middle Pennsylvanian, Buck Mountain #5 Coal Seam, Upper Sharp member. Pottsville series. St. Clair (excellent flora with *Alethopteris serlii* abundant). ● Permian, Upper Washington limestone, and Lower Greene formation. Dunkard group. Off Pennsylvania Route 186, Washington Stone Co. Quarry at Vance (fish fauna *Xenacanthus, Hybodus, Ectosteorhachis, Sagenodus, Moningahela;* Amphibia *Diploceraspis, Lysorophus;* several types of unidentified fishes).

South Carolina

Upper Cretaceous, Peedee formation. Approximately 5 miles south of North Myrtle Beach, Horry County, along Highway 17, on the west side of the road there is a large spoil bank of Peedee clay (weathered-out macrofossils, *Cucullaea, Trigonarca, Exogyra ponderosa, E. costata* and *E. spinosa, Placenticeras placenta* and, with luck, *Eutrephoceras dekayi*). ● Eocene, Santee limestone and Oligocene, Cooper marl. Giant Portland Cement Co. quarry, 2 miles north-northeast of Harleyville, Dorchester Co. (Santee fauna; vertebrae of *Basilosaurus* and teeth of *Zygorhyza*; many invertebrates, pectinids, bryozoans, some molluscan casts, pycinodont oysters, shark teeth, the bivalve *Chlamys cocoana,* and a large foraminiferal assemblage). ● Eocene-Pliocene. All the Duplin, Yorktown, and equivalent formations are now placed in the Pliocene. Martin Marietta Quarry at Crosse (typical Eocene-Pliocene echinoids, Mollusca, some Bryozoa). ● Oligocene, Cooper marl. Spoil banks of the old Bolton Mine. 0.3 mile south of the James Island railroad station, 9 miles southwest of Charleston, on Route 17 (Bryozoa, bivalves, cirripides, bone fragments, and shark teeth). ● Pleistocene, Canepatch formation. Right bank of Intracoastal Canal, immediately behind the Shrine Club on U.S. Highway 17, north of Myrtle Beach, Horry County (mostly bivalves, rare pectinids); along both banks of the Intracoastal Canal, 0.5 mile west of Myrtle Beach, Horry County, exposures on both sides of the Highway 51 bridge, crossing the canal (well-preserved *Polinices, Terebra, Rangia, Turritella, Noetia, Busycon, Conus* and *Astrangia*. Ref. *Atlantic Coastal Plain,* Geological Association 12th Annual Field Conference, Myrtle Beach, 1971). ● Pleistocene, Younges Island. Excellently preserved marine invertebrate fossil bed in mud flat at low tide. A lower, richer bed is available at Springtide.

South Dakota

Jurassic. Sundance, Unkapa, and Morrison formation. Cretaceous. Belle Fourche shale, Niobrara, Pierre, Fox Hills, and Hell Creek formations. The Black Hills of South Dakota, which take in the Fall River, Custer, Pennington, and Lawrence counties in the southwestern part of the State, provide some of the richest and most diversified fossil exposures in the world. From bones of triceratops, abundant in the sandstones south of Buffalo, to giant ammonites and bivalves in exposures north of Belle Fourche, to the prized bones and teeth of tyrannosaurus found in exposures south of White River. In and around Timber Lake, the Fox Hills formation offers a wealth of invertebrate fossils, ammonites, baculites, bones of reptiles and giant dinosaurs. The Fox Hills outcrops were popularized in the scientific literature by the field observations and collections of Meek and Hayden during their survey work in the Upper Cretaceous of the Dakotas from 1853 through 1859.

Tennessee

Upper Cambrian. Nolichucky and Maryville formations. Outcrops along Big Creek, south of U.S. route 11-W, 6½ miles northeast of Rogersville, Hawkins County (primarily trilobites, *Aphelaspis, Pseudagnostus, Dytremacephalus, Blountia, Coosia, Mayvilia, Tricrepicephalus;* the Maryville formation consits of *Coosella, Modocia, Norwoodia, Genevievella*). Road cut exposures on east shore of the Three Springs embankment of Cherokee Reservoir, Hamblen County (trilobites *Aphelaspis, Paraphelaspis, Pseudagnostus, Dytremacephalus*). ● Silurian. Waldron shale, Wayne group, Niagaran. Outcrops along Interstate 40, near Pegram, Davidson County (large brachiopod, coral, cephalopod, crinoid, and trilobite beds); Brownsport formation. Niagaran. Exposures both sides of State Road 13, north of Gilmore bridge 0.65 mile north of bridge over Marrs Branch Creek, Perry County; also, east side of Perryville-Decaturville road, 1.2 miles south of Perryville, Decatur County (typical brachiopod and bryozoan fauna, scarce trilobites, and straight ammonoids). ● Silurian, Decatur limestone; Devonian, Ross and Harriman formations; Cretaceous, Coffee Sand formation. Excellent, diverse fauna at the Vulcan Materials Co. Parsons Quarry located on Tennessee Highway 69, 11.5 miles south of the intersection with Interstate 40, and 3 miles north of the town of Parsons (fauna for the Decatur limestone, *Astraeospongium, Favosites, Halysites, Atrypa, Phipidomella, Stropheodonta, Cypricardinia;* for the Ross formation, *Isorthis, Levenea, Leptostrophia, Gypidula, Icodema, Hallopora, Monotrypa, Dalmanites,* and *Phacops*). ● Upper Devonian. Chattanooga shale. Outcrops 2 miles south of Eidson on Tennessee Highway 70 (ganoid fish plates, teeth, and associated invertebrates). ● Lower Mississippian, Maury shale. 3 miles east of Dowelltown on Tennessee Highway 26. Exposures offer fish

fragments and teeth, including the chimaeriform *Synthetodus*).
● Upper Cretaceous, Coon Creek formation. Dave Weeks
property, 3.5 miles south of Enville and 7.5 miles north of
Adamsville, McNairy County (fauna very extensive with large series
of fish and reptiles remains: shark vertebrae and teeth, skates,
Ischyriza; fishes *Anomoedus, Saurodon, Enchodus;* turtle *Toxo-
chelys;* mosasaurs *Mosasaurus, Prognathodon, Plioplatecarpus;*
invertebrate fauna mostly unreplaced Mollusca). ● Paleocene,
Cooper Pit formation. Clay mine on the Hollow Rock-Buena Vista
Road about 1.5 miles south of U.S. 70 and town of Hollow Rock,
Carroll County (contains largest flora deposits of Upper Cretaceous–Lower Tertiary in U.S., now known to contain teleost
fishes). ● Pleistocene, Wisconsin stage. About .07 mile north of
Darks Mill, Maury County on the west side of Carter Creek Road in
a phosphate pit (snapping turtle *Chelonia;* proboscidean *Mam-
muthus americanum* and *Megalonyx jeffersoni*).

Texas

Upper Ordovician. Montoya formation (equivalent to the
eastern Cincinnatian). Hueco Mountains, Long Canyon, 4 miles
east of Helms West well and 9 miles southeast of Hueco Tanks
(typical Cincinnatian fauna of brachiopods, sponge *Receptaculites,*
corals). ● Lower Permian. Bone Springs limestone. Northwest
side of road cut on U.S. Highway 62, near BM 4367, 1.8 mile
northeast of junction with State Highway 54, Culberson County
(this locality produces large quantities of ceratiloid ammonites,
including slabs covered with specimens of *Paraceltites elegans*).
● Upper Triassic. Truyillo formation. Exposure near head of
Sunday Canyon branch of the Palo Duro Canyon, near town of
Canyon (carbon-encrusted impressions of plants on light gray
mudstone, *Samnieguelia lewisii*). ● Jurassic. Malone formation-
Leonard formation of the Permian. Malone Mountains to Finlay
Mountains, near Torter Station, south-central Hudspeth County
(varied fauna, *Trigonia, Pleuromya, Idoceras, Kossmotia*).
● Lower Cretaceous, Edwards formation. Referred to as Goldth-
waite Reef, a hill, 7.9 miles southwest of Goldthwaite, Mill County
(abundant molluscan remains, echinoids, and the scleractinian
coral *Texastrea catenata*); Comanche series with the Goodland,

Duck Creek, Fort Worth, Weno, and Pawpaw formations. Exposures all along U.S. Highway 67 between Stephenville and Glen Rose provide a wealth of well-preserved fossils, including many casts and molds form massive ammonites, to echinoids, and sponges. Almost every outcrop, stream bed and cemetery provides weathered-out specimens (fauna extremely abundant, index forms, bivalves *Exogyra, Lima, Pecten, Gryphaea;* gastropods *Lunatia, Turritella;* echinoids *Hemiaster, Phymosoma, Enallaster;* sponge *Porocystis globularis*). Glen Rose formation. Garner Ranch, 7 miles west of Kerrville and 13 miles north of the Kerrville-Junction Road, Kemble County; Hondo Creek 2 miles downstream and 2½ to 3 miles upstream from Tarplay, Medina County (the Glen Rose exposures have some of the largest and most varied fauna beds in Texas; along roadsides, quarries, and stream beds are found large ammonites, bivalves, reef corals, sponges, foraminifers, and dinosaur bones). ● Upper Cretaceous. Burditt marl. Lower Campanian. Just above the bridge across Little Walnut Creek, Highway 291, Travis County (typical ammonites, molluscs and echinoids); Anachacho limestone. Campanian. Along Seco Creek, north of D'Hanis, Medina County (echinoid and ammonite fauna); Dessan chalk. Campanian and Santonian groups. along San Gabriel River, 1 mile above the bridge on Highway 104, Williamson County (ammonites, echinoids, and molluscs); Austin chalk. 2 miles southeast of Watters Park on Little Walnut Creek, Travis county (ammonites and molluscs); Corsicana marl. Navarro group. Exposures along highways, rock pits, creek beds, near San Antonio, Castroville, Bexar County (typical echinoids, vermes, sponges, molluscs. Ref. University of Texas Publication 4101, 1941); Nacatoch sand, Navarro group. Exposures in all directions from Corsicana, Navarro County (large, well-preserved fauna beds of vermes, molluscs, cephalopods). ● Eocene. Weches formation. Roadside exposure 20.7 miles east of Nacogdoches on the San Augustine Road, Nacogdoches County (molluscan fauna). ● Middle Eocene, Claiborne, Cook Mountain, and Stone City formations. Bluffs along Little Brazos River, both sides of Route 21, west of the courthouse in Bryan, Brazos County (scaphopods, gastropods, bivalves, serpulid worm tubes, ostracods, foraminifers, bryozoans, hexacorals, teeth, bone, scale, otoliths, and dermal plates of several species of fish); Stone City beds. Type locality. Stone City Bluff on south bank of the Brazos River at the bridges of the Southern Pacific Railroad and of State Highway 21 (Bryan-Caldwell Road) 11.4 miles west of courthouse in Bryan, Brazos County (classic site for a very extensive molluscan deposit, specimens well-preserved and abundant. Ref. University of Texas Publication 5704, 1957). ● Middle Pliocene. Blanco formation. 3 miles southwest of Mendota, ½ mile west of east line of Hemphill County, north of Red Deer Creek (large mammal collection, *Hypparion, Paracamelus, Stegomastodon,* and many more vertebrates excellently preserved). ● Upper Pliocene. Named the Beck Ranch local fauna of Blankan age. James Beck Ranch, 10 miles east of Snyder, Scurry County. Exposures from ranch house to highway, named the Beck Ranch local fauna (molluscs, fishes, amphibians, birds, reptiles, and mammals, particularly remains of the three-toed equid, *Nannupis beckansis*).

Utah

Middle Cambrian, Marjum and Wheeler shales. Millard County. Exposures and peaks from Rainbow Peak to Marjum Pass; and Swasey Peak to Wheeler Amphitheatre, in the House Range (trilobite fauna, *Marjumia, Olenoides, Modocia, Peronopsis, Asaphiscus, Zacanthoides;* Brachiopoda, *Prototreta, Lingulella, Acrothele, Nisuria;* Mollusca, *Pelagiella, Hyolithes, Helcionella, Stenothecoides;* Porifera, *Chancellaria, Choia*). ● Lower Pennsylvanian. Oguirrh formation. Bridal Veil Fall member. Morrowan. Provo Canyon, near Provo (crinoids); 1 mile northwest from Cedar Fort, on east-west spur north of rodeo grounds, central Utah (conodonts and trace fossils in sandstone; cruziana facies contains trace fossils and arthropod trails, *Neonerites, Scalarituba, Spirophycus, Zoophycos,* and *Skolithos*). ● Lower Cretaceous. Cedar Mountain formation. 5 miles southeast of Castle Dale. Channel sands along San Rafael River just north of Rock Canyon Creek (dinosaur egg fragments, *Oolithes carlylensis*). ● Upper Cretaceous. North Horn formation. Wasatch Plateau, between Salina and Thistle (entire dinosaur eggs have been found in association with sauropod and hadrosaur bone fragments).

Vermont

Notable exposures of Cambrian trilobites and other invertebrate fossils are found in the northwestern part of the state near Highgate Springs. Maps and information can be obtained from the Vermont Geological Survey, East Hall, University of Vermont, Burlington. ● Ordovician. Day Point formation and Crown Point formation. Middle Chazyan. Goodsell and Fisk quarries, southern Isle La Motte (stromatoporoid corals).

Virginia

Paleocene. Aquia formation. Accokeek Creek member. Belvedere Beach (formerly listed as Eocene, this locality has a typical Paleocene-Eocene fauna with index brachiopods and molluscs). ● Miocene. St. Mary's formation. High bluff on south bank of James River, 0.8 mile northwest of Claremont, Surry County. Shell bed 8-10 feet above base of bluff (typical molluscan fauna, large pectinids, coral, vertebrate fragments, and shark teeth). ● Upper Miocene. Yorktown formation. Hunt Club, south bank of James River, 0.65 mile east-southeast of FHA-AFF girls camp at Mogart's Beach, Isle of Wight County. Excellent molluscan exposures along base of cliffs and ravines leading to shore of James River (bivalves, gastropods, corals, cirripides, echinoids, and shark teeth); Zook's Pit on northwest side of Virginia Highway 238, 0.5 mile west of Yorktown, York County (classic molluscan fauna); Rice's Fossil Pit and Museum, off Harris Creek Road, Hampton. Owners Mr. and Mrs. W. Macon Rice. Classic locality for regional collectors (typical Miocene fauna with massive corals, cetaceans); FHA-AFF girls camp, 3.6 miles north-northeast of Smithfield, south bank of James river, Isle of Wight County (Mollusca, shark teeth, cirripides, and echinoids *Echinocardium orthonotum* and *Psammechinus philathropus*). ● Pleistocene. Kempsville formation. Womack Pit, ¼ mile southeast of the intersection of Kempsville and Indian River roads, Virginia Beach, Princess Anne County (gastropods, bivalves, fish fragments, cetaceans, sharks, and other vertebrates).

Washington

Cambrian. Quarries of Lehigh Portland Cement Co. ½ mile southeast of Metaline Falls, Pend Oreille County (trilobites and brachiopods). ● Orodvician. Road cuts along King Road, 2.1 miles northwest of its junction with McKern Road east of Rice, Stevens County (graptolites, *Phyllograptus* and *Didymograptus*). ● Triassic. Hillside exposures above and on east side of the Kettle River, immediately north of White Creek, 3.5 miles north of Curlew on Highway 4-A (fossils abundant but unknown to the authors). ● Tertiary formations. Sandstones and shales along Chuckanut Drive, south of Bellingham, Whatcom County; Banks of Olequa and Stillwater Creeks at Vader, in Lewis County (Ref. *Fossils in Washington,* for longer listing of fossil locations). ● Pliocene, Ringgold formation, and Pleistocene, Delight formation. On the bluffs along the Columbia River upstream from Pasco, as well as at the classic Delight site north of Lake Kahlotus, in Franklin and Adams counties in central Washington (large mammalian assemblage with equids, mammoth, cats, ground sloth, and several species of deer, including a large antlered form; also amphibians, reptiles, and fishes). ● Pleistocene through Cambrian. (List of periods with locations for fossiliferous exposures in *Geologic History and Rocks and Minerals of Washington,* Washington Department of Natural Resources, Division of Mines and Geology, Information Circular No. 45, 1969.)

West Virginia

Pennsylvanian. Lower Freeport coal. Allegheny group. Spoil banks of abandoned coal strip mine near Gladesville, Monongalia County (plants and rare myriopods, *Acantherpestes clarkorum*). ● Permian, High Greene limestone. Dunkard group. Channel deposits along Interstate 70 near Elm Grove (vertebrate fauna, *Diploceraspis, Edops*-like labyrintodont and *Lysorophus*); Waynesburg coal in the Washington formation. Dunkard group. Lemley Strip Mine of the Dippel and Dippel Coal Co., Mount Morris (large deposits of paleoflora).

Wisconsin

Upper Cambrian. Lodi sandstone. Road cuts along State Highway 44, near Kingston, Green Lake County (brachiopods and trilobites); Eau Claire formation. Outcrops on Mt. Washington at Eau Claire, Eau Claire County (quarries contain abundance of brachiopods and trilobites); Jordan formation. Quarry located near Tunnel City, Monroe County (fauna as above); Eau Claire formation. Croixian series. Dresbachian stage. Abandoned quarry at east side of County Trunk Highway "D," 0.2 mile north of its junction with Highway 10, at the north edge of the village of Strum, Trempeleau County (trilobites and brachiopods). ● Ordovician. Oneota formation. Canadian series. Prairie du Chien group. Exposures along the west bluffs of Perrot State Park east of the mouth of Trempeleau on the river road, Trempeleau County. Follow Brady's Bluff trail eastward to the top of the bluff (Ordovician fauna, but unknown to this author); Galena formation. Quarry at Duck Creek, 3 miles northwest of Green Bay (trilobite *Encrinurus*). ● Middle Ordovician. Platteville formation. Quarry, 3.6 miles northwest of Fannimore, Grant County (typical Ordovician fauna with crinoids); Galena formation. Trentonian. Road cut about 3.5 miles northwest of Dickeyville, Grant County along Highways 35 and 61 (brachiopods, sponges, ostracods); Road cut on Main Highway west of junction of Highways 92 and 69, 3 miles north of New Clarus, Green County (trilobites, brachiopods, ostracods, gastropods). ● Silurian. Niagara dolomite. Racine group. Quarries in the vicinity of Valders and Reedsville, west of Manitowoc, Manitowoc County (trilobites, corals, brachiopods, stromtoporoids); Outcrops and quarries in the banks of the Milwaukee River between Cedarburg and Crafton, Ozankee County (brachiopods, gastropods, trilobites, corals, bryozoans, and crinoids); Railroad cut on the north side of the Rapid Transit tracks along the north side of the Menominee Valley in Milwaukee, Milwaukee County (corals, stromatoporoids, bryozoans, brachiopods, molluscs, trilobites); Several quarries along State Highway 83, between Waukesha, Waukesha County, and Burlington, Racine County (crinoids, large trilobite, *Bumastus imperator*).

Wyoming

Upper Ordovician. Bighorn formation. Beds exposed along south and east side of bluff extending eastward from Hunt Mountain, facing Wallrock Creek Canyon, Sheridan County, south of Highway 14, between Burgess Junction and Medicine Wheel (crinoids and brachiopods, similar to Maysvillian of Ohio, with *Ectocrinus, Dendrocrinus, Cupulocrinus, Macrostylocrinus*). ● Paleocene. Evanston formation. Torrejonian. Outcrop of variegated strata between Bell and Little Muddy creeks, close to south boundary of Lincoln County (primarily multitubercultes, Insectivora, primates, creodonts, and condylarths). ● Eocene. Upper Bridger and Wasatch formations. Northern Green River Basin, east and west of Marbleton and Big Piney, along U.S. 189, east of U.S. 187, at Tabernacle Butte, and south of Boulder, east and west of U.S. 187 and New Fork River (large mammalian assemblage in exposures, including skulls and disarticulated bones). ● Oligocene, Brule formation. White River series. Bald Mountain located on Swope's Ranch, near Whitman, Niobrara County (unusual occurance of fossil mammal tracks on the slopes of Bald Mountain, credited to *Mesohippus;* Camelidae vertebrae also have been found); West part of Beaver Divide, on escarpment forming the northern margin of the Sweetwater Plateau, 4 miles south of Sand Draw Oil Fields, in the vicinity of Wagon Bed Spring, Fremont County (mammals and molluscs).

CHAPTER 8

MUSEUMS WITH MAJOR FOSSIL EXHIBITS

Over six thousand museums throughout the United States and Canada display fossil collections, dinosaurs, or earth science information. Several major museums' fossil holdings and exhibitions are so extensive that their listing of collections would be meaningless to the collector, as the exhibits are intended primarily for educational purposes. The numerous research collections throughout the country are in part available to the serious collector and researcher upon request. A one- to three-star rating system is used here to determine the research and/or exhibition value of each museum listed.

Alabama

Alabama Museum of Natural History ★
P. O. Box 5897
University, AL 35486
(205) 348-5061

Alaska

University of Alaska Museum ★
Department of Geology
Fairbanks, AK 99701
(907) 479-7505

Arizona

Museum of Northern Arizona ★
Route 4, Box 720
Flagstaff, AZ 86001
(602) 774-5211

Laboratory of Paleontology ★ ★
University of Arizona
Tucson, AZ 85721
(602) 884-1819

California

Museum of Paleontology ★ ★ ★
Earth Sciences Building
University of Calif. at Berkeley
Berkeley, CA 94720
(415) 642-1821

George C. Page Museum of La Brea
   Discoveries ★ ★ ★
5801 Wilshire Boulevard
Los Angeles, CA 90036
(213) 933-7451

Paleontology and Stratigraphy
   Branch ★ ★
U.S. Geological Survey at Menlo Park
345 Middlefield Road
Menlo Park, CA 94025

University of California at
   Riverside ★
Department of Geological Sciences
Riverside, CA 92502

Sacramento Science Center and
   Junior Museum ★
4500 Y Street
Sacramento, CA 95817
(916) 456-6417

Calif. Division of Mines and
   Geology Museum ★
Ferry Building, Room 2022
San Francisco, CA 94111
(415) 557-0633

Santa Barbara Museum of Natural
   History ★
2559 Puesta del Sol
Santa Barbara, CA 93105
(805) 963-7821

Natural History Museum of Los
   Angeles County ★ ★ ★
900 Exposition Boulevard
Los Angeles, CA 90007
(213) 746-0410

Geology Museum ★ ★
University of Calif. at Los Angeles
Geology Building – 405 Hilgard Ave.
Los Angeles, CA 90024
(213) 825-3880

Morro Bay State Park Museum of
   Natural History ★
State Park Road
Morro Bay, CA 93442
(805) 772-2694

Riverside Municipal Museum ★
3720 Orange Street
Riverside, CA 92501
(714) 787-7273

San Diego Nat. History Museum ★ ★
Balboa Park
2518 San Marcos Avenue
San Diego, CA 92112
(714) 232-3821

Josephine D. Randall Junior
   Museum ★
199 Museum Way
San Francisco, CA 94114
(415) 863-1399

Colorado

University of Colorado Museum ★
University of Colorado at Boulder
Boulder, CO 80309
(303) 492-6165 or 492-6892

Paleontology & Stratigraphy Branch ★
U.S. Geological Survey, Denver
Box 25046, Denver Federal Center
Denver, CO 80225
(303) 234-4004

Colorado (cont.)

Denver Museum of Nat. History ★ ★
City Park
Denver, CO 80205
(303) 297-3923

Historical Museum and Institute of
   Western Colorado ★
Fourth and Ute Streets
Grand Junction, CO 81501
(303) 242-0971

Colorado School of Mines ★
16th and Maple Streets
Golden, CO 80401
(303) 279-0300

The College Museum ★
Trinidad State Junior College
Trinidad, CO 81082
(303) 846-5508

Connecticut

The Bruce Museum ★
467 Steamboat Road
Bruce Park
Greenwich, CT 06830
(203) 869-0376

Peabody Museum of Nat. Hist. ★ ★ ★
Yale University
170 Whitney Avenue
New Haven, CT 06520
(203) 432-4043

District of Columbia

National Museum of Nat. Hist. ★ ★ ★
Smithsonian Institution
Washington, D.C. 20560
(202) 628-4422

Florida

Florida State Museum ★ ★
University of Florida
Museum Road
Gainesville, FL 32611
(904) 392-1721

Georgia

Emory University Museum ★
Sociology Building
Atlanta, GA 30322
(404) 377-2411

Illinois

Museum of Ecology of the Chicago
   Academy of Science ★
2001 North Clark Street
Chicago, IL 60614
(312) 549-0606

Field Museum of Natural
   History ★ ★ ★
Roosevelt Road and Lake Shore Drive
Chicago, IL 60605
(312) 922-9410

Illinois (cont.)

Lizzadro Museum of Lapidary Art ★
220 Cottage Hill
Elmhurst, IL 60126
(312) 833-1616

Burpee Museum of Natural History ★
813 North Main Street
Rockford, IL 61103
(815) 965-3132

Department of Geology, Museum
  of Natural History ★ ★
University of Illinois
Urbana, IL 61801
(217) 333-2517

Fryxell Geological Museum ★ ★
Augustana College
Rock Island, IL 61201

Illinois State Museum ★
Spring and Edward Streets
Springfield, IL 62706
(217) 782-7386

Indiana

Department of Geology ★
Indiana University
Bloomington, IN 47401

Joseph Moore Museum ★
Earlham College
Richmond, IN 47374
(317) 962-6561

Children's Museum of Indianapolis ★
3000 North Meridian
Indianapolis, IN 46208
(317) 924-5431

Iowa

Sanford Museum and Planetarium ★
117 East Willow
Cherokee, IA 51012
(712) 225-3922

Historical Museum and
  Archives ★
East 12th and Grand Avenue
Des Moines, IA 50319
(515) 281-5111

Department of Geology ★
University of Iowa
Iowa City, IA 52242

Putnam Museum ★
1717 West 12th Street
Davenport, IA 52804
(319) 324-1933

Museum of Natural History ★
The University of Iowa
Macbride Hall
Iowa City, IA 52240
(319) 353-5893

Idaho

Idaho State University Museum of
  Natural History ★
P. O. Box 8096
Pocatello, ID 83209

Kansas

Sternberg Memorial Museum ★ ★
Fort Hays Kansas State College
Hays, KS 67601
(913) 628-4286

Geology Department ★
Kansas State University
Thompson Hall
Manhattan, KS 66506
(913) 532-6724

Mus. of Invertebrate Paleontology ★ ★
University of Kansas
Lawrence, KS 66045
(913) 864-3985

Fick Fossil and History Museum ★
700 West Third Street
Oakley, KS 67748

Kentucky

Owensboro Area Museum ★
2839 South Griffith Avenue
Owensboro, KY 42301
(502) 683-0296

Big Bone Lick State Park ★
Route 2, Box 92
Union, Boone County, KY 41091
(606) 384-3522

Maryland

The Peale Museum ★
225 Holliday Street
Baltimore, MD 21202
(301) 396-3523

Massachusetts

Pratt Museum ★
Amherst College
Amherst, MA 01002
(413) 542-2233

The Paleobotanical Laboratories ★ ★
22 Divinity Avenue
Cambridge, MA 02138
(617) 868-7600

Mus. of Comparative Zoology ★ ★ ★
Harvard University
Cambridge, MA 02138
(617) 495-2466

Museum of Science ★ ★
Science Park, Storrow & Memorial Dr.
Boston, MA 02114
(616) 723-2500

Botanical Museum ★
24 Oxford Street
Cambridge, MA 02138
(617) 868-7600

Granby Dinosaur Museum ★
194 West State Street, Route 202
Granby, MA 01033
(413) 467-7822

Michigan

Museum of Paleontology ★ ★ ★
University of Michigan
1109 Geddes Avenue
Ann Arbor, MI 48109
(313) 764-0478

Wayne State University Museum of
   Natural History ★
Department of Biology
Detroit, MI 48202
(313) 577-2555

Grand Rapids Public Museum ★
54 Jefferson Avenue, SE
Grand Rapids, MI 49502
(616) 456-5494

Kingman Museum of Natural
   History ★
West Michigan Avenue at 20th Street
Battle Creek, MI 49017
(616) 965-5117

Michigan State University
   Museum ★
West Circle Drive
East Lansing, MI 48824
(517) 355-2370

Minnesota

Geology Museum, Univ. of MN ★
109 Math-Geology Building
Duluth, MN 55812
(218) 726-7238

The Science Museum of Minnesota ★
30 East 10th Street
St. Paul, MN 55101
(612) 222-6303

Mississippi

Mississippi Museum of Natural
   Sciences ★
111 N. Jefferson Street
Jackson, MS 39202
(601) 354-7303

Mississippi State University Dunn-
   Seilers Museum ★
Department of Geology-Geography
Mississippi State, MS 39762
(601) 325-5926

Missouri

University of Missouri ★
Department of Geology Museum
Columbia, MO 65201
(314) 882-6673

Edward Clark Museum of Missouri
   Geology ★
Buehler Park
Rolla, MO 65401

Kansas City Museum of History
   and Science ★
3218 Gladstone Boulevard
Kansas City, MO 64123
(816) 483-8300

Montana

Blaine County Museum ★
P. O. Box 927
Chinook, MT 59523
(406) 357-2590

Corps of Engineers Fort Peck
   Powderhouse Museum ★
P. O. Box 208
Fort Peck, MT 59223
(406) 526-3411

Museum of Paleontology ★ ★
University of Montana
Missoula, MT 59801

Carter County Museum ★
Ekalaka, MT 58324

Northern Montana College
   Collections ★
Havre, MT 59501
(406) 265-7821

Nebraska

Cooke Museum of Natural History ★ ★
Agate, NE 69330

Scotts Bluff National
   Monument ★
Box 427
Gering, NE 69341
(308) 436-4340

Univ. of Nebraska Museum ★ ★ ★
212 Morrill Hall
14th and U Streets
Lincoln, NE 68508
(402) 472-2638

Nevada

The Nevada State Museum ★
Capitol Complex
Carson City, NV 89710
(702) 885-4810

New Jersey

Rutgers Geology Museum ★
Geology Hall, Queens Campus
Rutgers College
New Brunswick, NJ 08903
(201) 932-7243

Museum of Natural History ★ ★ ★
Princeton University
Guyot Hall, Washington Road
Princeton, NJ 08540
(609) 452-4102

The Newark Museum ★
43-49 Washington Street
Newark, NJ 07101
(201) 733-6600

New Mexico

University of New Mexico ★
Department of Geology Museum
Albuquerque, NM 87131
(505) 277-4204

New York

New York State Museum & Science
 Service ★ ★ ★
State Education Building
Albany, NY 12234
(518) 474-5877

Paleontological Research
 Institution ★ ★ ★
1259 Trumansburg Road
Ithaca, NY 14850
(607) 273-6623

The Am. Museum of Nat. Hist. ★ ★ ★
Central Park West at 79th Street
New York, NY 10024
(212) 873-1300

Rochester Mus. & Science Center ★ ★
657 East Avenue
Rochester, NY 14604
(716) 271-4320

Buffalo Museum of Science ★ ★ ★
Humboldt Parkway
Buffalo, NY 14211
(716) 896-5200

Childs Frick Collection of Fossil
 Vertebrates ★ ★ ★
The American Museum of Natural Hist.
Central Park West at 79th Street
New York, NY 10024
(212) 873-1300

Vassar College Geology Museum ★
Ely Hall
Poughkeepsie, NY 12601
(914) 452-7000

Petrified Creatures Museum ★
U.S. Route 20
Warren, NY 13439
(315) 858-0855

Ohio

Cincinnati Museum of Natural
 History ★ ★ ★
1720 Gilbert Avenue
Cincinnati, OH 45202
(513) 621-3889

The Cleveland Museum of Natural
 History ★ ★ ★
Wade Oval, University Circle
Cleveland, OH 44106
(216) 231-4600

Warren Co. Historical Society Mus. ★
105 South Broadway
Lebanon, OH 45036
(513) 932-1817

Univ. of Cincinnati Geology Mus. ★ ★
Old Tech Building
The University of Cincinnati
Cincinnati, OH 45221
(513) 475-3732

Orton Geological Museum ★
Ohio State University
125 South Oval Mall
Columbus, OH 43210
(614) 422-4473

The Allen Co. Historical Society ★
620 West Market Street
Lima, OH 45801
(419) 222-9426

Ohio (cont.)

Miami University Geology Museum ★
Shideler Hall
Oxford, OH 45056
(513) 529-4729

Oklahoma

No Man's Land Historical
  Museum ★
Panhandle State College
Goodwell, OK 73939

Stovall Museum of Science & Hist. ★ ★
University of Oklahoma
1336 Asp Avenue
Norman, OK 73069
(405) 325-4711

Oregon

Museum of Natural History ★ ★
University of Oregon
Eugene, OR 97403
(503) 686-3033

Rock, Mineral and Fossil Museum ★
State of Oregon Dept. of Geology
  and Mineral Industries
1069 State Office Building
Portland, OR 97201
(503) 229-5580

OR Mus. of Science & Industry ★ ★ ★
4015 SW Canyon Road
Portland, OR 97221
(503) 248-5900

Prehistoric Life Museum ★
U.S. Route 101
Yachats, OR 97498
(503) 547-3836

Pennsylvania

William Penn Memorial
  Musuem ★ ★
3rd and North Streets
Harrisburg, PA 17108
(717) 787-4978

Pennsylvania Academy of Natural
  Sciences ★ ★ ★
Nineteenth and the Parkway
Philadelphia, PA 19103
(215) 299-1000

Wagner Free Institute of Science ★ ★
Montgomery Avenue and 17th Street
Philadelphia, PA 19121
(215) 763-6521

Carnegie Museum of Nat. Hist. ★ ★ ★
4400 Forbes Avenue
Pittsburg, PA 15213
(412) 622-3243

Lackawanna Historial Society ★
232 Monroe Street
Scranton, PA 18504

South Dakota

Museum of Geology ★ ★
SD School of Mines and Technology
2nd Floor, Administration Building
Rapid City, SD 57701
(605) 394-2467

The W. H. Over Museum ★
The University of South Dakota
Vermillion, SD 57069
(605) 677-5228

Tennessee

Memphis Pink Palace Museum ★
3050 Central Avenue
Memphis, TN 38111
(901) 454-5603

Texas

Texas Memorial Museum and Archives
  for Geological Research ★ ★
2400 Trinity
Austin, TX 78705
(512) 471-1604

Lamar University Geology Museum ★
Lamar University Station
Beaumont, TX 77710
(713) 838-8228

Panhandle-Plains Historial Museum ★
West Texas Station
Canyon, TX 79016
(806) 655-2567

Shuler Museum of Paleontology ★
Southern Methodist University
Dallas, TX 75275
(214) 692-2743

Houston Museum of Natural
  Sciences ★
Hermann Park
Houston, TX 77004
(713) 526-4273

The John K. Strecker Museum ★
Sid Richardson Science Museum
Baylor University
Waco, TX 76703
(817) 755-1110

Utah

Earth Sciences Museum ★
Brigham Young University
Provo, UT 84602
(801) 374-1211

Utah Museum of Natural History ★ ★
University of Utah
Salt Lake City, UT 84112
(801) 581-6927

Virginia

Museum of Geological Sciences ★
VA Polytechnic Institute & State Univ.
2062 Derring Hall
Blacksburg, VA 24061
(703) 951-6521

Dinosaur Land ★
On U.S. 522, 340 and 277 between
  Winchester and Front Royal
White Post, VA 22663
(703) 869-2222

Washington

Thomas Burke Memorial Washington
State Museum ★
University of Washington
Seattle, WA 98195
(206) 543-5590

Ginkgo Petrified Forest State
Park ★
Ginkgo State Park
Vantage, WA 98950
(509) 856-2700

West Virginia

Marshall University Geology
Museum ★
Marshall University
Huntington, WV 25701
(304) 523-3411

WV Geological Survey Museum ★
310 Mineral Industries Building
West Virginia University
Morgantown, WV 26506
(304) 293-0111

Wisconsin

Greene Memorial Museum ★
University Wisconsin-Milwaukee
Department Geological Sciences
Milwaukee, WI 53201
(414) 963-4794

Milwaukee Public Museum ★ ★
800 West Wells Street
Milwaukee, WI 53233
(414) 278-2700

Wyoming

Univ. of WY Geological Museum ★ ★
Geology Building
Laramie, WY 82071
(307) 766-3386

Canada

Drumheller District Museum ★
Box 560
Drumheller, Alberta
(403) 823-2593

Dept. of Geology Museum ★
University of Alberta
Edmonton, Alberta T6G 2E1
(403) 432-3266

Nova Scotia Museum ★
1747 Summer Street
Halifax, Nova Scotia B3H 2A6
(901) 429-4610

Geological Sciences Museum ★
Queen's University
Kingston, Ontario K7L 3N6
(613) 547-6903

Redpath Museum ★ ★
McGill University
Montreal 101, Quebec
(514) 392-5994

Niagara Falls Museum ★
5651 River Road
Niagara Falls, Ontario L2E 6V8
(416) 356-2151

Geological Survey of Canada ★ ★ ★
601 Booth Street
Ottawa, Ontario L1A 0E8

National Museum of Nat. Sciences ★ ★
Metcalfe and McLeed Streets
Ottawa, Ontario K1A 0M8
(613) 996-3102

Canada (cont.)

Museum of Geology & Mineralogy ★ ★
University of Laval
Department of Geology
Quebec, Quebec G1K 7P4
(418) 656-2195

New Brunswick Museum ★
277 Douglas Avenue
St. John's, New Brunswick E2K 1E5
(506) 693-1196

M. Y. Williams Geological Museum ★
University of British Columbia
Department of Geological Sciences
Vancouver, B.C. V6T 1W5
(604) 228-5586

Museum of Natural History ★
Waskana Park
Regina, Saskatchewan
(306) 527-6608

Royal Ontario Museum ★ ★ ★
100 Queen's Park
Toronto, Ontario M5S 2C6
(416) 978-3674

Mexico

Instituto de Geologia ★ ★
Univ. Nacional Autonoma de Mexico
Ciudad Universitaria
Mexico 20, D.F.

Geological Museum ★
Cipres 176
Mexico City, D.F. 20

Prehistoric Museum of the Valle
  de Mexico ★ ★
On Laredo Road
Tepexpan

Alfred Duges Museum ★
Universidad, Guanajuato

Museum of Natural History ★
Chapultepec Park
Mexico City, D.V.

NATIONAL AND STATE PARKS WITH FOSSIL EXHIBITS

Arizona

Petrified Forest National Park
Located on the southern portion of the Colorado Plateau Privince, in the Little
Colorado River drainage. The Painted Desert entrance is on U.S. 66/I-40, 27 miles
northeast of Holbrook, Arizona. The Rainbow Forest entrance is on U.S. 180, 19
miles southeast of Holbrook, AZ 86028

Colorado

Dinosaur National Monument
Dinosaur, CO 81610

Florissant Fossil Beds National Monument
Box 185
Florissant, CO 80816

Colorado National Monument
Fruita, CO 81521

Connecticut

Dinosaur State Park
West Street, ¾ mile east of Interstate 91, Exit 23
Rocky Hill, CT 06115

Idaho

Massacre Rocks State Park
American Falls, ID 83211

Nebraska

Agate Fossil Beds National Monument
and Scotts Bluff National Monument
Box 427
Gering, NE 69341
(308) 436-4340

Nevada

Berlin-Ichthyosaur State Park
Park is located 23 miles east of Gabbs via Nevada State Route 91. The Ichthyo-
saur quarry is in Union Canyon, just east of Berlin, covered by an enclosed shelter.
Gabbs, NV 89409

New Mexico

Carlsbad Caverns and Guadalupe Mountains National Park
3225 National Parks Highway
Carlsbad, NM 88220

Oregon

John Day Fossil Beds National Monument
Box 415
John Day, OR 97845

South Dakota

Badlands National Monument
Box 36
Interior, SD 57750
(605) 433-5631

Texas

Dinosaur Valley State Park
Box 396
Glen Rose, TX 76034
(814) 897-4588

Washington

Ginkgo Petrified Forest State Park
Vantage, WA 98960

Wyoming

Como Bluff Dinosaur Graveyard
Medicine Bow, WY 82329

Fossil Butte National Monument
The Butte is located just north of U.S. 30N and the Union Pacific Railroad.
Kemmerer, Wy 83101

CHAPTER 9

GEOLOGICAL SURVEYS AND THEIR PUBLICATIONS

This listing provides addresses of all the State Geological Surveys, their latest catalogs of publications and maps, and a brief listing of recommended paleontological pamphlets and brochures of interest to the fossil collector.

Alabama

Publications Sales Office
Geological Survey of Alabama
P. O. Drawer O
University, AL 35486
(205) 349-2852

Index and List of the Publications of the Geological Survey of Alabama and the State Oil and Gas Board, 1979.

Copeland, Charles W., *Curious Creatures in Alabama Rocks: A Guidebook for Amateur Fossil Collectors.* Circular 19, 1963. $1.50

Toulmin, Lyman D., *Stratigraphic distribution of Paleocene and Eocene fossils in the eastern Gulf Coast region.* Monograph 13, 1977. $10.00

Alaska

State of Alaska
Department of Natural Resources
Division Geological & Geophysical Surveys
Box 80007
College, AK 99701

State of Alaska
Division of Geological Survey
Pouch M
Juneau, AK 99801

List of reports issued by the Division of Geological & Geophysical Surveys, Information Circular 11, 1976.

Arizona

State of Arizona
Bureau of Geology and Mineral Technology
845 North Park Avenue
Tucson, AZ 85719
(602) 626-2733

List of Available Publications, 1980.
Fieldnotes, issued Quarterly. Some issues contain fossil notes.

Arkansas

Arkansas Geological Commission
Maps and Publications Section
3815 West Roosevelt Road
Little Rock, AR 72204
(501) 371-1646

List of Maps and Publications, 1979.
Freeman, Tom, *Fossils of Arkansas.* Bulletin 22, 1966. $2.50

California

California Division of Mines & Geology
P O. Box 2980
Sacramento, CA 95812
(916) 445-5716

List of Available Publications, 1979.
California Geology, issued monthly. Many issues contain fossil notes.
Savage, Donald E. and Theodore Downs, *Cenozoic land life of Southern California.*
  California Division of Mines Bulletin 170, 1954.

Canada

Geological Survey of Canada
601 Booth Street
Ottawa, Ontario K1A 0E8

Monthly and weekly list of publications and maps.

Ministere de L'Energie et des Ressources
Secteur des Mines
1620 Boulevard de l'Entente
Quebec G1S 4N6

Montly list of publications and maps.

Colorado

Colorado Geological Survey
1313 Sherman Street, Room 715
Denver, CO 80203
(303) 839-2611

Publications Geology, 1980.

Connecticut

State of Connecticut
Department of Environmental Protection
State Office Building
Hartford, CT 06115
(203) 566-3540

List of Publications of the Connecticut Geological and Natural History Survey, 1980.
Lull, Richard Swann, *Triassic Life of the Connecticut Valley.* Bulletin 81, 1953
(Revised). $4.00
Colbert, Edwin H., *Fossils of the Connecticut Valley.* Bulletin 96, 1970. $1.00

Delaware

Delaware Geological Survey
University of Delaware
Newark, DE 19711

Geological Survey List of Publication, 1980.
Pickett, T. E., *Guide to Common Cretaceous Fossils of Delaware.* Report of
Investigations No. 21, 1972.
Windish, D. C. and T. E. Pickett, *Delaware: Its Rocks, Minerals, and Fossils.* n.d.

Florida

Florida Bureau of Geology
Publications Office
903 West Tennessee Street
Tallahassee, FL 32304

Bureau of Geology List of Publications, 1980.
Richards, Horace G. and Katherine V. W. Palmer, *Eocene mollusks from Citrus and
Levy counties, Florida.* Bulletin 35, 1953.
DuBar, Jules R., *Stratigraphy and paleontology of the late Neocene strata of the
Caloosahatchee River area of southern Florida.* Bulletin 40, 1958.
Olsen, S. J., *Fossil Mammals of Florida.* Special Publications 6, 1959.
Olsen, S. J., *Vertebrate Fossil Localities in Florida.* SP 12, 1965.

Shaak, Craig, *Catalogue of Invertebrate Fossil Types at the Bureau of Geology: List of collecting localities.* SP 24, 1980.

All publications are priced at $1.00 per publication, plus postage.

Georgia

Georgia Geologic Survey
19 Dr. Martin Luther King Jr. Drive
Room 400
Atlanta, GA 30334

List of Publications and maps, 1977.

Idaho

Idaho Bureau of Mines and Geology
Morrill Hall, Room 332
University of Idaho Campus
Moscow, ID 83843
(208) 885-7991

List of Publications, 1980.
Ross, Sylvia H. and Carl N. Savage, *Idaho Earth Science: Geology, Fossils, Climate, Water, and Soils.* 1967. $4.00

Illinois

Illinois State Geological Survey
Natural Resources Building
615 East Peabody Drive
Champaign, IL 61820

List of Publications, 1980.
Collinson, Charles W., *Guide for Beginning Fossil Hunters.* Educational Series 4, Reprinted 1966.
Collinson, C. W. and Romayne Skartvedt, *Field Book – Pennsylvanian Fossils of Illinois.* Educational Series 6, Reprinted 1966.
Leonard, A. B., J. C. Frye and W. H. Johnson, *Illinoian and Kansan Molluscan Fauna of Illinois.* Circular 461, 1971.

Indiana

Publications Section
Indiana Geological Survey
611 North Walnut Grove
Bloomington, IN 47405
(812) 337-7636

Geologic Publications of Indiana, 1979. Addenda June 1980.
Shaver, R. H., *Adventures with Fossils*. Circular 6, 1959. $1.00
Perry, T. G., *Fossils: Prehistoric Animals in Hoosier Rocks*. Circular 7, 1959. 50¢

Iowa

Iowa Geological Survey
12 N. Capitol Street
Iowa City, IA 52242
(319) 338-1173

List and Index of Publications, 1976. Recent publications, 1980.
Iowa Geology, Issued periodically on January of each year.
Fossil collecting areas of Iowa, Educational Materials 4. Free

Kansas

University of Kansas Paleontological Institute
The University of Kansas
Lawrence, KS 66045

Paleontological Contributions Series. Issued periodically. List of titles in series may
   be ordered from Library Sales Office, University of Kansas Libraries, Lawrence,
   KS 66045.

Kansas Geological Survey
1930 Avenue A, Campus West
The University of Kansas
Lawrence, KS 66044
(913) 864-3965

Available Publications Kansas Geological Survey, 1979.
Williams, Roger B., *Ancient Life Found in Kansas Rocks*. Educational, 1975. $2.50
Merriam, Daniel F., *The Geologic History of Kansas*. Bulletin 162, 1963. $3.50

Kentucky

Kentucky Geological Survey
University of Kentucky
311 Breckinridge Hall
Lexington, KY 40506
(606) 257-3896

List of Publications, 1980.
U.S. Geological Survey Reports obtained from the Kentucky Survey: Ross, R. J.,
   Calymenid and Other Ordovician Trilobites from Kentucky and Ohio. 1967. 55¢
Pojeta, John (editor), *Contributions to the Ordovician Paleontology of Kentucky
   and Nearby States*. Professional paper 1066-A-G, 1979. $4.50

Louisiana

Louisiana Geological Survey
Room 153, Geology Building
Louisiana State University
P. O. Box G, University Station
Baton Rouge, LA 70893
(504) 342-6754

Publications of the Louisiana Geological Survey, 1980.
McGuirt, James H., *Louisiana Tertiary Bryozoa.* Bulletin 21, 1941. $2.00

Maryland

Maryland Geological Survey
The John Hopkins University
Merryman Hall
Baltimore, MD 21218
(301) 338-7001

List of Publications, 1980.
Vokes, H. E., *Miocene fossils of Maryland.* Bulletin 20, 1957. $1.00
Glaser, J. D., *Collecting fossils in Maryland.* Educational Series 4, 1979. $1.00
McLennan, J. D., *Dinosaurs in Maryland.* Leaflet, 1973. Free
McLennan, J. D., *Miocene Shark's Teeth of Calvert County.* Leaflet, 1971. Free
Pliocene and Pleistocene. Systematic Reports, 1906 reprinted. $4.00
Miocene text, 1904 reprinted, $5.00. *Miocene* plates, $4.50. *Eocene,* 1901
    reprinted, $7.00

Michigan

Geological Survey Division
Michigan Department of Natural Resources
Box 30028
Lansing, MI 48909
(517) 373-1220

Available GSD Publications and Map List, 1980.
Kelley, R. W., *Guide to Michigan Fossils.* Pamphlet 3, 1962. 25¢
Wilson, S. E., *Collecting Rocks, Minerals and Fossils in Michigan.* 1976. 25¢

Minnesota

Minnesota Geological Survey
1633 Eustis Street
St. Paul, MN 55108
(612) 373-0223

List of Publications, 1980.

Hogberg, R.K., R. E. Sloan and S. P. Tufford, *Guide to Fossil Collecting in Minnesota*. 1967. Revised edition, 1979. $1.00

Mississippi

Mississippi Department of Natural Resources
Bureau of Geology and Energy Resources
P. O. Box 4915
Jackson, MS 39216
(601) 354-6228

List of Publications, 1980.
Mississippi Geology. Issued September (Vol. 1, No. 1) and December (Vol. 1, No. 2), 1980. Contains fossil articles of interest.
Dockery, David T., *The Mollusca of the Moodys Branch Formation, Mississippi*. Bulletin 120, 1977. $3.00
Dockery, David T., *The Invertebrate Macropaleontology of Clarke County, Mississippi*. Bulletin 122, 1980. $4.00

Missouri

Missouri Department of Natural Resources
Division of Geology and Land Survey
P. O. Box 250
Rolla, MO 65401
(313) 364-1752

List of Publications, 1980.
Mehl, Maurice G., *Missouri's Ice Age Animals*. Educational Series 1, 1962. $3.00
Fact Sheets, No. 9, *Crinoids and Brachiopods*. No. 14, *Fossil Collecting Localities*.

Montana

Publications Office
Montana Bureau of Mines and Geology
Montana Tech, Main Hall
Butte, MT 59701
(416) 792-8321

Publications and Maps, 1981.

Nebraska

Conservation and Survey Division
The University of Nebraska
113 Nebraska Hall
Lincoln, NE 68588
(402) 472-3471

List of Publications, 1976; Additions, 1978.

Pabian, R. K., *Record in Rock, Handbook of Invertebrate Fossils of Nebraska.*
  Educational Circular, 1970. $1.00
Condra, G. E. and C. O. Dunbar, *Brachiopoda of the Pennsylvanian System in
  Nebraska.* Geological Survey Publications 5, 1932. $2.00
Pabian, R. K. and J. A. Fagerstrom, *Late Paleozoic trilobites from southeastern
  Nebraska.* General Publications 8, 1972. 25¢

Nevada

Nevada Bureau of Mines and Geology
Publications Office
University of Nevada
Reno, NV 89557
(702) 784-6691

Publications of the Bureau, 1980.

New Jersey

Bureau of Geology and Topography
Department of Environmental Protection
P. O. Box 1390
Trenton, NJ 08625

List of Maps and Publications, 1980.
Richard, Horace G., *The Cretaceous fossils of New Jersey.* Bulletin 61, 2 Parts,
  1958-1962. Set $10.00
Yolton, James S., *Fossils of New Jersey.* Report No. 2. $2.00. n.d.

New Mexico

New Mexico Bureau of Mines and Mineral Resources
Socorro, NM 87801
(505) 835-5410

Publications Available, List 14, 1980. Large numbers of miscellaneous fossil study
  papers listed in Memoirs series.
New Mexico Geology. Issued Quarterly, Vol. 1, Nos. 1-4, 1979; Vol. 2, Nos. 1-4,
  1980. Annual subscription $3.00; 1981 subscription $4.00. Not many fossil
  notes.

New York

Geological Survey, State Science Service
New York State Museum
State Education Department
Albany, NY 12230

Empire State Geogram: List of Geological Publications, 1979.

Clarkge, J. M. and Rudolf Ruedemann, *The Eurypterida of New York.* 2 Vols., Memoir No. 14, 1912. Set $20.00

Bell, B. M., *Study of North American Edrioasteroids.* Memoir 21, 1976. $7.00

Weinman, P. L., *An Introduction to Invertebrate Fossils of New York.* Educational Leaflet 19, 1966. 25¢

New York State Newsletter. Issued periodically. Free distribution.

Empire State Geogram. Issued periodically. Free distribution.

North Carolina

Natural Resources and Community Development
Geological Survey Section
P.O. Box 27687
Raleigh, NC 27611
(919) 733-3833

List of Publications, 1980.

North Dakota

North Dakota Geological Survey
University Station
Grand Forks, ND 58202

Hainer, John L., *The Geology of North Dakota.* Bulltin 31, 11th edition, 1961. 75¢

Folsom, C. B., *A History of the North Dakota Geological Survey.* Miscellaneous Series No. 58, 1980.

Ohio

Division of Geological Survey
Department of Natural Resources
Building B
Fountain Square
Columbus, OH 43224
(614) 466-5344

List of Publications, 1979. New Publications List, 1980.

Stewart, Grace A., *Fauna of the Silica Shale of Lucas County.* Bulletin 32, Reprinted 1966. $1.00

La Roqque, Aurele and Mildred Marple, *Ohio Fossils.* Bulletin 54, Reprinted 1977. $2.00

La Rocque, Aurele, *Pleistocene Mollusca of Ohio.* Bulletin 62, 3 parts, 1966-1968. Set $9.00

Sturgeon, Myron T. and Richard D. Hoare, *Pennsylvanian Brachiopods of Ohio.* Bulletin 63, 1968. $3.00

Smyth, Pauline, *Bibliography of Ohio geology, 1755-1974.* Information Circular 48, 1979. $6.25

Oregon

State of Oregon Department of Geology & Mineral Industries
1069 State Office Building
Portland, OR 97201
(503) 229-5580

List of Available Publications, 1980.
Fossils in Oregon. Bulletin 92, 1977. $4.00
Oregon Geology. Issued monthly. $4.00 per year
Also recommended: Bones, Thomas J., *Atlas of Fossil Fruits and Seeds from North Central Oregon* (The Clarno Flora). OMSI Occasional Papers in Natural Science, No. 1, 1979. May be obtained from the Oregon Museum of Science and Industry, Portland, OR 97221.

Pennsylvania

Pennsylvania Geological Survey   For Free publications.
Department of Environmental Resources
P.O. Box 2357
Harrisburg, PA 17120

Department of General Services   For priced publications.
State Book Store
P.O. Box 1365
Harrisburg, PA 17125

Hoskins, D. M., *Fossil Collecting in Pennsylvania.* General Geology Reports 40, 1976. 50¢
Pennsylvania Geology. Bimonthly publication, contains fossil articles. Free distribution.

Rhode Island

Department of Environmental Management
Office of the Director
83 Park Street
Providence, RI 02903

Quinn, Alonzo W., *Rhode Island Geology for the Non Geologist.* May be obtained by writing the above. 50¢

South Carolina

South Carolina Geological Survey
Harbison Forest Road
Columbia, SC 29210
(803) 758-6431

Catalog of Geologic Publications, Circular 1, 1980-81.

Geologic Notes — see below.

South Carolina Geology. A biannual publication containing many articles on the fossils of South Carolina. Beginning with Vol. 24, No. 1, 1980, titled *South Carolina Geology.* Subscription $5.00 per year

Holmes, F. S. and M. Tuomey, *Pleiocene Fossils of South Carolina.* 1857. Reprinted by the Paleontological Research Institution, 1259 Trumansburg Road, Ithaca, New York, 14850. $10.00

Supplement above with Campbell, Lyle D. and Sarah C. Campbell, *Revision of Tuomey and Holmes' Pleiocene Fossils of South Carolina.* In the South Carolina Division of Geology, *Geologic Notes,* Vol. 20, No. 3, Fall, 1976.

South Dakota

South Dakota Geological Survey
Science Center
University of South Dakota
Vermillion, SD 57069

Publications, 1980.

Tennessee

Department of Conservation
Division of Geology
G-5 State Office Building
Nashville, TN 37219

List of Publications, 1977.

Miller, Robert A., *The Geologic History of Tennessee.* Bulletin 74, 1974.

Corgan, James, *Vertebrate Fossils of Tennessee.* Bulletin 77, 1976.

Texas

Bureau of Economic Geology
The University of Texas at Austin
Box X, University Station
Austin, TX 78712

List of Publications, 1977.

Utah

Utah Geological and Mineral Survey
606 Black Hawk Way
Salt Lake City, UT 84108
(801) 581-3056

List of Available Publications, 1980.

Hintze, L. F., *Lower Ordovician Trilobites from Western Utah and Eastern Nevada.* Bulletin 48, 1952. $2.00
Fossil Localities in Utah. Circular 45, 1964. Free
Stowe, C. H., *Rockhound Guide to Mineral and Fossil Localities in Utah.* Circular 63, revised edition. $2.50

Vermont

State of Vermont
Department of Libraries
Montpelier, VT 05602

List of Publications, 1976.

Virginia

U.S. Geological Survey
Branch of Distribution
1200 South Eads Street   or 604 South Pickett Street
Arlington, VA 22202   Alexandria, VA 22304

New Publications of the Geological Survey issued monthly. U.S.G.S. Professional Papers series contain numerous fossil publications during the year.

Virginia Division of Mineral Resources
Natural Resources Building, McCormick and Alderman Roads
Charlottesville, VA 22903
(804) 293-5121

List of Publications and Maps, 1980.
Butts, Charles, *Geology of the Appalachian Valley in Virginia.* Bulletin 52, Reprinted 1973, 2 parts. $4.25

Washington

Department of Natural Resources
Division of Geology and Earth Resources
Olympia, WA 98504

Geologic Publications, 1980.
Geology of Washingon. Reprint 12, n.d. 50¢
Geologic Time, Rocks, Fossils, and Minerals in Washington. General Information Pamphlet. Free

West Virginia

West Virginia Geological and Economic Survey
P. O. Box 879
Morgantown, WV 26505
(304) 292-6331

Publications, 1980.
Gillespie, W. H., J. A. Clendening, and H. W. Pfefferkorn, *Plant Fossils of West Virginia*. Educational Series 3A, 1978. $3.00
Cardwell, Dudley H., *Geologic History of West Virginia*. Educational Series 10, 1975. $2.00

Wisconsin

Wisconsin Geological and Natural History Survey
1815 University Avenue
Madison, WI 53706
(608) 262-1705

List of Publications, 1979.
Ostrom, M. E., *Fossil Collecting in Wisconsin*. Educational Series 4, 1962. 50¢
The Geology of Wisconsin. Educational Series 14, 1977. 25¢
Part 2, 1977, 25¢; Part 4, 1978, 25¢

Wyoming

Geological Survey of Wyoming
P. O. Box 3008, University Station
Laramie, WY 82071
(307) 742-2054

List of Publications, 1980.
Hager, Michael W., *Fossils of Wyoming*. Bulletin 54, 1970. $3.00
Blackstone, D. L., *Traveler's Guide to the Geology of Wyoming*. Bulletin 55, 1971. $3.00
Grande, L., *Paleontology of the Green River Formation, with a review of fish fauna*. 1980. $12.50

CHAPTER 10

PALEONTOLOGICAL LIBRARIES AND SOCIETIES

LIBRARIES

Library collections of books, periodicals, and reprints on paleontology vary from several odd volumes in the smaller museums or departmental offices to the extensive libraries containing over ten thousand volumes.

While fossil reference materials may be found in almost every geology department, or museum library, the following collections are suggested for their wealth of reference materials.

Arizona

University of Arizona Laboratory of Paleontology
Tucson, AZ 85721
Excellent reference library.

California

University of California Museum of Paleontology
Berkeley, CA 94720
Over 50,000 volumes in the Earth Sciences Library, extensive reprints.

University of California Department of Geological Science
Riverside, CA 92503
Over 40,000 volumes in the Physical Science Library.

University of California Geology Library
Los Angeles, CA 90024
Excellent research facilities with private reprint collections of paleontology curators.

Natural History Museum of Los Angeles
Los Angeles, CA 90007
7,000 volumes, plus reprint collection.

Colorado

Denver Museum of Natural History
Denver, CO 80205
Very large fossil library.

University of Colorado Museum
Boulder, CO 80302
Reprint collection numbers over 7,000 titles.

Connecticut

Yale Peabody Museum of Natural History
New Haven, CT 06520
Very extensive paleontological library, including large foreign periodical series.

District of Columbia

Smithsonian Institution (U.S. National Museum) Library
Washington, D.C. 20242
Library contains over 45,000 volumes and over 25,000 reprints.

Florida

Florida State Museum Library
Gainesville, FL 32611
Over 44,000 volumes, including reprints.

Idaho

Idaho State University Museum
Pocatello, ID 83209
Over 10,000 reprints, plus bound volumes.

Illinois

Field Museum of Natural History
Chicago, IL 60605
Library has over 17,000 volumes.

Kansas

University of Kansas Museum of Natural History
Lawrence, KS 66045
Research library adequate.

Fort Hays Kansas State College — Sternberg Memorial Museum
Hays, KS 67601
Fossil library fair, mostly reprint collection.

Massachusetts

Pratt Museum of Geology of Amherst College
Amherst, MA 01002
Adequate reference materials.

Harvard University Museum of Comparative Zoology
Cambridge, MA 02138
Fossil library begun with collection of Louis Agassiz. Over 50,000 reprints, unsurpassed foreign serial publications, very extensive reference materials.

Michigan

University of Michigan Museum of Paleontology Library
Ann Arbor, MI 48104
Reprint collection with over 18,000 titles, bound library adequate.

Michigan State University Museum
East Lansing, MI 48824
Library adequate, mostly private collections of the curators.

Minnesota

Science Museum of Minnesota
Minneapolis, MN 55401
Over 15,000 reprints.

Missouri

University of Missouri Geology Department Library
Rolla, MO 65401
Library adequate.

Montana

University of Montana Museum of Paleontology
Missoula, MT 59801
Library adequate.

North Carolina

University of North Carolina Geology Department Library
Chapel Hill, NC 25514
Departmental library adequate.

Duke University Geology Department Library
Durham, NC 27706
Older department collections, excellent holdings.

New Jersey

Princeton University Museum of Natural History
Princeton, NJ 08540
Over 22,000 reprints, better than average bound reference holdings.

New York

American Museum of Natural History — Osborn and Frick Libraries
New York, NY 10024
Excellent with over 10,000 reprints and uncounted bound volumes.

Ohio

Cleveland Museum of Natural History
Cleveland, OH 44106
Adequate for size of museum and collections of fossils.

Pennsylvania

Carnegie Museum Library
Pittsburg, PA 15213
Large reprint and bound collection.

South Dakota

South Dakota School of Mines Library
Rapid City, SD 57701
Holdings adequate.

Texas

Texas Memorial Museum — University of Texas at Austin
Austin, TX 78705
Over 90,000 volumes in University Library.

Wyoming

University of Wyoming Geology Museum Library
Laramie, Wy 82071
Over 15,000 reprints, bound volume collection adequate.

SOCIETIES

Most State Geological Surveys, as well as the U.S. Department of Interior Geological Survey (Ruston, Virginia) contain invaluable libraries, as do such institutions as the various

Academies of Science and the regional museums of natural history.

While the paleontological societies listed here are primarily for the professional, amateur collectors and students often are invited to become members, but must be sponsored by current members.

Colorado

Geological Society of America
3300 Penrose Place
Boulder, CO 80301
(303) 447-2020

Founded in 1888 to promote the science of geology by issuing scholarly publications in the earth sciences and paleontology, holding meetings, both national and regional, and by aiding geological research. There are six regional sections and six topical divisions. Issues numerous publications, the most valuable of which are *Treatises of Invertebrate Paleontology*, and the *Memoirs*.

Iowa

Mid-America Paleontology Society
Dennis Sievers, Secretary
2323 W. 10th Street
Davenport, IA 52803
(319) 342-6113

An amateur oriented society organized about 1978, currently enjoying a membership of several thousand collectors, students, and museum curators. Issues *Mid-America Paleontology Society Digest.*

Oklahoma

Society of Economic Paleontologists and Mineralogists
P. O. Box 4756
Tulsa, OK 74104
(918) 936-1602

Founded in 1926 as a section of the American Association of Petroleum Geologists to promote the science of stratigraphy, paleontology, sedimentary petrology, and related disciplines. Six regional sections cover the United States. Publishes the *Journal of Paleontology* and the *Journal of Sedimentary Petrology,* as well as special publications, the reports of symposia held at the annual meetings, and a new reprint series of earlier publications.

Texas

Society of Vertebrate Paleontology
The Texas Memorial Museum
Route 4, Box 189
Austin, TX 78705
(512) 836-0440, ext. 253

Founded in 1934 as a part of the Virginia-based Paleontological Society, becoming a separate society in 1941. Publications include the *News Bulletin* and the quarterly *Bibliography of vertebrate paleontology*. Organized in the interest of uniting vertebrate paleontologists and all others interested in vertebrate history and evolution.

Virginia

Geoscience Information Society
The American Geological Institute
5205 Leesburg Pike
Falls Church, VA 22041
(703) 379-2480

Founded in 1965 to initiate and improve the exchange of earth science information through the mutual cooperation of librarians, earth scientists, editors, and information specialists. Publications are a union list of field trip guidebooks, proceedings volumes, and a Geoscience Information Society Newsletter.

Paleontology Society
The American Geological Institute
5205 Leesburg Pike
Falls Church, VA 22041
(703) 379-2480

Founded in 1908 to promote the science of paleontology. Issues the *Journal of Paleontology* and the *Paleontological Society Memoirs,* as well as periodic *News and Notes.*

Aside from these major societies of interest to the fossil collector, there are also numerous local and regional collectors' clubs based in many natural history museums and universities, e.g. the "Dry Dredgers," a group of collectors sponsored by the University of Cincinnati. Several other clubs in California are under the sponsorship of the regional University of California branches and museums. Fossil collectors' clubs are also busy in east coast cities and throughout Florida, but the names and addresses of these have not come to this author's attention.

Glossary of Paleontological Terms

The names and definitions given here relate in most part to North America, and may well come to the attention of the fossil collector either in the literature or on museum labels. The terminology has been abbreviated into brief and clearly definitive forms.

Allosaurus   Recently renamed *Antrodemus,* this carnivorous dinosaur ranged over our western states during Jurassic time.

Ammonoids   Extinct cephalopods similar to the modern nautilus. These forms of the Mollusca branched from the nautiloids during early Devonian times, becoming very abundant until the close of the Cretaceous. The Jurassic of Europe and the Cretaceous deposits of North America contain varied and abundant ammonite fauna.

Angiosperms   Flowering plants with broad leaves and complex seeds, which began during the Triassic Period and expanded during the Cretaceous to become the dominant flora of our planet. The growth and spread of this form of vegetation during the early Cenozoic may have helped give rise to the mammals.

Ankylosaurs   A dinosaur whose body was completely covered with bony plates and a club-like tail. Possessed a massive jaw, but the teeth were singularly weak and small, indicating that these creatures fed upon plants. Ranged our western states during the Upper Cretaceous.

Apatosaurus   A new name for our old friend *Brontosaurus,* whose massive sauropod body averaged 70 feet in length and weighed over 30 tons. Lived during the Middle and Upper Jurassic over several western states.

Archaeozoic   The oldest known geologic era, going back some 3.6 billion years and more. The Archaeozoic is the earliest interval of the twofold subdivision which covered Pre-Cambrian time. This term is also synonymous for the term "Archean." During this vast period of time there was little evidence of life on earth, although prior to the Pre-Cambrian Period, complex compounds of possible organic nature have been found. Metamorphism, the extreme compacting of sedimentaries and the altering of volcanic rocks, obscures evidence of Archaeozoic life, although scientists have recently discovered microscopic organisms of 3.5 billion years ago, in rocks found at Figtree, South Africa.

Archaeopteryx   This is the earliest known bird, found primarily in the Upper Jurassic of Germany. About the size of a crow, with a long neck and elongated tail. The skull, teeth, and general bone construction are considered reptilian. The impressions of feathers in the lithographic limestone in which the specimens have been found give a clue to the fact that these birds were warm-blooded.

Arthrodires   The arthrodires were the armored, joint-necked fishes of the Devonian. They became extinct by the end of the Devonian Period.

Arthropods   The phylum of segmented animals, containing the crustaceans, insects, trilobites, and horseshoe crabs, and dating from the Lower Cambrian through the present.

Artiodactyl   These are most of the hoofed mammals, e.g. pigs, camels, giraffes, cattle, sheep, goats, etc. They are also known as the even-toed ungulates, beginning before the Oligocene Epoch to the present.

Authochthonous   Referring to a fauna restricted to a specific place, or being indigenous to a given place.

Belemnite   An Upper Cretaceous cephalopod with a straight, tube-like, pointed body. Abundant in the Upper Cretaceous of New Jersey and South Dakota, and found at other locations.

Biostratigraphic Unit   A group of rock strata that is identified by its fossil content. Such identification may be based on a single species or upon a distinctive assemblage of fossils. Zones may be included within biostratigraphic units composed of rock groups formed during the time of a specific type of fossil or group of fossils.

Bivalves   A mollusc with two hinged shells, of the class Bivalvia, or "lamp-shell" brachiopods.

Blastoids   Abundant during Mississippian times, these echinoderms were related to the crinoids, having a column and calyx, but without arms. The mouth was in the center of the calyx, surrounded by five spiracles, or openings. Appearing first during the Ordovician, they became extinct by the end of the Permian.

Brachiopods   Bivalves distinguished from others by the dissimilarity of the two shells. Known popularly as "lamp shells," these forms ranged in the geologic column from the Cambrian down to the present. During the Ordovician, Silurian and Devonian times, they were prominent and extremely abundant, both as to populations and species. The Permian reefs of west Texas are built of brachiopods. The Phylum Brachiopoda is divided into two classes. Class Inarticulata includes the primitive, "unhinged" brachiopods, while the Class Articulata possess a well-developed hinge structure for articulation of the valves.

Brachiosaurus   A sauropod who rose in height to some 40 feet, weighing to 50 tons and certainly one of the largest reptiles to walk our continent. It is regarded as an unusual type of dinosaur as its front legs were longer than those in back, with the body sloping down to a proportionately short tail. Ranged over North America during the Middle and Upper Jurassic.

Bryozoans   Commonly referred to as "moss animals" and living today in temperate waters, these microscopic branched and encrusting animals grow together in a variety of forms, from single branching clusters to massive colonies. They were abundant during Ordovician times, particularly in the Cincinnati region.

During Mississippian times, these forms assumed lace-like branching or spiral colonies, as in *Archimedes*. Today there are 2000 species worldwide, including freshwater and sea water species.

Cambrian   Oldest period of the Paleozoic Era. Begun some 600 million years ago, it lasted for about 100 million years. During Cambrian times as much as 30% of North America was submerged, with such primitive life forms living in the Cambrian seas as stalked echinoderms, arthropods, sponges, annelid worms and brachiopods. The trilobites were the most prolific and varied organism of the time. The classic fauna of the Middle Cambrian are found in the Burgess shale of Canada. The delicate impressions of worms and other forms have been preserved in the black shale. Blue-green algae formed calcareous reefs on the Cambrian sea floor, and these lime secreting rock masses may be seen in Montana and Wyoming.

Carboniferous   In European usage, a designation for the combined Mississippian-Pennsylvanian periods, the term is seldom used by American paleontologists. It was during this combined era that the great coal deposits were laid down in North America to provide the abundance and variety of fossil plants collected today. The Carboniferous began about 345 million years ago and ended about 280 million years ago.

Carbonization   A type of fossilization by distillation. As organic matter slowly decomposes under water or sediment, the oxygen, nitrogen, and hydrogen are lost in the distillation process. When these liquids and gases have been completely removed, a thin film-like carbon remains. Through this carbonization process, the wings of insects and the structure of leaves have been preserved. While plants are the most common fossils to be found in the carbonized state of replacement, graptolites, insects, and even fish, have been preserved by this process. Coal, of course, if the best-known result of carbonization.

Carnivorous   Any mammal or reptile which feeds upon other mammals or reptiles. Plants may also be carnivorous, e.g. the Venus Fly Trap plant.

Cartilaginous   Having a skeleton composed mainly of gristle or elastic tissue, as in most vertebrates.

Casts and Molds   While not representing the actual remains of organisms, casts and molds of prehistoric life are considered fossils. This mode of preservation contains little, if any, of the original organic matter. A mold is the life-sized impression of an actual organism, such as a clamshell, snail, plant, bone, or even an entire skeleton. The cast is the positive reproduction of the organism, which is made in the mold. A cast occurs when a natural mold is filled while embedded in the surrounding sedimentary or volcanic deposit.

Catastrophism   The hypothesis which assumes that differences between fossils occurring in successive formations were the result of extinction of the earlier forms by natural catastrophes followed by the introduction of new organisms. This hypotheses advances the literalist Biblical idea of a young earth and a brief period of creation by explaining geologic and evolutinary changes in terms of violent cataclysms such as floods and volcanic eruptions. During the late 18th and 19th centuries, the catastrophic hypothesis was replaced by the principle of uniformitarianism, which states that the natural processes now modifying our planet and its inhabitants operate uniformly and continuously with the geologic periods of the past.

Cenozoic   The most recent geological era which occupies the last 70 million years. This era includes the Tertiary and Quaternary periods, which brought forth the rise of mammals, many of which became extinct by the close of the Pleistocene Epoch. Many of the mammalian families which began in the Eocene Epoch continue today, represented by the equids, primates, camelids, carnivores, proboscideans, and others.

Cephalopods   Along with the bivalves and gastropods, these are members of the phylum Mollusca, class Cephalopoda. The group includes the squids, octopuses, and pearly nautilus. While the squids lack hard parts, the ammonites and nautiloids possessed calcareous shells which were abundantly preserved in the fossil record. The ammonoids and belemnoids were extinct by the end of the Cretaceous, but extremely numerous and varied in the shallow seas which covered much of the Mesozoic world. The cephalopods are key index fossils to many formations, particularly in the European, African, and Asiatic Mesozoic Era. In North America they are most numerous in the Comanchean series of Texas and the Fox Hills-Pierre shales of the Dakotas.

Ceratopsians   These are the horned dinosaurs, the best known being *Triceratops,* a three-horned herbivore, some thirty feet long and weighing in the neighborhood of six to eight tons. Found in the Upper Cretaceous deposits of our West. *Styracosaurus* and *Torosaurus* were related genera.

Chalichotheres   Perissodactyls of the Tertiary which roamed the grasslands of North America. Noted for their clawed, three-toed feet without hooves.

Class   A taxon more inclusive than an order, but less than phylum. Members of a class may share basic structural similarities even though they may have undergone adaptive changes.

Cnidarians   The phylum *Cnidaria* contains the corals, sea anemones and jellyfishes, of the classes Hydrozoa or hydroids, Scyphozoa or jellyfishes, and Anthozoa, the corals and sea anemones. The stony corals of the class Anthozoa are the most commonly found fossil corals. Jellyfishes from the Pre-Cambrian through Cretaceous have been found preserved by carbonization, as casts and molds in finely-grained sedimentary deposits, as the Ediacara fauna of Australia and in the Solnhofen limestone of Germany. Corals range from Ordovician times to the present, where they are found in most temperate and tropical waters as reef-forming organisms, the Great Barrier Reef of Queensland, Australia, being an excellent example. Paleotemperatures of ancient seas are studied via fossil corals.

Coccoliths   Tiny photosynthetic organisms, part of the plankton found in warm, low-latitude waters. Coccolithophons are important constituents of prehistoric chalk deposits, and compose deep-sea sediments called calcareous ooze.

Coelurids   Small, upright dinosaurs which were carnivorous predators, of which *Coelophysis* is an example that lived during the Upper Triassic. The saurischians had their origin during the Triassic, but this order carried on until the Jurassic and Cretaceous periods.

Conodonts   Small tooth-like fossils believed to represent the hard parts of extinct fishes. Conodonts first appeared in the Ordovician and were abundant in some areas until the early Mesozoic, becoming extinct during the Permian. Many genera and species of Ordovician, Devonian, and Mississippian conodonts are valuable as index or guide fossils to the micropaleontologist.

Correlative   Designation of any two or more rock units as similar from the fossil or stratigraphic evidence.

Creodonts   The primitive carnivore mammals of the order Creodonta, appearing during the late Cretaceous Period. Developing through the Tertiary, they became specialized in tooth and claw. Closely resembling the felines and canines of the period, they were of considerable size and much fiercer. *Andrewsarchus*, a giant creodont from Mongolia, had a skull more than three feet long. *Patriofelis*, a lion-sized carnivore roamed North America during the Eocene, becoming extinct by early Pliocene time.

Cretaceous   The last period of the Mesozoic Era, beginning approximately 135 million years ago and ending about 70 million years ago. During this period many new forms of reptiles appeared, *Tyrannosaurus, Triceratops, Ankylosaurus,* the hadrosaurs, and others of the giant reptiles, as well as the flying and swimming reptiles, all of which became extinct with the close of the period. Cretaceous formations are widely distributed and may be found in all continents, in both marine and nonmarine sediments. Throughout Europe, the Cretaceous sediments are extremely fossiliferous, although in England, the USSR, and northern Germany, formations are largely freshwater or of continental origin. In North America, the Cretaceous appears in the Rocky Mountains and Great Plains area with the famed Kansas Niobrara chalk, and along the eastern seaboard from New Jersey to Florida. The Comanchean series of Texas is known for its very abundant fossil assemblage, particularly the large ammonites, some of which reach six feet in width.

Crinoids   The class Crinoidea of the phylum Echinodermata, popularly known as "sea lilies," and resembling long-stemmed flowers. The crinoid is composed of a stem, calyx or body, and the arms. Many fossil crinoids had stalks as much as 50 feet long. Some living crinoids are stemless and free-living during the adult stage. Appearing widely during the Ordovician, their fossilized remains are particularly abundant during Paleozoic times. They continue today in considerably smaller numbers as usually stemless (a few species in temperate waters do possess stalks), free-moving "feather stars."

Crossopterygians   Rather primitive lobe-finned fishes of the Devonian Period. Since they possessed respiratory organs, they are considered forerunners of the modern lungfishes. In Upper Devonian time the crossopterygians were abundant in the waters covering parts of Quebec. The only living member of this order is the coelacanth taken live from the southeast coast of Africa, identified as *Latimeria*.

Cycads   A large group of semi-tropical, primitive plants of the order Cycadales. The Cretaceous species, with their short, pithy trunks and woody covering, with naked seeds carried in simple cones, and leaflets arranged on either side of a common stem, differ from the living species. The latter have cylindrical, erect trunks and large fern-like leaves, on short, thick stems. These primitive plants may have had their origin during late Permian times.

Cystoids   Members of the class Cystoides of the phylum Echinodermata, these forms have a globular or saclike calyx composed of numerous calcareous plates. The calyx was usually attached to the sea bottom by a short stem. They ranged from the Cambrian to the Devonian, being especially aundant during the Ordovician and Silurian. Many forms occur in the Ordovician-Silurian of North America, and are found equally abundantly in the early Paleozoic of Bohemia and the USSR.

Devonian   Beginning about 345 million years ago in the Paleozoic Era, the formations of this period, particularly in New York, Iowa, and Montana, are fairly complete and the rocks contain an abundant faunal assemblage of crinoids, brachiopods, molluscs, and trilobites. Devonian beds occur throughout the world. In North America, the close of the period was climaxed by the Acadian orogeny, or mountain-building movement. Land climates appear to have been mild and moderate, the period being characterized by the growth and expansion of land plants, which developed from small, leafless species, to giant tree ferns. The marine organisms were extremely abundant, consisting of brachiopods, trilobites, and other invertebrates. The insects and vertebrates made their first appearance. Among the vertebrates, both freshwater and marine fishes underwent an almost explosive development and inhabited most bodies of water. Among these primitive fishes were the jawless ostracoderms, the jawed and armored placoderms, and shark-like arthrodires. New forms of armored fishes appeared, like *Bothriolepis,* lung-fishes as *Scaumenacia,* and the air-breathing *Eusthenopteron,* all three being found in the Miller Cliffs, Scaumenac Bay, Quebec. Of greater importance in the evolution of the chordates was the appearance of the earliest tetrapods, or four-footed amphibians, that appear to have evolved from the crossopterygians.

Diceratherium   Small rhincero from the Miocene of North America, having a pair of transverse horns on the front of the skull.

Diplocaulus   An exotic amphibian from the Lower Permian of North America belonging to the order Nectidia. This bizarre creature had a large, flat, broad skull shaped much like an arrowhead.

Diplodocus   The longest sauropod of the Upper Jurassic from western North America. From the Morrison beds of Wyoming and other western states, quarried specimens of this giant dinosaur reaching 90 feet in length are on display in museums. This creature had a long, snaky head and whip-like tail. It is believed that diplodocus spent much of its time in the water.

Echinoderms   Members of the phylum Echinodermata which is divided into two subphyla: the Pelmatozoa, which included the classes Cystoidea, Blastoidea, and

Crinoidea; and the Eleutherozoa, which contains the classes Stelleroidea, Echinoidea, and Holothuroidea. The echinoderms ranged from the Cambrian through the present. Fossil forms from all the classes of this order are found in marine formations on all the continents.

Echinoids   Belonging to the class Echinoidea of the phylum Echinodermata. These are free-moving animals with exoskeletons, or tests, of globular, heart, or biscuit shapes, covered with large numbers of moveable spines. These spines serve as a means of locomotion, as well as protection from predators. Although occurring in the Ordovician, the echinoids began to flourish during the Mesozoic, with a great variety of genera and species occurring during the Cretaceous. The echinoids are still very abundant in today's oceans.

Edaphosaurus   One of the most bizarre reptiles of the Lower Permian, this plant-eating pelycosaur, abundant in Texas, carried a row of vertical spines across its back, studded with horizontal crossbars of bone, much like a sailing ship.

Edentates   Numerous and varied from Tertiary times to the present, these placental mammals consist of the anteaters, sloths, and armadillos.

Endocast   Mold of the interior of a fossil braincase, common in fossil mammals, as braincasts of oreodonts. Rare in fossil man-apes.

Eocene   The second epoch in the Early Cenozoic Era, which saw the development of many of today's mammals and primates. The epoch lasted from 60 to 40 million years ago. In North America, Eocene beds of marine and nonmarine origin are exposed along the Atlantic and Gulf Coastal plains, from Maryland to Florida. They reappear on the Pacific Coast in California, Oregon, and Washington. The vertebrate beds of western North America, particularly the Wasatch and Green River formations, contain a varied mammalian fauna. The climates during the Eocene were warm, almost subtropical, as far north as Canada. Besides the large number of species of invertebrates, marine animals included many species of bony fishes (as in the Green River shales of Kemmerer, Wyoming), sharks, and whale-like mammals, zeuglodonts. The plant life of the Eocene was widespread and related to such modern forms as walnut, elm, and beech trees. Birds and primitive mammals made their appearance and ranged in form from dog-like condylarths, to the larger uintatheres, to tiny three-toed horses, to equally small, tusked elephants.

Eohippus   A seldom-used name for *Hyracotherium,* one of the earliest horses of the Eocene.

Evolution   The process by which groups of organisms change, through the passage of time, from primitive forms to more sophisticated forms differing morphologically from their ancestors. The historical development of related groups is called phylogeny. Evolution may be either a gradual process through the passage of time or it may be explosive (in terms of millions of years).

Eurypterid   Lower Paleozoic marine arthropods characterized by having pairs of broad, winglike appendages or paddles. Occurring in some Silurian and Devonian formations, some species possessed a scorpion-like stinger and possibly a poison gland. In the New York State Silurian, the species *Pterygotus* reached a length of some nine feet. Related to the modern horseshoe crab, these arthropods were believed to have swum on their backs.

Family A taxon more inclusive than a genus, but less than an order. In a family, members may have many structural differences, as in the family Proboscidea, which includes mammoths, mastodons, and elephants.

Faunal Assemblage Any specific group of animals, vertebrates or invertebrates, living in a specific region at a specific time.

Foraminifera One-celled organisms that secrete chambered or unchambered shells or tests capable of preservation, possessing numerous pores through which pseudopodia extend. Member of the order Foraminifera of the phylum Protozoa, they are found in most marine fossiliferous deposits, and ranged from the Cambrian to the present.

Formation In stratigraphy, this is the primary unit, consisting of a succession of rock layers which have been either separated or combined. Formations can be combined into groups or "members."

Fossilization Briefly, this is the process by which an animal or plant or any trace of its existence is preserved in rock or as a single unit. A fern on a piece of shale, an agatized shell, an unreplaced mollusc, trace fossils (tracks of all kinds), gastroliths (dinosaur gizzard stones) and coprolites (fish or animal dung) are all examples of fossils.

Gastrolith Polished, rounded stones belived to have been used by dinosaurs for grinding the food in their stomachs. *Plesiosaurus* remains invariably contain several pounds of these stones in their stomach cavities.

Gastropod A univalve of the class Gastropoda, which contains all the snail forms, limpet shells, and slugs, or nudibranchs. Originating during the Early Cambrian and continuing through the present, their remains are found in nearly all the marine deposits where Mollusca is present. The shells, being composed of aragonite, dissolve quite easily after death, causing an abundance of casts and molds of these forms in some formations.

Genus A taxonomic category above a species but below a family, e.g. *Atrypa* would be the generic designation, followed by the Latin adjective *formosus* as the species, in the family Atrypidae.

Geologic Range The duration of geologic time that any organism lived, and during which specific fossils became index fossils or guides to those periods of time. Certain genera or species were shortlived only in a given period, thereby becoming useful as a guide fossil to that particular time unit, while other genera or species ranged through two or more time periods.

Gondwanaland This was the southern hemispheric portion of postulated land masses during Permian time, and included South America, Africa, India, Antarctica, and Australia (with New Zealand and Tasmania).

Graptolites A group of colonial animals consisting of chitinous exoskeletons composed of a series of tubes growing along a branching stalk. These stalks could float or become attached to shells, rocks or any other solid feature. Presently considered chordates, they began during the Cambrian and saw considerable development during the Ordovician, becoming extinct by the end of the Silurian.

Hadrosaurus A member of the duck-billed ornithopods which grew to large size, possessing a shovel-type mouth. This group of fossil reptiles have the honor of being the first dinosaurs excavated in the United States, in 1858, in New Jersey. The Hydrosauridae ranged in herds over much of western America, Canada, and Asia during Late Cretaceous times.

Hesperornis Resembling a modern loon, this large Cretaceous bird is found in the Niobrara chalk of Kansas.

Hipparion A three-toed equine that originated in North America during the Pliocene, and spread into the Old World.

Holocene The most recent geological epoch, beginning about 10,000 years ago, and believed to continue into the present. This is the last epoch of the Quaternary Period, and includes all the time since the last Ice Age.

Hominidae A family within the super-family Hominoidea comprising the man-like beings. This includes all the species of *Homo,* from *Homo sapiens* back to *Homo erectus* of Europe, Indonesia and Africa, and 1.9 million year-old *Homo habilis* of East Africa.

Hominoidea The super-family which contains both the apes and man.

Hypohippus A rare three-toed equine ranging through the Miocene-Pliocene period, across North America and Asia. Unlike the *Hipparion,* this form retained certain primitive features, as low-crowned teeth.

Hyracodon A small, harmless rhinoceros from the Oligocene of western America.

Hyracotherium The earliest equine, in older literature referred to as *Eohippus.* This very small perissodactyl had four toes on the front feet and three on the hind feet. Remains are known from the Eocene of North America and Europe.

Ichthyosaur Short-necked marine reptiles, not unlike modern dolphins, reaching a length of 25 to 40 feet. These forms possessed a long, knife-like jaw filled with teeth. Their geologic range was from the Middle Triassic to Late Cretaceous, being prominent some 190 millions of years ago in the U.S. and Europe.

Insectivores Considered the most primitive of the placental mammals, having their beginning during the Cretaceous and continuing to the present. Common forms today are shrews, hedgehogs, and moles.

Interglacials The periods between two glacial epochs. Three interglacial stages are known in the U.S., the oldest being the Aftonian interglacia, followed by the Yarmouth and the Sangamon. In Europe, the three interglacials were the

Gunz-Mindel, Mindel-Riss and Riss-Wurm. While the last three are considered equivalent in time to the North American stages, Neanderthals and Cro-magnons were known to have lived during these interglacials, hunting the Holocene mammals, particularly the mammoth, mastodon, cave bear, and deer groups.

Jurassic   The second oldest period of the Mesozoic Era, beginning about 190 to 195 million years ago and lasting some 55 million years. This period gave rise to the giant carnivorous theropods which walked upright on their hind legs, as well as the giant sauropods, such as the *Brontosaurus*. During this period the *Stegosaurus* and the bird-like *Ornitholestes* were numerous. Rocks from the Jurassic Period are exposed over many major portions of the earth's surface, with formations throughout our western states containing a wealth of dinosaur remains, as the Dinosaur National Monument and Como Bluffs. Some marine deposits are known out West, but most of the Jurassic Period consists of continental deposits representing windblown desert sand sediments laid down by streams and flash floods. On the land portions, plants were numerous, notably the conifers and cycads. The predominant plants were the cycad and ginkgo.

Labyrinthodonts   Beginning in the Upper Devonian and ending with the Triassic Period, these amphibians of the fossil class Stegocephalia were the oldest dominant group of air-breathing, four-legged animals.

Laurasia   This was the northern portion of the super-continent Pangea which consisted of the land masses that became North America, Asia, and Europe.

Mammoth   An extinct member of the Proboscidea, or elephant, family, having long, curved tusks and massive hair. The mammoth is easily distinguished from the mastodon by the shape of its teeth, the molars being massive, flat, and plate-like, compared to the conical teeth of the mastodon. The lower jaws do not carry tusks as in the mastodons. Originating during Oligocene time, mammoths developed from Asia, the Middle East, and throughout North America. They were common in Europe during the Ice Ages.

Mastodons   Another member of the Proboscidea, elephant-like mammals, whose molars were pointed and not as deep as in the mammoth. These proboscideans had a pair of upper tusks.

Megafossils   All forms of invertebrate and vertebrate remains that are readily visible to the naked eye, unlike microfossils. Another term used to describe these larger fossil forms is 'macrofossils.'

Megatherium   The gigantic ground sloth from the Pleistocene. Recorded in some abundance in several states, their fossilized dung has been found deposited many feet thick in some western caves. It is believed that paleoindians knew and hunted the ground sloth, which partially contributed to the extinction of *Megatherium*.

Merycoidodon (also Mioniochoerus)   Commonly known as an oreodont, this is the four-toed artiodactyl whose bones and skulls are found so abundantly in the Oligocene of the Badlands. Collected in great abundance in Wyoming, Nebraska, and South Dakota.

Mesohippus   The small, three-toed equine from the Oligocene of western America.

Mesozoic   This era is composed of the Triassic, Jurassic, and Cretaceous periods. Beginning with the close of the Paleozoic, some 225 million years ago, it ended with the beginning of the Cenozoic some 70 million years later. The Mesozoic is generally called the Age of Dinosaurs, from the vast array of marine, flying, and land reptiles that existed throughout this era. Mesozoic formations are exposed along both eastern and western coastal areas, and on portions of all other continents. At the closing of the Mesozoic, the Andes and Rocky mountains underwent major uplifting.

Microfossils   Includes all fossils which can be examined only under a microscope, regardless of phyla, e.g. pollen, spores, ostracods, forams.

Miocene   This is the fourth oldest epoch of the Tertiary Period, from about 25 to 12 million years ago, when many mammals developed and ranged across the continents. In the seas, cetaceans were becoming modern in appearance. Marine Miocene exposures surface throughout Europe and parts of the Caribbean. In North America, fossiliferous deposits occur along the Atlantic Coastal Plain, being particularly attractive to the fossil collector in North Carolina, Virginia, and Maryland. On the Pacific Coast, the Miocene is restricted largely to California. Beds are known from Washington and Oregon, while nonmarine deposits occur from the Rocky Mountains to the Mississippi River, and from South Dakota to Texas.

Mississippian   Beginning some 345 million years ago, this period, considered the lower part of the Carboniferous, has widespread exposure in Europe and the USSR. Marine deposits are known also from China, Australia, Africa, and South America. In Canada, continental deposits contain fossil plants and freshwater fishes. Marine fossils continued in appearance not unlike earlier Upper Devonian forms, with the crinoids and blastoids becoming numerous. Large swamp-forests covered much of the land, with amphibians having an explosive evolution. Ferns and water plants flourished. Fishes were abundant, including some 300 species of sharks.

Molds   (see Casts and Molds)

Moropus   A clawed perissodactyl from the Miocene which roamed Nebraska, in association with *Oxydactylus* (a camel), and *Parahippus* (another three-toed horse).

Mosasaur   A carnivorous marine lizard known to have inhabited the Cretaceous seas of Kansas and other regions. Considered the major marine predators of the time, they grew up to 50 feet long, and possessed great, gaping jaws with sharp teeth that curved backward.

Multituberculates   Rodent-like mammals which had their origin in the Jurassic and continued to the Paleocene. Abundant in western deposits, easily recognized by their teeth, bearing numerous cusps on their cheek teeth.

Mylodon   Another large sloth which ranged over parts of the U.S. during the Pleistocene.

Neogene   A seldom-used term for the upper division of the Tertiary, the Miocene and Pliocene epochs.

Notochord   A cylindrical sheath forming a flexible support in chordates.

Oligocene   An epoch within the Tertiary which saw the rise of large mammalian faunas in the West, particularly in the Badlands of South Dakota and Nebraska. The period covered 40 to 25 million years ago. Oligocene outcrops of marine deposits are exposed along the Gulf Coast and the southern Atlantic Coastal Plain. Similar deposits are found along the Pacific Coast extending from Alaska to lower California. Besides the typical invertebrate fauna of the Tertiary, rays, sharks, and bony fishes were numerous. On land, grass-like plants filled prairies which helped develop a rapidly expanding mammalian biota. Many earlier mammals died out, while modern groups, as the horse, camel, rhinoceros, cats, and deer, became abundant and continued to the present in modified forms.

Order   That taxonomic category of animal or plant division which ranks above the family designation but below the class designation.

Ordovician   The second oldest period of the Paleozoic Era, begun some 500 million years ago. During its 75 million-year history, shallow seas covered much of the Mediterranean, Britain, Scandinavia, and parts of the USSR. The climates and widespread seas appeared favorable for the development and growth of marine life, the Ordovician seas teeming with vast numbers of invertebrates. The trilobites and brachiopods beginning in the Cambrian, became more numerous and complex at this time, being joined by corals, crinoids and other echinoderms, and molluscan forms. Some species of cephalopods, bearing straight, cone-shaped shells, reached lengths of 15 feet. The Bryozoa also developed many new genera and species. During this period the vertebrates were represented by the ostracoderms, one of the earliest armored, jawless fishes. Their bones, plates, and scales are collected in Ordovician sediments of Colorado and neighboring states.

Oreodonts   These artiodactyls, which roamed over parts of western America from the Eocene to the Pliocene resembled sheep, but in reality were closer to the camels. Their remains are found in the greatest abundance in Oligocene deposits, as in the Brule formation of Nebraska and South Dakota. This form is so common it is found in most museum collections, while the Frick Mammal Collection of the American Museum of Natural History in New York contains thousands of skulls and skeletons of this mammal.

Ornithischians   The extinct order of Archosaurs, one of the two (the other is Saurischia) which make up the dinosaurs. The Ornithischia are the "bird-hipped" reptiles which have a pelvis reminiscent of that in birds. These appeared during middle Triassic time, but disappeared late in the Cretaceous.

Ostracoderms   The primitive jawless fishes of the class Agnatha, appearing during the late Ordovician. These oldest of the vertebrate animals have been found in Norway, Greenland, Britain, and Canyon City, Colorado. Their bony armor plates, spines, and teeth have been found in some abundance, although by the close of the Devonian they already were becoming extinct.

Paleogene   A seldom-used term containing the lower divisions of the Tertiary, the Paleocene, Eocene, and Oligocene epochs.

Paleocene   The oldest epoch of the Tertiary Period, beginning at the close of the Cretaceous, some 70 million years ago, and lasting about 10 million years. By this period, the last of the dinosaurs had passed and the invasion of the mammals now began. Insectivore-mammals lived in the trees, leading to the primates and hominoids of today. Fossil-bearing Paleocene deposits have been worked in France and England, while fossiliferous sandstones and limestones of the Paleocene have been found in some western states, the Pacific Coast, and the Atlantic and Gulf Coastal areas. Marine invertebrates were locally abundant, including Mollusca, the echinoderms, Foraminifera, and many types of fishes. During this epoch considerable volcanic activity took place in Colorado, Montana, and New Mexico.

Paleopathology   The study of diseased and injured conditions of fossil organisms. Shell or bone injury and repair is a common indicator of pathological conditions, as well as worm infection, sponge boring, regeneration of arms in starfish, dwarfing, deformation of shell structure, regeneration in crinoid spines, and evidence of preying bacterial organisms.

Paleontology   The science which studies extinct forms of life, existing in former geologic periods of time, represented by their fossilized remains. Various disciplines within paleontology are paleobotany, which treats with fossil plants; paleoclimatology, or the study of ancient climates; and paleoecology, the association of plants and animals of the geologic past, examined in relationship to their environments.

Paleozoic   The vast era of geologic time which opened after the close of the Pre-Cambrian some 600 million years ago, and lasted until the beginning of the Mesozoic, some 225 million years later. The Paleozoic contains seven major time units: Cambrian, Ordovician, Silurian, Devonian, Mississippian, Pennsylvanian, and Permian. With the beginning of the Paleozoic, the earliest fossil record begins, ushering in the explosive development of many types of marine life, including representatives of most major phyla. Paleozoic rocks and their fossil contents cover much of North America.

Pangea   The name given in plate tectonics theory to the huge land mass which included all the modern continents on earth during the late Paleozoic. Upon breaking up, the land masses became the separate continents as we know them today.

Parallel Evolution   Identical courses of evolution followed by two unrelated groups of animals, e.g. the Australopithecines and *Homo*.

Pelycosaurs   The order of reptiles containing *Dimetrodon* and *Edaphosaurus* which are considered to be in a line of direct ancestry to the mammal-like reptiles of the Permian-Triassic. Beginning during the late Pennsylvanian, these reptiles were characterized by the large snail-like structure on their backs, supported by elongated spines along the vertebral column. Pelycosaurs were both carnivorous and herbivorous.

Pennsylvanian   The coal measures of North America and Europe are found from the Pennsylvanian Period which began 320 million years ago. While sediments of this period were widespread throughout Alaska and the U.S., the bulk of fossil plants collected come from the coal field regions of Ohio, West Virginia, Pennsylvania, Illinois, Indiana, and Kentucky. The earliest known Pennsylvanian amphibians were the dominant vertebrates, while fossil plants as ferns, giant scale trees and rushes, developed abundantly in the mild, humid, subtopical temperatures. Marine life teemed with molluscs, crinoids, brachiopods, and corals, as well as sponges and fusulinids. The coal deposits of Illinois provide the collector with countless thousands of nodules containing plants, arthropods, worms, and other bizarre animals.

Perissodactyla   This group, consisting of odd-toed hoofed mammals, contains the titanotheres, chalicotheres, rhinoceroses, and equids, the horse family.

Permian   About 280 million years ago, the Permian seas covered vast areas of Europe, Asia, South America, Australia, and the East Indies. Permian rocks best exposed in the American mid-continent region, the western states and the northern Appalachian region. Among the vertebrates, amphibians and reptiles were numerous and highly specialized. This was the age of the pelycosaurs, mammal-like theraspids and reptiles which were the forerunners of the dinosaurs. Many of the coal-age plants disappeared and were replaced by the conifers. The long line of the invertebrates continued to develop, with bivalves and ammonites being more numerous and varied.

Phylum   The major subdivision of the animal kingdom which denotes the placement of the organism into its key classification, and separates that group of organism from all others, e.g. phylum Brachiopoda from phylum Arthropoda.

Placoderms   An extinct class of fishes, the Placodermi, which lived from the Silurian to the Permian. This group had well-developed, massive, bony, articulating jaws with pointed, tooth-like projections and sharp cutting edges. The well known *Dinichtys*, a Devonian arthrodire, grew to a length of over 30 feet.

Pleistocene   The early epoch of the Quaternary Period which contained the four glacial ages of North America, ranging from about 2 million years ago to about 11,000 years ago. The Pleistocene saw the disappearance of the mastodons, mammoths, and giant ground sloths. During the glacial and interglacial times, the seas rose and fell again and again. Invertebrate fossil deposits of this epoch are numerous along both the Pacific and Atlantic coasts, where deposits are found from Virginia to Florida, and Oregon to southern California. True man appeared during the early Villafranchian or Lower Pleistocene, and underwent rapid physical and cultural development. Many deposits in Europe, East Africa, Indonesia, and China contain their remains, artifacts, and fragments of the animals they hunted for food.

Plesiosaurs These were the long-necked marine reptiles with paddle-like flippers and turtle-like bodies, which were adapted to life in the open seas, from Middle Triassic to Late Cretaceous times. Their remains are known from the Cretaceous of Kansas and Alabama, and they occur in deposits of other regions.

Pliocene The last period of the Tertiary system, beginning about 5 million years ago and ending with the beginning of the Pleistocene, about 2 million years ago. The marine molluscan faunas were beginning to change from the earlier Eocene-Miocene biota. Approximately 60% of the Pliocene species carried into the Pleistocene. Fossiliferous Pliocene deposits are well-known in Europe, as well as in Asia. In North America, both marine and continental deposits are found in the Carolinas, Florida, and Gulf Coastal states. Mammals were extremely numerous, the present forms of horses, camels, deer, giraffes, and rhinoceroses being widespread. The proboscideans underwent some specialization, while the primates advanced to today's numerous species. A great many invertebrates and fishes resembled present-day forms.

Poebrotherium A small camel found abundantly in the Oligocene strata of South Dakota's Badlands, in Nebraska, and other areas.

Proboscideans The order of large mammals with long, flexible snouts. Proboscidea include our two living elephants (the African and Asiatic), the fossils *Moeritherium,* mastodons, mammoth, *Palaeomastodon,* and *Trilophodon.* Their geologic range extended from the Oligocene (particularly in the Fayum deposits of Egypt) to the Pleistocene and Recent.

Pseudofossils Objects of inorganic origin that resemble the forms of animals or plants. Concretions may be found in the shapes of sponges, algae, or the fern-like "dendrites." Pseudofossils occur in some geologic formations and have been taken for true fossils, particularly by the early collectors of the 17th and 18th centuries. Many present-day collections have pseudofossils labeled as true fossils by unsuspecting collectors.

Pterosaurs (Pterodactyls) During Triassic times, pterosaurs developed to become the winged reptiles or flying vertebrates, taking to the air. By the late Cretaceous, they were extinct. *Pteranodon* and *Rhamphorhynchus* are prime examples of pterosaurs. *Pteranodon* has been found with a wing span of twenty feet, and reached its evolutionary peak in Kansas beside the Niobrara seas. Possessing skin-covered wings, they were capable of gliding or soaring for great distances, much like today's hang-gliders.

Quaternary The most recent geological period which contains the Pleistocene and Holocene epochs. It was during Early Quaternary times that the great ice sheets spread over much of Europe and North America. The four major ice ages were separated by three interglacial stages. It has been suggested by glaciologists that our earth is today undergoing the fourth interglacial stage.

Saurischia One of the two orders of dinosaurs (the other is Ornithischia). In this group both herbivorous and carnivorous dinosaurs, the pelvis was three-pronged, resembling that of a crocodile.

Sauropods   This is the group of dinosaurs that walked on all four feet and reached gigantic size. Sauropods included the water-borne forms of *Apatosaurus* and *Diplodocus*. The sauropods reached their zenith in western America during the Jurassic Period, primarily in the Morrison formation.

Silurian   Beginning about 430 million years ago, the Silurian, third oldest period in the Paleozoic Era, lasted a short 30 million years. Excellent exposures of Silurian sediments may be seen in the gorge of the Niagara River in western New York. The mild temperatures of this period supported reef-building corals and widespread limestone deposits. Marine life saw an expansion of brachiopods, corals, molluscs, and bryozoans. The graptolites were fairly dominant in certain areas, while the trilobites had reached their peak of development and specialization. The scorpion-like arthropod *Eurypterus*, was the giant scourge of the Silurian seas, with some specimens found to reach seven feet in length. Air-breathing animals became established on land near the end of the period, with the earliest-known plants originating in Upper Silurian land areas of Australia. The fossil scorpions and centipedes of Wales are considered the first known air-breathing animals on earth. Primitive fishes continued to inhabit the Silurian seas.

Smilodon   The largest Pleistocene saber-toothed cat found in North America. The largest concentration of their remains occurs in the La Brea Tar Pits of Los Angeles. Recently designated the State Fossil of California.

Species   The basic taxonomic group of organisms which can interbreed and produce fertile offspring. In fossils, members of the same species can be recognized by taxonomic comparison and morphological gradations.

Stratigraphy   The classification, correlation, and analysis of stratified rocks. This branch of geology also deals with the description and interpretation of rocks to reveal their age, physical and chemical properties, distribution, and origin. Biostratigraphic units relate to faunal assemblages and zones.

Taphonomy   Events which influence the remains of an animal between the time that the animal dies and the time that the remains are discovered. Taphonomy depends on the interpretation of the orientation of the fossil deposits under study.

Taxon   A category of organisms classified according to common characteristics, ranging from distinctions between races and species, to differences between the animal and plant kingdoms.

Taxonomy   The science of classification of organisms.

Tertiary   The geological period which occupied the first portion of the Cenozoic, from about 70 million years ago to the beginning of the Quaternary, 2 to 3 million years ago. This period of time contains the Paleocene, Eocene, Oligocene, Miocene, and Pliocene epochs. The Tertiary deposits consist of some of the most fossiliferous strata, exposed and especially well-developed in the Paris and Vienna basins, Italy, Belgium, Holland, Germany, and Britain, and extending into North Africa. Extensive Tertiary deposits are also well-developed in both North and South America. In the United States, fossil exposures of Tertiary age extend along both the Pacific and Atlantic coasts, as well as the Gulf Coastal region.

Therapsids   Mammal-like reptiles that first appeared during Middle Permian times, only to disappear by the Middle Jurassic. Although not as well-developed as other primitive terrestrial animals, the therapsids occupied a niche in the mammalian evolutionary process.

Theropods   Suborder Therapoda, these are the carnivorous saurischians or dinosaurs that retained their bipedal mode of locomotion through their entire geological history. They ranged from the Upper Triassic through the Cretaceous.

Triassic   The first period of the Mesozoic Era, which saw the beginning of the mammal-reptiles leading to the development of the early dinosaurs and flying reptiles. These ranged from the primitive therapods, similar to *Coelophysis,* a bird-like land reptile genus six feet tall, to the phytosaurs, crocodile-like reptiles which were almost 25 feet in length. The Triassic Period contained considerable continental deposits, as witness the great fossil logs preserved in the Petrified Forest National Monument in Arizona. That the period had a subtropical climate is seen in the well-preserved plants and cone-bearing trees. Marine invertebrates were represented by the continuing lineage of ammonites, bivalves and gastropods, and reef-building corals. The vertebrates showed a remarkable increase in number and species. The reptiles developed into many unusual forms, with phytosaurs, and some of the earliest dinosaurs appearing. The famed dinosaur tracks found along the Connecticut Valley indicate a great number of dinosaurs inhabiting the region during this period. While the tracks are countless, their bones and skulls have rarely been found.

Trilobites   The most popular of all fossil arthropods, the trilobitomorphs began during Lower Cambrian times and developed into thousands of families, genera, and species, becoming extinct by the close of the Permian. Trilobites are found in most fossil-bearing deposits of the Paleozoic Era, ranging from simple tri-lobed structures, as in the *Agnostus,* to specialized forms such as *Terataspis,* the largest known trilobite, from the Middle Devonian of New York.

Type Locality   A geographical location designated as the precise area from which a type fossil specimen originates. There are five primary type categories for original description of any specimen: holotype—nominal species name based on a single specimen; syntype—if a new nominal species has no holotype, all the subsequent specimens of the type-series are "syntypes" and of equal value; paratype—after the holotype has been specified, all remaining specimens (if any in original lot) are "paratypes" and should be labeled as such; loctotype—if a species has no holotype or if the holotype is lost, any paleontologist can designate one of the syntypes as the "lectotype" and remaining syntypes then become "paralectotypes"; neotypes—a paleontologist may designate another specimen to serve as a "neotype" of a species if no member of the original type series (that is, any of the above) was in existence, as proven lost or destroyed. The type can be designated as the genotype (type species of a genus), holotype, or paratype, based on the original description and illustration of the specimen. Subsequent specimens from a type locality, if not the genotype or holotype, may be designated as paratypes or figured specimens.

Tyrannosaurs   Upper Cretaceous carnivorous dinosaurs which roamed western America and include the famous *Tyrannosaurus rex* and *Tarbosaurus*. *Tyrannosaurus* was the most highly evolved of all therapods and the terror of its day, standing some 18 feet tall, with an enormous head, and a possible length of 50 feet. Its mouth contained numerous daggerlike teeth from three to six inches in length, capable of tearing any smaller dinosaur apart. While its hind legs were massive and strong enough to carry the weight of the entire body in a standing position, its forelimbs were seemingly useless appendages.

Uintatherium   The giant herbivorous mammal from the Dakotas and Nebraska, having six horns on the skull. Large deposits of several species of this form have been found in the Eocene.

Ungulates   Mammals beginning in the Paleocene, having risen from insectivore ancestors. During Cenozoic times they evolved into fourteen orders, some becoming extinct and others continuing today. Among the condylarths, *Phenacodus* became extinct, while among the tubulidentates, the living aardvark is well-known.

Wurm Glacial   The final major Ice Age in the Pleistocene. Some geologists think that we are today living at the close of the Wurm Glacial period or in an early phase of the inter-glacial.

Recommended Reading

Here are suggested reading and reference works for the beginner as well as the advanced fossil collector. While some of these recent publications are of a general nature, several titles are necessary in the collector's library for the taxonomic, stratigraphic, or morphological interpretation of fossil materials.

Colbert, Edwin H. *The Age of Reptiles*. W. W. Norton Co., New York, 1965. This is a history of the reptiles from the late Paleozoic ancestry to the dinosaurs' demise at the close of the Cretaceous. The narration continues with the appearance of birds and mammals. Well-written in nontechnical language and of interest to every collector.

—————. *Men and Dinosaurs: The Search in Field and Laboratory*. E. P. Dutton Co., New York, 1968. An extensive and thoroughly enjoyable treatment of the history of vertebrate paleontology and of the men who discovered the giant reptiles in the field and recreated their forms in the laboratory and museum. A must for every collector interested in dinosaurs.

—————. *Wandering Lands and Mammals*. E. P. Dutton Co., New York, 1973. Interesting narrative of the geographical migrations of the mammals throughout geological time, including fossil vertebrates in the Antarctic and the story of continental movements.

Dockery, David T. *Mollusca of the Moody's Branch Formation, Mississippi*. Bulletin 120, Mississippi Geological, Economic & Topographical Survey, Jackson, 1977.

Desmond, Adrian J. *The Hot-Blooded Dinosaurs: A Revolution in Paleontology*. The Dial Press, New York, 1976. A narrative history of the dinosaurs from origins to extinction, with interesting sidelights of the lives of the many vertebrate paleontologists who opened up the field of dinosaur study and collecting.

Fairbridge, Rhodes W. and David Jablonski. *The Encyclopedia of Paleontology*. Academic Press, New York, 1979. A very expensive and technical encyclopedic treatment covering topics from Pre-Darwinian paleontology, to biostratigaphy, paleobiogeography of vertebrates and taphonomy. Of interest to the advanced collector.

Fischer, Jean-Claude and Yvette Gayrard-Valy. *Fossils of All Ages*. Grosset & Dunlap, New York, 1978. A sumptuously illustrated volume of invertebrate fossils in the collection of the Natural History Museum in Paris; expensive but recommended for the superb photography.

Fox, Sidney W. and Klaus Dose. *Molecular Evolution and the Origin of Life*. New York, Marcel Dekker, 1978. A textbook for the general reader, excellent in its treatment of life's origins.

Gillespie, William H. et al. *Plant Fossils of West Virginia*. West Virginia Geological & Economic Survey, Morgantown, 1978. An excellent, illustrated field guide.

Glut, Donald F. *The Dinosaur Dictionary*. Citadel Press, New Jersey, 1976. A comprehensive volume illustating the major forms of dinosaus. Practically every known type is illustrated. Covers the Saurischia and Ornithischia.

Hallam, A. A. *A Revolution in the Earth Sciences: From Continental Drift to Plate Tectonics*. Clarendon Press, Oxford, 1973. Of importance in delineating the geographical dispersal of biofaunas through plate tectonic movements of land masses and ocean bodies.

Hertlein, Leo G. and U. S. Grant. *The Geology and Paleontology of the Marine Pliocene of San Diego, California*. San Diego Society of Natural History, Memoir 2, Part 2B, 1972. Excellently illustrated summary of the bivalve fauna of Pacific coastal deposits.

Howard, Robert West. *The Dawnseekers: The First History of American Paleontology*. Harcourt, Brace, Jovanovich, New York, 1975. A relatively brief treatment of the history of American fossil hunters from colonial times to the Golden Age of western dinosaur hunts.

Lapedes, Daniel N. ed. *McGraw-Hill Encyclopedia of the Geological Sciences*. McGraw-Hill Publishing Co., New York, 1978. Highly recommended for all collectors, schools, and libraries.

Ludvigsen, Rolf. *Fossils of Ontario, Part 1: The Trilobites*. Royal Ontario Museum Miscellaneous Publications, 1979. A valuable handbook, illustrated, for the identification of eastern Canada trilobites.

McKerrow, W. S. ed. *The Ecology of Fossils: An Illustrated Guide*. The M.I.T. Press, Cambridge, MA, 1978. Somewhat technical for the average collector, but an interesting look into the living ecology of fossil groups throughout geological time.

McLoughlin, John C. *Archosauria: A New Look at the Old Dinosaurs*. The Viking Press, New York, 1979. An excellent study of the dinosaurs, for the general reader. Interesting drawings of the major dinosaurs.

————. *Synapsida: A New Look Into the Origins of Mammals*. The Viking Press, New York, 1980. Excellent reading into the early origins and development of the mammalia.

Nitecki, Matthew H. *Mazon Creek Fossils*. Academic Press, New York, 1979. Series of articles on the varied fauna found in the popularly collector Mazon Creek nodules. Expensive but necessary for the student of this fauna.

Ostrom, John H. and John S. McIntosh. *Marsh's Dinosaurs: The Collections from Como Bluff*. Yale University Press, New Haven, 1966. Excellent look into the background of the Como Bluff (Wyoming) dinosaur beds and the impact the dinosaurs taken from there made on museums all over the world. Should be used with Othniel C. Marsh's "The Dinosaurs of North America," 16th Annual

Report, U.S. Geological Survey, 1894-95, pp. 133-414. Valuable for a history, description, and illustrations of Marsh's Jurassic dinosaurs.

Plate, Robert. *The Dinosaur Hunters: Othniel C. Marsh—Edward D. Cope*. David McKay Co., New York, 1964. Of general interest for the collector.

Ratkevich, Ronald P. *Dinosaurs of the Southwest*. University of New Mexico Press, Albuquerque, 1976. A short volume, well-illustrated, briefly outlining the passage and range of dinosaurs from the Triassic through the Creteceous period in the American Southwest.

——————— and Neal La Fon. *Field Guide to New Mexico Fossils*. Dinograph Southwest Inc., Alamogordo, 1978. A handy field and lab guide illustrating the where and how of fossil collecting in New Mexico, with numerous localities listed.

Raup, David M. and Steven M. Stanley. *Principles of Paleontology*. W. H. Freeman Co., San Francisco, 1978. A handy textbook for the collector.

Romer, Alfred S. *Vertebrate Paleontology*. University of Chicago Press, Chicago, 1966. An invaluable reference work for the beginning student and advanced collector. Lists by order, family and genera, for all chordates, fishes, dinosaurs, mammals, etc. A very necessary tool for the collector of vertebrate material.

Schneer, Cecil J. ed. *Two Hundred Years of Geology in America*. University Press of New England, Hanover, NH, 1979. Interesting chapters on the early geologists and paleontologists working in North America from the 17th through 19th centuries.

Shimer, Harvey W. and Robert R. Shrock. *Index Fossils of North America*, revised edition. M.I.T. Press, Cambridge, MA, 1977. The most indispensible tool and a must in every collector's library. Illustrates the vast majority of North America's index fossils, and covers just about all the fossil phyla. Expensive but necessary.

Steel, Rodney and Anthony Harvey. *The Encyclopedia of Prehistoric Life*. McGraw-Hill Publishing Co., New York, 1979. An excellent summary of geological periods, the fossils, both invertebrate and vertebrate found in each period and a description of the major families and phyla. Numerous time charts, and brief biographies of early paleontologists. Certainly recommended for the beginning as well as advanced collector.

Tasch, Paul. *Paleobiology of the Invertebrates: Data Retrieval from the Fossil Record*. John Wiley, New York, 1973. A modern synthesis of historical geology for the advanced earth science student.

Thenius, Erich. *Fossils and the Life of the Past*. Springer-Verlag, New York, 1973. A handy paperback text covering technical aspects of paleontology.

Thomas, M. C. *Fossil Vertebrates: Beach and Bank Collecting for Amateurs*. Published by the author, 519 Harbor Drive, Venice, FL 33595, 1968. A reasonably-priced but brief outline on collecting fossils along coastal beaches. Good illustrations of mammal bones, shark and fish teeth.

Thompson, J. L. Cloudsley. *Why the Dinosaurs Became Extinct.* Meadowfield Press, Durham, England, 1978. Interesting paperback theorizing the possible causes.

Waddington, Janet. *An Introduction to Ontario Fossils.* Royal Ontario Museum, 1979. Paperback guide to Ontario fossil invertebrates. Nicely illustrated to help identify Ontario fossils.

Webb, S. David, ed. *Pleistocene Mammals of Florida.* The University Presses of Florida, Gainesville, 1974. A handy text with illustrations for the advanced collector interested in the taxonomy and distribution of mammals during the Pleistocene in Florida; also of interest for geographical distribution of similar mammal fauna throughout the South.

Serial Publications

Journal of Paleontology. Published bimonthly by the Society of Economic Paleontologists and Mineralogists, and The Paleontological Society, P. O. Box 4756, Tulsa, OK 74104. A highly technical journal for the professional, although a great many amateur fossil collectors are members of the Society. Excellent source of illustrations and fossil locality data.

Journal of Vertebrate Paleontology. Published at the University of Oklahoma, School of Geology and Geophysics, Norman, OK 73019. This publication will appear in the spring of 1981.

The U.S. Geological Survey offers a considerable library of reasonably-priced paleontological publications. See their 7-volume series of publication pamphlets listing hundreds of reports on fossils, which can be obtained *gratis* from the Branch of Distribution, U.S. Geological Survey, 1200 South Eads Street, Arlington, VA 22202, entitled *Publications of the Geological Survey from 1879 through 1975,* and subsequent monthly list of publications and maps.

For the beginning collector, student and museum curator, *Fossils Quarterly,* offers a variety of articles on fossil collecting, both in North America and abroad, fossil collectors, past and present, the systematics of fossils, museums with current fossil exhibits, fossils in the news, book reviews. Published by Geotech Archives, 3616 Garden Club Lane, Charlotte, NC 28210.

General Index

Index of Scientific Names of Genera and Species